Valerij Zisman
Criminal Law Without Punishment

Practical Philosophy

Edited by
Herlinde Pauer-Studer, Neil Roughley,
Peter Schaber and Ralf Stoecker

Volume 25

Valerij Zisman

Criminal Law Without Punishment

—

How Our Society Might Benefit From Abolishing Punitive Sanctions

DE GRUYTER

ISBN 978-3-11-221492-3
e-ISBN (PDF) 978-3-11-102782-1
e-ISBN (EPUB) 978-3-11-102802-6
ISSN 2197-9243

Library of Congress Control Number: 2023938944

Bibliographic information published by the Deutsche Nationalbibliothek
The Deutsche Nationalbibliothek lists this publication in the Deutsche Nationalbibliografie; detailed bibliographic data are available on the internet at http://dnb.dnb.de.

© 2025 Walter de Gruyter GmbH, Berlin/Boston
This volume is text- and page-identical with the hardback published in 2023.
Printing and binding: CPI books GmbH, Leck

www.degruyter.com

Acknowledgment

My interest in the topic of legal punishment started during my BA studies when I attended a year-long seminar on theories of punishment—ranging from classics to contemporary texts. Later, during my MA-studies, I attended a seminar on moral psychology at Georgia State University, where we looked at recent empirical research on what drives laypeople's punitive judgments.

This dissertation is the result of wanting to combine both these research traditions. On the one hand, the classical philosophical and legal debate on the moral justification of legal punishment, and on the other hand the empirical debate on what drives our punitive judgments, and whether these judgments are any good. I am happy that both philosophers who introduced me to the respective topics, Véronique Zanetti and Eddy Nahmias, ended up supervising this dissertation and helped at countless points along the way with the development of the arguments.

Many people have helped me sharpen the arguments in this dissertation and challenged me to specify how the normative debate on the moral justification of criminal punishment can learn from different empirical research traditions. I presented many versions of the chapters in this dissertation at the Colloquium at Bielefeld University and am thankful to Sylvia Agbih, Rüdiger Bittner, Verena Bergmann, Silvia Donzelli, Daniel Friedrich, Jonas Geske, Ina Herbst, Martina Herrmann, Nina Hirschmüller, Moritz Humberg, Ralf Stoecker, Roland Kipke, Alexandra Koch, Sandra Löhr, Niels Neier, Tim Niklas Nissel, Nele Röttger, Michaela Rehm, Konstanze Rosenbaum, Markus Rothhaar, Wolfgang Ruppert, Gesine Schepers, Ariane Schneck, Johanna Wagner, Almut von Wedelstaedt, Véronique Zanetti—and likely more participants that I have missed in this list—for their helpful comments. I am also thankful to Hanno Sauer and anonymous reviewers at De Gruyter for helpful comments.

Parts of this dissertation were presented at the *VIII. Tagung für Praktische Philosophie*, the *XXV. Deutsche Kongress für Philosophie* and at the *Center for Interdisciplinary Research* in Bielefeld—I am thankful to the audience of my talks for their helpful feedback. I also had the opportunity to present my ideas during my stay as *Junior Fellow* at the *Center for Interdisciplinary Research* in Bielefeld in the context of the research group *'Felix Culpa?' On the Cultural Productivity of Guilt*. I have had a lot of fun discussing the connection between guilt and punishment with all the members of the research group and enjoyed our vehement but friendly disagreements on the necessity of criminal punishment. I am especially thankful to Matthias Buschmeier and Katharina von Kellenbach for the opportunity to participate in this research group and all the opportunities to discuss my own ideas there.

The philosophy department at Bielefeld University was an ideal place to write a dissertation. The friendly and helpful environment there made working on such a lengthy project enjoyable despite all the challenges that it brings. I am especially thankful to Lea Bachus, Philippe Biermann, Tim Niklas Nissel, Marlo Passler, Paul Rehren, Ali Yasar, and Marko Wenzel for the company within and outside of the university and countless late-night debates on punishment and philosophy more broadly. Paul was especially helpful in helping me to assess the empirical research for the whole manuscript and what we can do with it in the context of normative debates—and in joining in on rants about armchair philosophy in moments of frustration.

Writing most of this dissertation during an ongoing pandemic was a challenge. I am very grateful to the *Studienstiftung des Deutschen Volkes* for funding this research. Despite all the chaos and challenges, the financial support made it possible to focus on the dissertation and finish the project in a timely manner.

Contents

Part I: The Problem of Punishment

Chapter 1
Another "New Perspective"? —— 3
1.1 Introduction —— 3
1.2 Outline of the Book —— 5

Chapter 2
Definitions, Theses, and Method —— 14
2.1 Introduction —— 14
2.2 Definition: Punishment and Other Types of Coercive Actions —— 15
2.3 Thesis: Rejecting the Punitive Rationale —— 30
2.4 Method: An Empirically Informed Approach to the Problem of Punishment —— 35
2.5 Conclusion —— 39

Part II: Backward-Looking Approaches

Chapter 3
Brute Retributivism —— 45
3.1 Introduction —— 45
3.2 The Normative Dimension —— 47
3.3 The Empirical Dimension —— 49
3.4 The Epistemic Dimension —— 59
3.5 Conclusion —— 63

Chapter 4
Fairness —— 64
4.1 Introduction —— 64
4.2 FBR: The Central Problems —— 66
4.3 Corrective FBR to the Rescue —— 69
4.4 The Benefits of Fairness Norms and the Condemnation Objection —— 81
4.5 Conclusion —— 87

Chapter 5
Penance and Censure —— 89
5.1　Introduction —— **89**
5.2　Penance —— **91**
5.3　Communicative Retributivism —— **101**
5.4　Consequentialist and Epistemic Communicative Theories —— **107**
5.5　Conclusion —— **117**

Chapter 6
Victims' Rights —— 118
6.1　Introduction —— **118**
6.2　Why Care about Victims? —— **120**
6.3　Why Care About Punishment? —— **128**
6.4　Conclusion —— **136**

Part III: Forward-Looking Approaches

Chapter 7
Deterrence —— 139
7.1　Introduction —— **139**
7.2　The Messiness of Testing Philosophical Theories —— **141**
7.3　Criminological Data —— **143**
7.4　Objections against Deterrence-Based Accounts —— **147**
7.5　Conclusion —— **160**

Part IV: Towards a Pluralistic Theory of Corrective Justice

Chapter 8
Weaving the Patchwork Rug —— 163
8.1　Introduction —— **163**
8.2　Hybrid Theories —— **165**
8.3　Unified Theories —— **167**
8.4　Non-Foundational Pluralism —— **171**
8.5　Objections to Pluralistic Theories in Criminal Law —— **174**
8.6　Conclusion —— **184**

Chapter 9
Objections to Corrective Approaches to Criminal Law —— 185
9.1 Introduction —— **185**
9.2 Problems with Corrective Approaches —— **185**
9.3 Conclusion —— **207**

Chapter 10
Epilogue —— 208
10.1 A Messy Conclusion —— **208**
10.2 It Is Not All about Sanctions —— **209**
10.3 It Is Not All about Philosophy —— **210**
10.4 Last Conclusion —— **212**

References —— 213

Index of Names —— 231

Index of Subjects —— 232

Part I: **The Problem of Punishment**

Chapter 1
Another "New Perspective"?

> This is a book about the justification of state punishment. Any writer starting out on this task must feel some need to explain to her readers why she has the presumption to inflict on the unsuspecting world yet another book on a subject to which so many books and articles, let alone years of academic effort, have already been devoted.
>
> Nicola Lacey, *State Punishment* (1988, xi)

1.1 Introduction

Nicola Lacey's assessment of the need to motivate writing yet another book on the justification of state punishment is even more pressing 30-odd years after her own publication. The topic of the moral justification of state punishment has occupied philosophers since the dawn of their discipline—and it never really fell off the table completely. Different theories came in and out of fashion, but the debate always continued.

I do not presume to reinvent the wheel in this book, and I happen to think that some of the books on the justification of punishment (or more precisely, the lack thereof), have already presented extremely convincing and somewhat comprehensive accounts of what I take to be the broadly correct view in the debate (Boonin 2008). But even if we were to agree on that, there is always some more tweaking of theories to be done and new objections to respond to. To me, however, tweaking theories and anticipating new objections does not seem to be a good enough motivation for such a book-length project.

What, then, does this book have to offer? The answer to this question begins with the observation that there has been a lot of *empirical* research on the topic of punishment in the recent decades. The main motivation for writing this book is my conviction that this empirical research needs accounting for in the *philosophical* debate. Up until now, only few philosophers had a crack at combining the empirical literature with the philosophical debate on the justification of punishment—and even fewer in a book-length project (but see Caruso 2021 for a similar project with a focus on the free will debate). This is partly also owed to the hesitance in the contemporary philosophical community to accept the relevance of such research for the philosophical debate in the first place (Berker 2009; Kauppinen 2014).

The research I allude to here comes from evolutionary psychology, behavioral economics, experimental philosophy, moral psychology, anthropology, and more areas that touch on the topic of punishment. The previous philosophical debate on punishment has of course already incorporated criminological and therapeutical research as long as such research has been around, especially in the first half of the 20th century. But the discussion within the tradition I am interested in has rarely gone beyond such criminological or therapeutic research in the philosophical debate.

Why should we care about these diverse areas of empirical research for the normative question whether (and for what reason, if any) criminal punishment is justified? This question leads me to the two related main objectives of the book.

The first objective of this book is to give an answer to that very question by pointing out all the debates and arguments in the discussion on punishment where empirical research is either directly or indirectly relevant for the success of the arguments.

The second objective of this book is to apply the empirical research we have to date in these areas to the debate on punishment. If the success of different theories directly or indirectly relies on yet largely unaddressed empirical questions, then a closer look at the research will help us either dismiss or strengthen said theories. In this book, I will argue that the empirical research gives additional strength to a position that is already around in the philosophical debate—though it has comparatively few supporters: We should not ground our criminal law institution on the principle that offenders should be punished for their crimes. Instead, we should ground our criminal law on a corrective rationale, that is, making offenders repair the harm done to the victims as much as possible.

The book thus promises to add interesting insights to the current debate in two respects: First, somewhat ambitiously, I want to improve the debate by pointing to all the areas in which empirical research is relevant to the problem of punishment. If that part of the argument is convincing, philosophers should work much more closely with relevant colleagues carrying out this empirical research. There will be much more need for further empirical research, since much of the research we have to date only scratches the surface of what we need to know to properly address the many different questions and problems in the debate on punishment. This, I think, would be a very important methodological contribution to the debate (see Pölzler 2018 for a similar project in the context of the debate on moral realism).

Secondly, this book uses the new methodology to defend a currently somewhat underappreciated position in criminal law. This will hopefully lead to a new, fruitful, and critical perspective on a very long-standing problem.

I will now sum up the structure of this book.

1.2 Outline of the Book

This book is divided into four parts. The first part introduces and clarifies the topic, problem, method, and theses of this book (Chapters 1–2). The second part looks at broadly backward-looking theories of the justification of punishment (Chapters 3–6). The third part looks at broadly forward-looking justifications of criminal punishment (Chapter 7). The fourth part aims to outline a pluralistic theory of corrective sanctions and addresses the objections that have been raised against such accounts (Chapters 8–10).

In contrast to some of the existing defenses of corrective sanctions (Boonin 2008; Golash 2005; but see Sayre-McCord 2001 for a similar strategy as mine), my aim in this book is not so much to show that punishment theorists got it all wrong. Rather, I think that most of them were quite right in wanting to emphasize the importance of justice, fairness, communicating censure, victims' rights, and deterrence. What they did get wrong, I think, is the idea that all these values can only (or even best) be realized by the intentional infliction of hard treatment on offenders, that is: Punishment. Instead, I want to suggest that these values are best realized by the infliction of corrective sanctions and sometimes the use of restorative justice procedures to address criminal wrongdoing.

Given that this work is interdisciplinary in spirit (though written by a trained philosopher), I will not be able to address all currently discussed theories of punishment in the depth that they might otherwise deserve. Such a comprehensive approach would probably also not fit very well with the methodological aim of this book. I want to discuss those kinds of punishment theories where empirical research can and does add something illuminating to the discussion. That is not necessarily the case for all justifications of punishment. I will thus not discuss all varieties and specific versions of retributivism, communicative theories of punishment, self-defense theories of punishment, and other variations of classical punishment theories. Rather, I will try to apply the empirical research to these types of theories generically, at least where it seems to me to be fruitful. I will also not touch the debate on free will and the justification of punishment, though of course it matters for the general debate on the justification of criminal law and sanctions. I would simply not be able to do all that I want to do in this book if I were to try to also adequately represent this specific debate (Caruso 2021 covers that debate quite well).

Some more important limitations are worth making explicit. Though I want to improve the debate by using research from various research areas, history and sociology fall somewhat short in my project. As I am mainly interested in research on our punitive attitudes and psychological accounts of how to best understand them, history and sociology would certainly improve such an understanding even more

—alas, learning about the research in these fields and applying them to the debate myself would have been too much for this specific project.

This book also only has a limited discussion of structural injustice and how it plays into the justification of criminal law. To a degree at least, it will come up in the discussion on fairness (Chapter 4) and my defense of the corrective approach against objections (Chapter 9). But there is of course much more to be said on the topic of structural injustice in criminal law, which those with more expertise in these areas than me have addressed for criminal law in general (for discussion of race, see Shelby (2022), for gender, see Goodmark (2018)). In the future, it would be interesting to see whether the same arguments also apply to a corrective approach to criminal law.

A last vice of my approach that I want to mention is that because I focus on the general reasons for imposing punitive or corrective sanctions, I do not talk about how to translate the arguments into specific policy proposals and sanctioning recommendations for each type of criminal wrongdoing. When I argue that we should prefer a system of corrective sanctions over a system of punitive sanctions, the details of such a system still need to be spelled out. How much restitution is adequate for which crimes? Are there any crimes where the corrective framework fails? If so, is that a reason to reject it entirely? Though I mention some specific crimes such as murder and sexual violence in Chapter 9, much more could—and in the future needs—to be said about the details of the corrective framework. But I hope that these general reasons to prefer corrective over punitive sanctions at least pave the way to the development of a more detailed corrective approach to criminal law.

With these caveats in mind, here is a rough outline of the content of the book.

Chapter 2 will lay out the central definitions, theses, and method of this project in more detail. For my central theses to be clearer, it will be important to emphasize the distinction between punishment and corrective sanctions as much as possible. Both types of sanctions have in common that they involve coercing the offender to do something they would otherwise probably not like to do. Nonetheless, there are important differences between punishment and corrective sanctions that are worth elaborating upon, as these differences have moral and practical importance. Moral, because punishment is typically taken to have a higher justificatory burden than corrective sanctions (or other types of coercive state actions for that matter), as punishment intentionally harms offenders for their wrongdoings while other coercive state actions do not intend to harm citizens. Corrective sanctions, in contrast to punishment, solely aim to make the offender repair the harm inflicted on the victim.[1] Thus, corrective sanctions should always be chosen in a way as to minimally infringe on the offender's rights or well-being while still adequately repairing the harm done to the victim. These conceptual differences have important practical implications, as a criminal law based on a corrective rationale will typically favor less harmful sanctions than a criminal law based on a punitive rationale.

The chapter will then go on to explain the details of the central theses of this book. First, empirical research is directly and indirectly relevant to the assessment of the success of arguments in the debate on punishment. Second, we should put the corrective rationale at the foundation of our criminal law and dismiss the punitive rationale.

Chapter 3 kicks off the second part of the book which focuses on broadly backward-looking approaches to justifying criminal punishment. I first take a closer look at a justification of retributive punishment that has sometimes been implicitly relied upon, but recently also been made more explicit: Brute retributivism. Brute retributivism states that the intuition, sentiment, or considered judgment that offenders deserve to suffer for their wrongdoings is a fundamental part of our moral psychology and should thus be awarded at least *pro tanto* moral consideration in criminal law.

The brute fact that people make retributive judgments will not convince critics of retributivism. Thus, the brute retributivist needs to clarify why we should care about such fundamental norms or judgments. Different explanations are possible, and in this chapter, I will not commit to any metaethical theory in particular, but rather focus on two dimensions of the brute retributivist's strategy that all different approaches have in common. First, the descriptive claim that people indeed uphold retributive norms or make retributive judgments. Second, the epistemic claim that such norms or the processes that lead to retributive judgments are reliable. I will argue that both claims are insufficiently supported to get the brute retributivist's argument off the ground. The research we have to date suggests that a purely retributive preference in laypeople is harder to find than many philosophers initially assume. Retribution seems to be largely driven by communicative intentions, not the philosophical idea of desert. Also, other forms of justice-restoring mechanisms such as corrective justice are often preferred to the retributive option by laypeople. The brute retributivists would thus need to have an independent argument for why retribution is a more adequate justice-restoring mechanism—but such an argument has yet not been presented and defended.

---

[1] See Chapter 9 for a more detailed discussion on indirect victims, more abstract victims, and the possibility of victimless crimes.

Lastly, there are many reasons to think that we should not trust retributive norms and judgments. Retributive judgments—or rather generically punitive judgments—are significantly more often made when crucial information which is deemed important when making sentencing recommendations about wrongdoing is missing from the description of a wrongdoing. When people have more of such information that are generally deemed necessary for well-justified sentencing recommendations, they tend to make less retributive or punitive judgments. Also, retributive norms might lead to all-considered bad outcomes, which should dampen our enthusiasm of retributivism when it comes to the question whether it is worth implementing retributive norms into criminal law.

All in all, brute retributivism fails on the empirical and the epistemic dimension of the argument.

The other chapters in the second part of the book try to make the justification of retribution dependent on broader normative principles. In Chapter 4, I will discuss a justification of retribution based on the fairness rationale. Such accounts start with the idea of society as a cooperative endeavor and then go on to argue that crime in such societies is best conceptualized as a disruption of the just distribution of benefits and burdens. The job of punishment, then, is to re-establish said balance by imposing additional burdens on offenders.

I will argue that fairness theories of punishment have two fundamental problems. First, they fail as a comprehensive theory of criminal law as they cannot adequately capture the wrongfulness of all crimes—and also not all that there is to criminal wrongdoing. In short: Not all crimes are crimes of unfairness, and even if that would be the case, unfairness is not the only reason why some crimes are wrong.

Secondly, fairness theories fail to show why punishment is a better response to wrongdoing than corrective sanctions for those crimes that do (partly) consist in unfairness. If crimes consist in the unfair distribution of benefits and burdens, it seems reasonable to think that crimes unfairly disadvantage victims whose rights should be protected by law. Corrective sanctions, not punitive ones, can hope to re-establish a just distribution of benefits and burden by lifting victims up from the unfair disadvantage they suffered.

But even if a corrective approach to fairness is correct, we need an additional motivation why the state should be tasked with re-establishing fair distributions of benefits and burdens in the society. Even though it might seem intuitive that fairness is a value that the state should be concerned with, the explicit and plausible reasons why that should be the case are harder to articulate than is often assumed. I will argue that we have some reason to suspect that upholding fairness expectations by inflicting corrective sanctions helps stabilize cooperation (at least in Western societies that we are typically concerned with in the debate on the justification of punishment). We can easily agree that upholding cooperative norms is something that is worthwhile pursuing, and if fairness norms and corrective sanctions can help with this, the state has good reasons to make it its business to uphold fairness norms.

Chapter 5 discusses the justification of punishment based on penance and the need to communicate censure to the offender. Some authors (Duff 2001; Garvey 1999; 2003) recently defended the idea that state punishment should be conceived of as a form of secular penance for offenders. By accepting a legitimate punitive sanction, offenders go through their deserved penance, but also reconciliate with the community whose values they violated with their wrongdoing. Communicative theories more broadly argue that offenders should be censured by the state imposing punishment on them. There are two motivations for why offenders should be censured. First, on the retributive model, because they deserve to be censured. Or second, on the consequentialist model, because censuring offenders has beneficial consequences for society.

There are several challenges for the penance theorists that I will discuss. First, aiming at a repentant recognition of wrongdoing with the imposition of punishment might overstep the authority of a liberal state. Second, sanctions based on the penance rationale might lead to disproportionate punishments, as different offenders might need different amounts of punishment for the same crime to experience repentant recognition of their wrongdoing. But lastly—and this is my main point—it remains unclear why the state should be concerned with penance in the first place. I will argue that there is no convincing argument to think that penance is intrinsically valuable, and little evidence to support the idea that punishing with the aim of penance will bring about good consequences. The penance account thus largely remains unmotivated.

A similar problem applies to broadly communicative theories. Even though intuitive, it is hard to spell out why offenders deserve to be censured—and even if they do, why censure should take the form of punishment. If we want to defend censure and punishment within a consequentialist perspective, we need data supporting this strategy. But such data is still lacking, as I want to argue.

Nonetheless, there is something to the idea that criminal sanctions should communicate censure and offer ways of coming to recognize one's wrongdoing. I will thus lastly argue that there are good reasons to adopt corrective sanctions and restorative justice in order to adequately communicate censure to offenders and reap the benefits of offering them ways of coming to recognize their wrongdoings.

Chapter 6 changes the perspective a bit and turns away from the offender to focus more centrally on the victims of wrongdoing. Here, I take a closer look at expressive retributivism. This version of retributivism claims, in a nutshell, that victims of crimes have a right to see the offender punished by the state. This right stems from the state's duty to express respect for the victim's moral value. Without punishment, the victim's moral value remains challenged by the offender's wrongdoing. Only by harming offenders can the demeaning message that wrongdoing expresses be accounted for.

I raise two central objections against such victim-centered defenses of retributive punishment. The first objection states that philosophers have failed to explain the intrinsic relationship between intentionally harming offenders and restoring the expressive harm done to the victim. Such a supposed relationship has been a common notion in the debate on punishment for some time, but the connection remains mysterious.

One way for the advocate of punishment to circumvent explaining the (supposed) mysteriousness of the connection is to make the connection conventional. That is, the victim's experience of moral worth and their perception of justice is diminished by the wrongdoing—and punishment is the conventionally best method to restore such a diminished feeling of moral worth and justice perception. This route, though more plausible, does not end up favoring retributive punishment, as I want to argue. The empirical evidence suggests that victims' moral value and perception of justice is not as dependent on the intentional infliction of harm on offenders as retributivists have suggested. Rather, corrective sanctions oftentimes do a better job at restoring the victims' sense of moral worth and the belief in the justice system. Additionally, restorative processes such as victim-offender mediation can additionally help reach such goals. That is not to say that victims never crave revenge and punishment—but that more often than not we do a better job of helping victims when we focus less on the punishment of the offender and more on directly trying to help the victims by restoring their sense of moral worth *via* corrective sanctions and other procedural mechanisms.

Chapter 7 looks at the main forward-looking theory of punishment—which constitutes the third part of the book. The main rationale behind forward-looking approaches, of course, is deterrence. In that chapter, I will first argue that the criminological data we have to date (or rather, which I was able to survey) is not well suited for investigating the efficacy of punitive *versus* corrective sanctions. That is so because the criminological research is typically not done with the conceptual distinction in mind that I have emphasized in this book. Thus, it is up to me to find at least some interesting difference in the data as to whether they solely support the efficacy of punitive sanctions, or of corrective sanctions (or of any at all, for that matter). I will argue that even though the data is far from clear, we are justified in having more confidence in the efficacy of corrective sanctions than punitive ones—especially given the costs that punitive sanctions typically have for the offender, the community of the punished person, and the taxpayers.

But the central philosophical question around deterrence theories also needs to be addressed. Is the state justified in pursuing deterrence as an aim of criminal law? Typically, both specific deterrence (that is, the deterrence of the offender) and general deterrence (that is, the deterrence of the public) are confronted with serious criticism: Offenders are treated with a lack of respect when the state offers them merely prudential reasons to adhere to the law. Furthermore, general deterrence faces the objection that offenders are used merely as means to deter other would-be offenders, which is unjustifiable. Lastly, deterrence might lead to the punishment of the innocent and disproportionate punishment.

I argue in this chapter that most of the objections are not as bad as they are presented to be by the critic. Giving people prudential incentives does not disrespect them, especially when the prudential incentives are motivated by a morally valuable goal—the prevention of wrongdoing. The same is true for using offenders as means. In principle, using people as means is not a serious moral problem. It is a problem when we intentionally harm people as a means to an end that they probably do not agree to. That is indeed a serious moral wrong, but it is not convincing to think that such a wrong should be forbidden under all possible circumstances. Rather, the deterrence theorists would have to show that the immorality of harming offenders as a means is proportionate to the benefits of deterrence. After all, simply allowing crimes to continue to happen is also morally problematic. We should thus specify the problem of deterrence and ask whether the benefits of punishment outweigh the moral costs of instrumentalization. And I will argue that they do not.

Lastly, it is unclear to what extent deterrence theorists are committed to disproportionate punishment and punishment of the innocent. No one has ever calculated whether the benefits of disproportionate punishment really outweigh the costs. Rather, critics focus on the mere possibility of punishment of the innocent and disproportionate punishment as a reason to dismiss the deterrence rationale. This, however, is not enough. I will argue that we should indeed be careful in accepting purely deterrent rationales in criminal law—but not because of the mere possibility of problematic punishment. Instead, we should be careful because of the high epistemic uncertainty with regards to serious wrongs such as the regular punishment of the innocent.

In sum, the critics have been correct in cautioning us in our praise for deterrence theories—albeit not for the right reasons, I think. But this conclusion is not sufficient to dismiss the deterrence rationale entirely. Rather the criticism only speaks against purely deterrent approaches to criminal law, but not hybrid or pluralist approaches. The discussion thus closes with the verdict that the deterrence rationale can sometimes influence the decisions about *which* corrective sanctions to prefer under specific circumstances.

Chapter 8 kicks off the last part of the book. I begin by bringing the results of the previous chapters together. After all, almost all these chapters concluded with the following findings: There is something right about the emphasis that we should care about the values discussed in the respective chapters, but the values are not best realized by the intentional infliction of harm on offenders. Rather, we are better advised to try to realize them *via* corrective sanctions and restorative approaches where possible. But if I acknowledge that there is something valuable in all these different accounts, I owe an approach to criminal law that has a place for all these different values. Therefore, I will argue for a non-foundational pluralist approach to criminal law. Such an account is somewhat rarer among those who accept that different values should play a role in criminal law. More popular in the debate are hybrid or unified theories, that either see only one value as justifying criminal sanctions (hybrid theories) or ground all different values in one fundamental unifying value (unified theories). I will argue that both these strategies fail. We are better off with a theory that acknowledges that all these values are independently justified, and all contribute to the justification of legal sanctions—even on pain of making the theory somewhat complicated.

A complicated theory opens the door for several objections. At worst, the theory is not just complicated, but inconsistent or incoherent. I will next argue that non-foundational pluralism in criminal law will not lead to inconsistent sanction recommendations. This is so because all the different values are best realized by very similar types of sanctions, namely corrective sanctions and (if possible) restorative justice procedures. There is indeed some wiggle room for sanctioning recommendations, given the different values we should ground our criminal law in. But such a wiggle room is actually useful in that it helps to adjust the sentence to whatever values we deem most important. Furthermore, some wiggle room is accepted in monistic theories, too, as it is in the practice of most jurisdictions. Pluralistic approaches as I envision them thus do not lead to vastly inconsistent sanctions.

Chapter 9 concludes the argumentation of the book with a chapter dedicated to different kinds of objections to corrective approaches to criminal law. When all of these objections have been addressed, the two main theses of the book will stand defended: The debate on punishment needs (and benefits from) incorporating empirical research, and when we take the empirical research into account a corrective approach to criminal law comes out on top.

In Chapter 10—The Epilogue—I will at least mention some of the different aspects of the debate that are equally important to what I have discussed, but which did not quite fit into the structure of this project. I will also conclude with some thoughts on future research on this topic, the necessity of collaboration between philosophy and empirical sciences, and what we can hope to realistically achieve with the research.

Chapter 2
Definitions, Theses, and Method

> This paper continues a debate about the following claim: an agent punishes someone only if she aims to harm him. In a series of papers, Bill Wringe argues that this claim is false, I criticize his arguments, and he replies. Here, I argue that his reply fails.
>
> Nathan Hanna, *The Nature of Punishment Revisited: A Reply* (2020, 89)

2.1 Introduction

As mentioned in the previous chapter, one of the central aims in this book is to defend the thesis that corrective approaches to criminal law are preferable to punitive approaches. This presupposes that there is an interesting and somewhat clear distinction to be drawn between corrective and punitive approaches in the first place—which is not uncontroversial in the literature. Several authors have suggested that corrective sanctions are in no interesting aspects different from punitive sanctions. Rather, corrective sanctions are considered to be merely less harmful or invasive types of punishments (Cholbi 2010; Duff 2002; Garvey 1999; Poama 2015; 2018).

I suspect that we will not find clear-cut definitions with necessary and jointly sufficient criteria for both punishment and corrective sanctions that everyone in the debate will agree on. This is exemplified by the long back and forth between Nathan Hanna and Bill Wringe (Hanna 2017; 2020; Wringe 2013; 2019) on just one criterion of punishment, namely whether or not it is intentional. The problem of finding a widely shared definition of punishment is complicated by the fact that the term "punishment" is used in a variety of circumstances and research areas. Psychologists, behavioral economists, evolutionary biologists, anthropologists, etc., all have different notions of punishment which are attuned to their respective research projects. Even if we can come up with a good understanding of legal punishment, we still need to make sure that our notion of legal punishment is close enough to other notions of punishment if we want to be able to draw from empirical research—as I think we should be. So, how should we approach these conceptual complications?

To get started, we need to get clear on what we expect from a definition, especially for the purpose of the project at hand. Following David Boonin, I think that we want the definition to be accurate, illuminating, and neutral on different justifications of punishment or corrective sanctions respectively (Boonin 2008, 4–6; also Lacey 1988, 7). Boonin took accuracy to entail necessary and jointly sufficient conditions, but I do not think that the bar should be that high for a good definition. I suspect that we will not find such a precise definition, so we should tone down this expectation anyway. Rather, we want the definition we use to cover as many instances as possible of those types of actions that are of interest. Also, the definition of punishment should not entail coercive actions that we do not deem to be proper punishments, such as taxation of the citizens or fees for getting married. If we manage to do that, the accuracy of our definition should be fine.

The definition should furthermore be illuminating in several respects. First, it should be illuminating regarding the question of why punishment has been so interesting to philosophers for so long. That is: It should explain the problem of punishment. If our definition of punishment is not illuminating in that regard, it will not be good. Also, similar to accuracy, the definition we use should be illuminating in that it enables us to distinguish punishment from other coercive state actions in the context of criminal law. Not all that the state coerces us to do or undergo in the context of the law are punishments. On the public health quarantine model developed by Caruso and Pereboom (Caruso 2016; 2019; Pereboom 2001; 2013; 2014), for example, the state has the right to restrict the freedom of offenders and potentially coerce them to undergo rehabilitative treatment, without punishment being justified. An illuminating definition of punishment should thus not lump punishment and sanctions based on the quarantine model together. In the same vein, I think, it should not lump together punitive and corrective sanctions (Lacey 1988, 11–12). But as this claim is more controversial, I will argue for it in more detail below.

Lastly, the definition of punishment we use should be neutral in that it does not preclude any justifications of punishment. If punishment were to be understood as a necessary evil, for example, it would exclude retributive accounts, as these see punishment as intrinsically morally valuable. Similarly, if punishment can never be inflicted on innocent people (on conceptual grounds), this would likely make utilitarian accounts of punishment impossible.

In the following, I will elaborate on a definition of punishment that is hopefully accurate enough, illuminating, and neutral (2.2). Then, I will lay out the central claims of this book (2.3) and motivate the empirically informed methodology (2.4).

2.2 Definition: Punishment and Other Types of Coercive Actions

In our search for an accurate, illuminating, and neutral definition of punishment we can begin with what is often seen as the standard definition of punishment—

the so-called Benn-Flew-Hart definition (Benn 1958; Flew 1954; Hart 1960; also Feinberg 1965 has later been added for the expressive dimension):

> Benn-Flew-Hart definition of punishment: Punishment is the (i) intentional (ii) infliction of harm (iii) on an (alleged) offender (iv) for a legal offense (v) which carries an expressive message of condemnation and (vi) is administered by a person other than the victim with the (alleged) authority to do so.[2]

My aim now is not to show that every instance of punishment will fall under this exact definition. Rather, I want to motivate that these criteria offer a roughly accurate, illuminating, and neutral understanding of punishment. I will argue that criteria (iii)–(vi) help to better illuminate important aspects of legal punishment. Both (i) and (ii) help to understand the problem of punishment, and criterion (i) furthermore will help to demarcate punishment from other types of coercive state actions. I will tackle the criteria in the order just mentioned.

Criteria (iii)–(vi): Offender, Offense, Expression, and Authority

The first two of these criteria state that punishment is administered on an (alleged) offender for a legal offense. These criteria help in several ways to better understand the phenomenon in question. Typically, legal punishment is inflicted only on supposed offenders, not on people that are known to be innocent. I think there is little point in debating whether a single instance of "punishment" of an innocent person really is punishment (for a short discussion see Hart 2008, 5–6). Rather, the first two criteria try to specify that a system of punishment which systematically aims to harm innocent people is no longer what we initially set out to capture when we asked what legal punishment is. This understanding of punishment is still neutral on utilitarian justifications of punishment. Utilitarianism might in some cases justify the imposition of "punishment" on people who are known to be innocent. But a system that "punishes" systematically only those who are innocent would cease to be the kind of system we wanted to describe in the first place. You could of course still call such a system "legal punishment", but then we would just be talking past each other. Accepting these two criteria thus improves accuracy and retains neutrality for the general purposes of the debate on criminal punishment.

---

[2] For some authors who mention this definition, see Burgh (1982, 193), Gert, Radzik, and Hand (2004, 79), Husak (2016, 51), Kasachkoff (1973, 363), Nino (1983, 298), Primorac (1981, 205), Stephenson (1990, 229), and Sverdlik (1988, 190).

Let us turn to the criterion which states that punishment is expressive—or, in other words, carries a message of condemnation. Feinberg emphasizes the importance of the expressive dimension in order to distinguish punishment from what he suggests should be seen as penalties:

> Imprisonment as hard labor for committing a felony is a clear case of punishment in the empathic sense; but I think we would be less willing to apply that term to parking tickets, offside *penalties*, sackings, flunkings, and disqualifications. Examples of the latter sort I propose to call penalties (merely), so that I may inquire further what distinguishes punishment, in the strict and narrow sense that interests the moralist, from other kinds of penalties. (1965, 398)

The criterion "condemnation" is illuminating in that it helps to demarcate criminal law from, for example, contract law or regulatory offenses. But the exact boundaries are fuzzy. Some regulatory offenses might warrant condemnatory responses. A regulatory offense such as public intoxication—if especially grave and annoying to people who are affected—might also legitimately be condemned in the sense Feinberg wanted to reserve for punishment. Also, anyone who has ever watched soccer with very engaged fans will know that there is no lack of a condemnatory dimension in demanding penalties for players. But at least in broad strokes, there seems to be something right about Feinberg's remark. Offenses such as fishing without a license often do not necessitate condemnation in any interesting sense of the term, whereas crimes such as assault do. I do not see any reason to think that there are clear boundaries between punishments and penalties—but in general the different categories capture something about our use of the terms. It is thus illuminating to include the criterion of condemnation to draw some (broad) distinctions with regards to different kinds of offenses that we will be primarily focusing on in this book.

Condemnation demarcates even more cases than just penalties, as Feinberg suggested. Taxation, for example, harms people and coerces them to do things they might rather not want to do. When you are taxed and your taxes are used to restore a statue that has been damaged, the taxation is not meant to be condemnatory. If you have to pay $1,000 to restore a statue that you have damaged yourself, however, condemnation is meant to be expressed by taking that money from you.

Furthermore, condemnation also helps with the accuracy of the definition of punishment. Laypeople who punish others in experimental settings do so with the intent of communicating a message (Cushman, Sarin, and Ho 2022; Dhaliwal, Patil, and Cushman 2021; Funk, McGeer, and Gollwitzer 2014; McGeer and Funk 2017;

Sarin et al. 2021).[3] If we described punishment in a way that lacks this dimension, we would miss an important aspect of why people want to punish. Both in everyday interactions and for legal punishment the condemnatory dimension thus seems of great importance.

So far, I have emphasized condemnation as an important aspect of punishment—but it is also a significant dimension of corrective sanctions. This will be a controversial issue throughout the book, so I will have plenty of opportunities to defend this claim in more detail later. Some authors think that corrective sanctions are not properly condemnatory, and it remains to be seen whether this is correct. But for now, we can say that at least in some form, corrective sanctions are also condemnatory. They are imposed on (supposed) offenders for legal offenses. This differentiates both punishment and corrective approaches from the quarantine model which I mentioned before. According to the quarantine model, the response to wrongdoing is not meant to convey blame or other forms of condemnation, as offenders are not strictly speaking blameworthy in such a model.

Lastly, let us take a look at the criterion which states that punishment is administered by an authority other than the victim. This criterion clearly helps to illuminate contemporary legal punishment. Such punishment is administered by people within an institution with the (alleged) authority to do so. The kinds of punishment which social psychologists, economists, and evolutionary biologists study are oftentimes inflicted by victims themselves. To better capture what we are after in the context of legal punishment, an authoritative dimension thus helps—at least for paradigmatic legal punishment.

Things are more complicated with corrective approaches, however. Restorative justice—which is one way of approaching corrective models—aims to give the criminal process back into the hands of the stakeholders of the conflict (the offender, victim, community, etc.). Such processes also sometimes entail that the stakeholders can come up with the appropriate punishment (or corrective sanction) themselves. If that is so, these cases would not fall under the criterion of authority. This would make punishment incompatible with restorative approaches—at least conceptually.

---

[3] "Expression" and "communication" are sometimes distinguished in the debate. In such cases, "expression" is a one-way street where the main aspect is to say or do something towards the offender. "Communication" is sometimes understood in a way to also include a specific response by the offender towards the expression. Whenever this conceptual difference is important, I will mention this explicitly. Otherwise, I will mostly be concerned with the communicative understanding of punishment as involving the victim, sometimes a broader community, and the offender of the wrongdoing.

The supposed conceptual incompatibility can be addressed, I think, by emphasizing that if we assume that the state has the legitimate authority to inflict punishment, it can also in turn authorize others to inflict said punishment. The state might thus be justified in allowing NGO's or victims to determine specific sentencing recommendations in accordance with legitimate guidelines of just sanctions. The criterion of authority thus does not exclude stakeholder-centered approaches to criminal law while still clearly demarcating contemporary institutionalized punishment by ways of emphasizing the necessity of (at least supposed) institutional authorization.[4]

Criterion (ii): Harm

Punishment typically is in some form bad for the people who are being punished—no big surprises here. But there is still need for clarification concerning how, specifically, to understand this dimension of punishment because different philosophers emphasized different dimensions of the "badness" of punishment. Flew, for example, takes punishment to "be an evil, an unpleasantness, to the [punished]. By saying 'evil'—following Hobbes—or 'unpleasantness' not 'pain' the suggestion of floggings and other forms of physical torture is avoided" (1954, 293). Here, we can already see that the specific understanding of the "badness" of punishment has implications for the kinds of actions that fall under the category of punishment. It does indeed seem to make a difference whether we say that punishment is about inflicting harm, a loss, suffering, unpleasantness, pain, or evil—as different punishments come to mind with the respective terms. But Flew's suggestion of taking punishment to be an evil or unpleasantness comes with a problem. One can inflict capital punishment without it being unpleasant in any direct sense; and using the term "evil" begs the question against the retributivist, who argues that what is done to the punished is morally valuable—not just all things considered, but the "badness" is, in fact, morally valuable (see also Boonin (2008, 6) for this point). Also, it is unclear why the definition of punishment should exclude the suggestion of especially gruesome acts of punishment (rather than rejecting them as legitimate punishments). After all, some philosophers take seriously the legitimacy

---

[4] In this book, I will not so much be concerned with the question whether any existing states actually do have such an authority. It might be the case, as some philosophers think, that legal punishment is in principle justifiable, but that contemporary states lack the legitimacy or authority (moral, not factual) to impose such punishments. For a discussion of such worries, see Hampton (1991, 22–23) and Hanna (2009).

of such punishments (Kershnar 2001), and some urge us to consider that corporal punishments might be morally preferable to prison sentences (Brennan 2017).

Boonin therefore suggests that it is

> more sensible to say that acts of punishment all, in some way, make the person who is punished worse off than she would otherwise be. [...] And so, a natural starting point [...] is to say that punishment *harms* the person who is punished, where harming someone means making her worse off in some way, which includes inflicting something bad on her or depriving her of something good. (2008, 7)

There will still be cases where understanding harm as making the offender worse off might not fit some instances of specific punishments. Imagine that an unhoused person who suffers from addiction is incarcerated in response to a wrongdoing. The imprisonment helps them to cope with the addiction and also with finding an apartment once they are released from prison. The prison also betters the sleeping situation of the unhoused person. In such cases, the punishment makes the offender better off—and it does not really seem to impose harm on them. Was the unhoused person punished after all, then?

First, we should clarify that the harm of punishment is neutral on its long-term consequences. Boonin takes the example of a parent who spanks a child, where the spanking ultimately has beneficial consequences for the child (let us assume), as the punishment does for the unhoused person just mentioned. To me, it seems reasonable to say that the spanking of the child was a punishment in the sense that it was harmful (also Boonin 2008, 8). But there could also be cases where even the direct act of punishment is not harmful to the offender. The unhoused person might benefit from having a bed, a roof over the head, and even appreciates not having to ask for food. In such cases, it might appear counterintuitive to some to say the unhoused person has been punished at all by the incarceration.

But as we have given up on the idea of finding a definition with necessary and jointly sufficient conditions for punishment, this should not worry us too much. If we have reasons to think that certain sanctions are systematically pleasant for offenders, it feels like these sanctions do not deserve the label "punishment." Nonetheless, punishments can happen not to be harmful to individual offenders. As long as they are systematically seen as harmful, the sanctions can be properly labeled "punishments" (Wringe 2019).

Even though most authors in the debate agree that harm is a crucial component of punishment, some have argued that it is counterproductive to build harm into the definition of punishment (Coverdale 2013; 2018; 2020; Poama 2015). Helen Coverdale argues that "[w]hat is needed is a definition of punishment that is open to the existence of non-harm practices, including, but not limited to, restoration, honesty about the risk of morally significant harms [as side effects of the punishment] and alertness to the dangers of ignoring these harms" (2013, 59). If we focus too much on the harmful dimension of punishment, we miss that the offenders (might) deserve care and help—and that caring for and helping offenders potentially has beneficial consequences such as rehabilitation and reintegration which we all should welcome. The argument here is essentially pragmatic, in that even though harmfulness better captures how we would intuitively understand punishment, it is unreasonable to build it into our legal understanding of punishment as this would bias sanctions towards being more harm-oriented and less focused on helping offenders.

I agree with Coverdale's worries about focusing too much on the harm of punishment, and too little on care and help for offenders. Nonetheless, I want to emphasize that it is still useful not to disregard the harmfulness of punishment, and especially to draw distinctions between punitive and corrective approaches. It is true that punitive sentences can both be harmful and try to help offenders, care for them, and try to restore their standing within the community. But if our responses to wrongdoers would systematically not aim to harm them, there seems to be no point in calling them punishments. This is what the quarantine model of Caruso and Pereboom would suggest. They suggest taking the focus off of harm and instead trying to help offenders to do better in the future. But by doing that, the quarantine model drops a crucial component of punishment, as the authors very well agree it should.

Corrective approaches also show important differences to punishment in that regard. They focus on what helps repair the harm done to the victim, not whether or not the offender should be harmed during the process. Instead of opting for a broad definition of punishment, I would thus suggest differentiating between punitive and corrective approaches. As we will see with the next criterion, both might entail some form of harmfulness, but the harmfulness of punishment is intended, whereas the harmfulness of corrective sanctions and quarantine models is not.

So, harm helps make our understanding of punishment more accurate. But it also helps getting closer at the problem of punishment. If we do things of which we know that they will reliably be harmful to offenders, we better have a good justification for it—especially if the harm to the offender is the very point of the sanction. But harm alone does not seem to be sufficiently illuminating. Taxing people, forcing them to correct the harm they have done to victims, or quarantining them also imposes harms on them. We do indeed need a good justification for each of these coercive state actions. But the problem of punishment seems to be more specific. Punishment is typically seen as demanding a better justification than taxing people etc. We thus need an additional criterion to describe this difference more precisely.

Criterion (i): Intentional Harm and the Principle of Least Infringement

Harm is not just an accidental feature of punishment—it is constitutive for an act to be punishment. When the state inflicts punishment on offenders, the harm is intentional rather than merely foreseen—it is not an unfortunate side-effect. It might be somewhat misleading to label this aspect of punishment "intentionality." Some philosophers take the criterion to literally mean that punishment needs to be administered by persons having the intention to harm the offender (Boonin 2008; Hanna 2017). Others, such as Hart, use it to exclude so-called "cosmic punishment" (Hart 1960, 5). If an offender is hit by a brick after committing a crime, this might be a deserved cosmic punishment, but it is not the phenomenon we are interested in.

I want the criterion to do another job. To me, whether judges or other authorized personnel actually intend to inflict harm on the offenders they sentence should not interest us so much. Rather, there is something that distinguishes corrective sanctions and quarantine models from proper punishment which can be captured by noting that the harm is intentional in the case of punishment. "Intentional" here is understood to describe that the harm is constitutive for something being punishment—harm is not an accidental feature of it. What the intentionality requirement comes down to for the moral debate, essentially, has already been explained within the quarantine model by Caruso and Pereboom and has been coined the *principle of least infringement*.

To clarify this principle, let us focus again on the quarantine model. A special quirk of the quarantine model is that offenders ought to only be detained as long as it is necessary to contain the danger they pose to society. If an offender will likely be dangerous for a year (let us assume we know that for the sake of the discussion), the quarantine model justifies incarcerating the offender for that time only. And we need to be even more precise here: According to the quarantine model, we should choose the least burdensome method of keeping society safe from the offender. Incarceration is a very burdensome method, as it restricts the freedom of movement of the offender, often times the freedom to have contact with friends and family members, access to the internet, to their jobs, etc. If the safety of the community could be guaranteed with house-arrest of the offender, in which they have less restrictions imposed on them, this should be preferred as a response to this specific wrongdoing. If there are even less burdensome ways, such as phone tracking, which would allow the offender some mobility but still guarantee safety, then even that should be preferred to house-arrest. To put it simply: We should choose those types of actions that reach the aim of self-defense (in the case of the quarantine model) with the least infringement on the rights or well-being of the offender.

Punishment—as it is typically understood in the philosophical debate—is not committed to the principle of least infringement. A certain amount of harm is deserved, serves an important communicative function, expresses condemnation, is the right of the victim, is needed for deterrence, etc. This is what the intentionality criterion tries to capture. The harmfulness matters, it should not be reduced as much as possible.

Of course, almost every theory of punishment has a certain built-in limit to the legitimate amount of punishment. Retributivism for example wants *proportional* harm inflicted on the offender—and no more than that. But in such a case, the harm is still *constitutive* for the act to count as an adequate form of punishment. With the principle of least infringement, in contrast, the moral demand would be to make the sanction the least harmful as is virtually possible while still trying to realize the value that the sanctions aim at (for example re-establishing fairness, providing adequate penance, respecting the victim's rights, etc.). Theories of punishment as understood here cannot say so. Retributivists, again, would agree that the punishment should not be disproportionate, but their very point is that there needs to be harm. If someone is to propose a proper theory of punishment, harm always plays an important moral role; it would simply be a misunderstanding of a theory of punishment to say that the aim should be to reduce the harm to the offender as much as possible.

Corrective theories as I want to understand them do not have this moral evaluation of the burden to the offender. Whenever there is a type of sanction that realizes the value in question with little amount of harm, we should go for it. If there are ways for offenders to be sanctioned that they themselves would systematically not consider to be harmful, that is even better. The harm is by no means morally valuable, but rather an unfortunate part of making someone provide restitution to a victim.

Both punishment and corrective sanctions *as sanctions* are means of realizing a certain value in criminal law. In this book, we will especially look at the values of justice, fairness, penance and censure, respecting victims' rights, and deterrence. Theories of punishment argue that in order to realize these values, we need to harm offenders. We need to sanction them in a way that we know will make them worse off. Such intentional harm either restores justice, fairness, offers penance and censure, expresses respect for the victim, or is essential for deterrence. Corrective theories argue that in order to realize the values in question, we do not put any moral value on the harm towards the offender. That is simply not the point of the sanction. The point is to make them do something that realizes these values, and for corrective theories this is providing some form of restitution to the victim and potentially participating in restorative processes. This will certainly make them worse off compared to how they were before, but that is not the point from a moral perspective. And because it is not the point, we are required to choose the type of restitution that is the least harmful to the offender, that is, the sanction which makes them the least worse off.

It is also important to note that only deontological theories of criminal law are committed to the view that only punishment realizes the values in question. For retributivism, the intentional infliction of harm simply *is* the restoration of justice. In the case of a retributive victim's rights theory, the intentional infliction of harm constitutes the restoration of the victim's moral worth. If you have a deontological theory of criminal law, punishment is constitutive in realizing these different values.

A point that is sometimes overlooked in the debate is that consequentialist theories of criminal law are not necessarily theories of punishment. Utilitarianism is not committed to thinking that punishment is needed in order to optimize deterrence, or even care about deterrence in the first place. Utilitarianism simply wants to maximize happiness and minimize suffering, and whatever state actions achieve this aim best with the least amount of harm should be chosen. Be it punishment, restitution, rehabilitation, or investment in the health care system. Or take a communicative theory of criminal law with its aim of communicating censure towards the offender. In its consequentialist version, the criminal law should realize the value of communicating censure to the offender because doing so has beneficial consequences for the society at large. But it is an open question which state action best communicates censure towards the offender. If only punishment achieves adequate communication of censure, then we should have a communicative theory of punishment. But if simple verbal communication is enough to express censure, the communicative theory should be happy without a theory of punishment.

Because of that, consequentialist theories are in a way always already committed to the principle of least infringement. If communicating censure is our aim, we should choose those types of actions that communicate censure with the least amount of harm. If both punishment and restitution adequately communicate censure, we should prefer restitution in such a framework as it typically involves less harm for the offender, while still realizing the value of expressing censure.

To sum this point up: Punishment is the intentional infliction of suffering on offenders. A proper theory of punishment insists on the harmful treatment of offenders. Corrective sanctions do not intend to harm offenders. Of course, paying restitution and participating in restorative justice settings typically are harmful things, but that is not morally valuable for corrective sanctions. That is why a corrective framework follows the principle of least infringement and should make the corrective sanctions as minimally harmful as is possible.

Does the intentionality criterion violate the neutrality requirement we proposed for a good definition of punishment? As just mentioned, consequentialist theories of criminal law are typically not conceptually committed to the view that the intentional infliction of harm, i.e., punishment, is what we should aim for. If you are a utilitarian, and you happen to think that the criminological data does not support the conclusion that punishment deters crime, then you will not have any problem rejecting punishment (Bentham 1789, chap. XIII). This is a general facet of consequentialist theories of punishment. But this does not exclude them from offering theories of punishment, and thus the neutrality requirement is not violated.

Throughout this text I have alluded to the claim that punishment has a higher justificatory burden than corrective sanctions, or for example quarantine orders for that matter. As mentioned above, punishment, corrective sanctions, and quarantine are all in need of justification because they involve harmful treatment of offenders. But punishment has a higher justificatory burden because it entails the intentional infliction of harm, or, to put it differently, because it disregards the principle of least infringement. While corrective and other frameworks typically aim to make the sanction the least harmful, for proper punishment theories some amount of hardship is intentional and should thus not be evaded.

Sayre-McCord makes this point regarding different burdens of justification in the context of the intentionality criterion specifically:

> If there is something right about the doctrine of double effect—so that intentionally inflicting pain or harm is worse in itself than merely knowingly causing pain or harm—then punishment (unlike reparations) stands on the wrong side of the contrast and requires special considerations in order to be justified, if it can be justified at all. (2001, 507)

If you either buy into the doctrine of double effect (which most people do, see Awad et al. 2020) or accept that punishment is not committed to the principle of least infringement, you should conclude that punitive approaches—all other things being equal—have a higher justificatory burden than corrective approaches in criminal law (or quarantine models, for that matter). Drawing this distinction with regards to the intentionality criterion is not new. But elaborating on it with the principle of least infringement additionally helps to sidestep some of the objections against the proposed definition of punishment and also the proposed difference to other coercive actions.

Michael Cholbi, for example, rejected the difference between punishment and corrective sanctions because he does not buy that corrective sanctions do not intend the harm imposed on offenders: "As such, anyone whose end is to compensate victims for their losses and who recognizes that harming offenders is the *in-*

dispensable means to achieving that end must rationally endorse harming offenders, and in so acting, intentionally harms the offender" (2010, 92, my emphasis). Similarly, I think, Cholbi would also need to hold that quarantine models and taxation aim to harm offenders. But rejecting the difference of punishment and corrective sentences based on that argument is unhelpful, I think, as it does not explain the punishment's disregard of the principle of least infringement.

Even if we accept Cholbi's account of what intentional actions are, we can still note that corrective sanctions and the quarantine model should opt for the least burdensome treatment of offenders. As I already said, there is nothing about calling the difference-making criterion "intentionality," especially if one disagrees on what intentional actions are. In this context, this does not seem to amount to more than philosophical nitpicking that masks the relevant differences between theories that uphold the principle of least infringement and those that do not. If Cholbi's point was rather focused on showing that corrective sentences are not committed to the principle of least infringement, then we would need to rethink the supposed distinction between corrective and punitive rationales. But nothing he argued suggests this—he solely seems to make a conceptual argument concerning the term "intentional." Thus, even if harming offenders is indispensable for corrective actions (which is open to debate), we should choose the least harmful coercive action that repairs the harm done to the victim—which clearly demarcates a relevant difference to punishment. If Cholbi chooses to call a system of sanctions that solely extracts compensation for the victim as "punishment," then he is of course free to define his concepts as he sees fit. I do not think there is much point in arguing how we should call these sanctions, as long as we establish that—in Cholbi's terminology—there is a morally significant difference between some forms of punishments and others.

Bill Wringe (2013; 2019) has two further worries regarding the proposed differentiation between punishment and corrective sanctions. First, he argues that the intentionality requirement is superfluous as the condemnatory dimension is sufficient to differentiate punishment from other sanctions such as quarantine. Secondly, and more importantly, he disagrees with the claim that punitive and corrective sanctions have different justificatory burdens. If we are systematically coercing offenders to undergo treatment of which we foresee that it will harm them, then this is in no way morally better than doing the same thing to intentionally harm offenders.

Both his points have some appeal but can also best be accounted for with reference to the principle of least infringement. Let us address the expressive point first. As mentioned above, there has been some debate among Boonin, Hanna, and Wringe whether and for what reasons the moral evaluation of something like the coerced incarceration of psychologically unstable people is different from punitive incarceration. Boonin and Hanna tend to explain it with reference to the missing intention to harm the psychologically unstable person. Wringe, however, argues that the condemnatory dimension is missing when quarantining a psychologically unstable person. If that is true, we can distinguish punishment from preventive incarceration by solely including the criterion of condemnation and we do not need the intention to harm the offender.

Wringe's response sounds promising, but it misses an important perspective, I think. When we incarcerate a person for preventive reasons, we should make the infringement of the freedom the least burdensome as is possible given the aim of protecting others. But with punishment, this is not the case—and the condemnatory dimension alone cannot explain this. Feinberg (1965) has emphasized that condemnation is only conventionally harmful, that is, we can express condemnation without harming people—but in most human societies, both things typically go together. If only condemnation were to be our aim, we would have moral reasons to make the condemnation the least burdensome as possible—maybe we should even express condemnation without burdening the offender at all if that is feasible (Günther 2014). This is at odds with paradigmatic understandings of punishment. Punishment should be burdensome. If we were to make it systematically non-burdensome, as the principle of least infringement would require, it would not really be the type of phenomenon we are interested in explaining or justifying in the first place. Condemnation, alone, cannot do the job of distinguishing punishment from other types of coercive actions in that regard. Including the intentionality criterion into our definition of punishment thus makes it more accurate and illuminating.

The same holds for Wringe's second point. It is true that if the same people who think that punishment is unjustified would nonetheless argue that it is unproblematic to systematically foresee severe harm imposed on offenders, something would be off. Wringe instead suggests that we should simply ask what kinds of sanctions are justified, instead of differentiating between punitive and corrective sanctions. If there is a problem with imprisonment, then that problem will always be there, regardless of whether the imprisonment is justified as punishment or as part of repairing the harm done to the victim.

Again, I think that Wringe is right in warning us against being blind to the justificatory burdens of corrective sanctions—but he misses that corrective justice has certain limitations built in by the principle of least infringement. The principle allows us to demand that the corrective sanction should be the least burdensome for the offender while still repairing the harm done to the victim. If we thus think that in order to repair the harm done to the victim, the offender needs to be taken off the grid for some time, we do not thereby have a justification to incarcerate the offender in prisons under terrible conditions. Rather, we would have reasons to quarantine the offender at home until the victim's justified feeling of security is restored (to just take one possible example). To describe this point adequately, we can use the intentionality requirement and the principle of least infringement. Nonetheless, even in cases where we take the least infringement corrective sanction into consideration, we still need a good justification for it. That much is uncontroversial. Wringe's worries can thus be set aside.

And again, there is nothing in principle wrong with Wringe's suggestion that we should simply ask: "What sanction should we use in this case (or cases like this), given that we want to realize values x, y, z…?" We could, in principle, go through every value and ask with what type of sanction it is best realized, and whether realizing the value with the imposition of the sanction is morally justified. There is nothing wrong with this methodology—but it will be somewhat messy. Maybe for one value, we need sanctions x, and for another value, we need sanctions y, and so on. Introducing a rough difference between punitive and corrective sanctions is a methodological device in order to make the approach somewhat more streamlined. If I am right that only broadly corrective sanctions are justified, we have a rough outline of what types of sanctions to choose from, and which moral guidelines they should follow. That is, the sanctions should minimize the burden to the offender. With that in mind, it should indeed be useful to distinguish punitive from corrective sanctions along these lines.

As for a last remark: I argued that the fact that punishment involves the intentional harm of offenders while corrective sanctions do not make corrective sanctions easier to justify, all else being equal. But the "all else being equal part" is important here. If we were to find out that corrective sanctions would, for example, put more psychological stress on offenders—and therefore involve more harm—than paradigmatic punitive sanctions, then corrective sanctions might be morally more demanding than punitive sanctions, even though the former does not involve the intention to harm offenders. To date, I do not know of any systematic evidence in that regard. The fact that corrective sanctions might feel like punishments to offenders alone does not undermine the morally relevant difference between the two (though this observation, if true, might be used to market the corrective approach as somewhat punitive to the public, which might be important, as I will discuss in Chapter 9).

Restitution and Reparation as Corrective Approaches

Now that we hopefully arrived at an accurate, illuminating and neutral definition of punishment, we also need to clarify in more detail the main alternative to punitive sanctions I discuss in this book: Corrective sanctions. I have already highlighted several aspects of corrective sanctions along the way of clarifying punishment. Corrective sanctions are imposed on (supposed) offenders for legal offenses. They involve foreseeable harmful treatment inflicted by an authority, which expresses condemnation for the wrong action. Nonetheless, corrective sanctions are committed to the principle of least infringement. Even with all that out the way, there are still various types of corrective sanctions we can distinguish for the sake of clarity. Also, the different kinds of corrective sentences might come with varying justificatory burdens. Broadly, we can distinguish three kinds of corrective approaches that vary in how demanding they are supposed to be on offenders.

The first is what we can call *simple compensation* (compensation for short). According to compensation, the main purpose of the reaction to the wrongdoing is to provide material compensation to the victim, no matter whether it is provided by the offender, the state, an insurance company, etc. (Radzik 2009, 47). Sometimes corrective approaches are criticized because they are thought to be committed to compensation. Such an account would indeed be problematic as it ignores the central role the offender ought to play in the response to wrongdoing. But this understanding of corrective approaches can be ignored for the purpose of this book. I will be interested in those accounts which take the offender to be accountable for repairing the harm done to the victim.

The second type can be referred to as *compulsory victim restitution* (restitution for short) which states "that the state should compel people who break the law to compensate their victims for the harms they have wrongfully caused them" (Boonin 2008, 218; similarly Barnett 1977). Even though, rather unfortunately, Boonin uses the term "compensation" to explain what the aim of restitution is, we can ignore this conceptual confusion here and stick with "restitution" for those types of coercive actions where the offender has to offer restitution for the harm inflicted on the victim. Restitution can be provided in the form of monetary payments, but it can also involve work for the victim (as in the form of community service), and in some instances even incarceration (Boonin 2018). Which type of restitution is most adequate depends on the harm that has been done to the victim. Minor wrongdoings might be accounted for with monetary payments. If, however, the wrongdoing has a greater impact on the victim or broader community—and potentially even involves secondary victims, i.e., other people being affected by the wrongdoing in addition to the direct victim—then more demanding sanctions are necessary. If the community does not feel safe because of the wrongdoing, the wrongdoer might owe community service that serves the purpose of restoring trust—thereby providing restitution for the loss of the feeling of security. In some cases, the only adequate way to restore the feeling of security might be some form of house arrest or even incarceration. But such sanctions are only justified in extreme cases where they are necessary to address the harm done to the community (thereby adhering to the principle of least infringement).

A third type of corrective approach puts more emphasis on the relationship of the offender to the victim and the broader community: *Restorative justice* (or *legal reparations* in some terminology used in the literature). Restorative justice conceptualizes the harm done to the victim in a different manner than restitution does. Restitution (at least in Boonin's and Barnett's versions) takes a libertarian approach that focuses on the violation of the victim's rights which, in turn, should be restored as much as possible by the offender.

Restorative justice, on the other hand, is often described as taking a more holistic approach to wrongdoing. The wrongdoing is not only a violation of the victim's rights, but also a disruption of the relationship between all stakeholders of the conflict. "Relationship" cannot be taken literally as sometimes the offender and victim might not have met before. But even if they have not met, some philosophers claim that wrongdoing violates a fundamental moral relationship (Radzik 2009, 81)—that is, a relationship of moral equals in a supposed egalitarian society.

Because of this additional dimension of wrongdoing, restitution is sometimes thought to be insufficient to adequately address wrongdoing. Rather, restorative justice proponents suggest methods of addressing wrongdoing such as victim-offender-mediations or family counseling, in which stakeholders of the conflict have the opportunity to come together and resolve the conflict that resulted from the wrongdoing. This entails giving the victim the opportunity to tell the offender how the crime has impacted them. It also entails giving the offender the chance to explain their actions or in the best case apologize for the wrongdoing. In some versions of restorative justice, the stakeholders can also make recommendations for corrective sanctions which address the harm inflicted on the victim—even though such recommendations still stand under the authority of the state who has the final word.

There are several such restorative approaches, but for now, it is sufficient to have clarified the differences between compensation, restitution, and restorative justice for the purpose of the discussion in this book. When I talk about corrective approaches as opposed to punitive approaches, I mean such accounts that entail restitution and potentially restorative justice.

2.3 Thesis: Rejecting the Punitive Rationale

Now that I have laid out what I take to be a useful definition of punishment and corrective sanctions, and also differentiated the relevant types of corrective approaches, I want to clarify the main thesis of this book. In short, it is this:

Main Thesis of the Book: All major justifications that have been brought forward to justify criminal punishment fail to plausibly show why punishment should be preferable to corrective sanctions. In fact, corrective approaches better realize the values in criminal law such as fairness, censure and penance, victims' rights, and deterrence. We should thus opt for corrective rather than punitive approaches in criminal law.

That is the general claim. But the details are more complicated—as always. A benchmark of corrective approaches is that they are committed to the principle of least infringement. The principle entails that whatever coercive action we chose should be minimally infringing on the offender's rights or well-being while still adequately addressing the victim's harm. Now, what that entails in detail depends on how we conceptualize the harm done to the victim (i.e., in a libertarian or holistic fashion)—but it also hinges on the type of justification that we put forward. And that is where the complications begin.

As mentioned in Chapter 1, I will discuss the following values in criminal law: Justice, fairness, penance and censure, victims' rights, and deterrence. As the main thesis states, we should opt for corrective approaches to criminal law. But of these mentioned rationales—which all ultimately favor corrective approaches—victims' rights and deterrence make a convincing case for the claim that the corrective approaches' adherence to the principle of least infringement has to be overridden in some cases. Let me elaborate on that.

According to corrective rationales, the sanction should aim to make the offender repair the harm done to the victim as much as possible, but at the same time, do so with the least infringement of the offender's rights or well-being. Two of the rationales mentioned above—the victims' rights and deterrence considerations, however, give us some reason to depart from that principle. I will argue for this in more detail in the respective chapters (Chapter 6 and Chapter 7), but the gist of the arguments is the following: In order to convincingly communicate to the victim that the state takes their rights or interests seriously, and in order to guarantee some degree of deterrence, we might (at least sometimes) opt for those corrective sanctions that are not the least infringing on the offender's rights or well-being. To put it in another way: There are epistemic and consequentialist reasons to sometimes depart from the principle of least infringement.

These reasons are on the one hand epistemic, because to some extent, the harmfulness of sanctions is a reliable way of communicating honest signals to the victim that the offender takes the wrong seriously and promises to respect the victim in the future. Such sanctions also communicate that the state takes the violation of the victim's well-being seriously. These signals are not *necessarily* epistemically reliable, but making the offender undergo some form of hard corrective action (rather than preferring the least harmful one) is at least a relatively more reliable way to communicate such honest intent. For the offender, simply demanding the least burdensome sanction appears to communicate that they do not grasp the full extent of their wrongdoing. According to the victims' rights-based argument, we might have reasons to opt for the more harmful corrective sanction in order to reach this more reliable communication. In cases where the honest intentions of the offender are clear, however, the principle of least infringement applies. In such cases, there is no good moral reason to opt for harsher sanctions than is necessary for repairing the harm inflicted on the victim.

On the other hand, there might be consequentialist reasons to sometimes depart from the principle of least infringement. This depends on whether always opting for the least infringing corrective sanction will reliably deter offenders in the future. This point will remain somewhat speculative, as the criminological data is unclear. Also, there are likely better ways to reach law-abidingness than the imposition of harm, as I will suggest in Chapter 7. Nonetheless I want to acknowledge that there might be good reasons to diverge from the principle of least infringement and opt for harsher corrective sanctions if we can plausibly hope for deterrent effects of doing so.

But does the fact that we sometimes might want to choose a more burdensome corrective sanction than is strictly necessary for pure restitution mean that we resort to punishment? I think that we should not make the jump back to the punitive rationale, even if we think that there are good reasons to not always go for the least burdensome corrective sanction.

The corrective rationale always comes with a variety of possible approaches to address the harm done to the victim. The offender can be made to write a check to the victim, can be sentenced to work for the victim to repair the harm done to them, to participate in a mediated process with the victim and other stakeholders of the conflict, and/or be sentenced to rehabilitative treatment in order to restore the loss of feeling of security of the community. The latter types of sanctions typically involve more harm to offenders. Listening to the victim's story can be tough on offenders and rehabilitative treatment as well as community service surely are more harmful than simply writing a check to the victim.

Even if the harm done to the victim could be accounted for by simply writing a check, we will often want to opt for the more demanding corrective sentences because of the epistemic and consequentialist reasons mentioned above. But here is the important point why I think it is worthwhile to emphasize that the theory defended here is not punitive in nature. If a case of criminal wrongdoing is such that the communicative or deterrent dimension is certain to have been established without the sanction, then there is no justification for imposing any hardship on the offender but repaying the loss of the victim. Imagine there is an offender who immediately after the wrong realizes the consequences their action had, and the victim sees no reason to doubt that the offender truly acknowledges their wrong. Imagine further that it is established that the offender poses no further threat. A proper theory of punishment per definition has to say that the offender still needs to receive a punitive sanction. Otherwise, a certain value will not be properly realized. But a corrective theory can happily accept that in such a case, nothing more has to be done than simply providing restitution to the victim.

Most cases will certainly not be so clear. And because of that, more burdensome corrective sanctions than mere repayment might be preferable in various kinds of cases. The important theoretical point stands, nonetheless. According to the corrective theory, there is no reason to impose hardship in these ideal epistemic and consequentialist circumstances. The values have been realized without corrective sanctions, and that is fine. But proper punitive theories cannot say so. As they are defined, some form of hardship is constitutive for the realization of such values.

But are more infringing corrective sanctions not simply punishments? As argued above, some philosophers think so. Given that I argue that we should use corrective sanctions and restorative justice processes over simple restitution, the critic might say: "Ha! So, you are not choosing the least infringing sanction. You are defending a theory of punishment after all!" If that is what the critic of corrective approaches means by punitive theories, then so be it. At this point, the dispute might be more verbal than substantial. If some philosophers want to call corrective sanctions that use restorative justice or community service rather than mere repayment in order to address the harm done to the victim "punishment", that is fine. My main thesis stands: Paradigmatic punitive sanctions such as fines paid to the state or incarceration typically do not do a good job at realizing the values in question. Rather, paradigmatic corrective sanctions do a better job at realizing these values.

Let us close this section with an example often mentioned by proponents of corrective approaches:

The case involves an offender, Mr. Clotworthy, who inflicted six stab wounds and a collapsed lung on the victim in an assault and attempted robbery. The victim and the offender agreed to participate in a restorative justice conference and worked out a solution that was acceptable to both. The offender would pay $15,000 to the victim to cover cosmetic surgery and additionally do 200 hours of community service. If he would not abide, he might be forced to serve a two-year prison sentence.[5] The court thought that the victim's sentence was too leni-

---

5 It is an open question whether the threat of imprisonment in case of non-compliance with corrective sentences is compatible with corrective approaches. In the case of Mr. Clotworthy, the judge

ent—even though the victim emphasized that restitution was most important to him, and that he thought that a longer prison sentence would neither help him nor the offender. But the court ruled against this suggestion, and instead of the required amount of compensation and community service sentenced the offender to four years in prison. In Braithwaite's account of the story, the victim "got neither his act of grace nor the money for his surgery. Subsequently, for reasons unknown, the victim committed suicide" (2002, 162).

According to the corrective rationale, the initial suggestion for an adequate sanction would have been perfectly fine, assuming that the offender indeed does not pose any threat to society. The community service could have been argued for on several grounds within the corrective rationale. On the one hand, it might have been the case that the victim would not have thought that the offender is honest about the apology (in the example, however, it seems that the victim was certain about the honesty of the offender because of the restorative process). On the other hand, one could also argue that the offender has to undergo some form of more burdensome corrective sanction in order to give an honest signal to the community that he will not be dangerous in the future.

What the court ruled, however, does not seem to be compatible with the corrective approach—especially with the principle of least infringement. The sanction proposed by the court has no clear connection to the aim of correcting the harm done to the victim. If that is correct, we lack a plausible justification for such a sanction according to my main thesis. Such an example hopefully clarifies that it is indeed useful to distinguish paradigmatic punishment from corrective sanctions—even those that violate the principle of least infringement. If I can make a convincing case that only corrective sanctions are justified—and that we should diverge form the principle of least infringement only in those cases where there are good epistemic or consequentialist reasons to do so—we will be able to rule out vast amounts and types of punishment that are administered in most states (and also thought to be justified by many philosophers). This, I think, would be a relevant research finding.

---

of course did not have these conceptual differences in mind, and we should thus not be surprised that the sentence might entail both corrective and punitive aspects. It still serves as at least an approximation of corrective models in that the corrective sentence is the main aim of the sanction. More on the possibility of imprisonment within corrective approaches in Chapter 9.

2.4 Method: An Empirically Informed Approach to the Problem of Punishment

Whatever your opinion on the recent empirical turn in some areas of philosophy, empirically informed philosophy—particularly ethics—is on the rise. I happen to think that this development should be welcomed, and in this section, I want to motivative this claim at least for the philosophy of punishment—I will then exemplify this motivation in most of the rest of the book. (For broader discussions concerning the role of empirical research in philosophy and ethics, see Nadelhoffer, Nahmias, and Nichols 2010; Sinnott-Armstrong 2008a; 2008b; 2008c; 2014; Tiberius 2015).

Empirical research in the form of criminology at least has been relevant in the debate on punishment for quite some time. For most of the first half of the 20th century, broadly utilitarian theories of punishment—especially rehabilitative theories—overshadowed retributive theories of punishment. These broadly utilitarian approaches were later rejected on philosophical grounds in the second half of the 20th century. Mainly, philosophers objected that such theories could not account for the dignity of the offender (Morris 1968). But rehabilitative theories—a branch of the utilitarian approach—also fell in disfavor because of the (supposed) "nothing works" conclusion that was drawn from the criminological data of that time (Martinson 1974; Lipton, Martinson, and Wilks 1975). If punishment makes the promise to lower the crime rate by rehabilitating the offender, and if the empirical data does not back such claims up, then the philosophical accounts need to be dismissed on such grounds as well.

But besides criminological data alone, the last decades of empirical research in other areas such as social and moral psychology, behavioral economics, evolutionary biology, anthropology, etc., have provided a plethora of data that waits to be made fruitful for the normative debate in punishment theory. But how can such data be interesting for the normative debate? In the following, I want to outline why empirical research matters in the debate that I will be interested in in this book. The respective chapters will then make a more comprehensive case for the relevance of such research.

Retribution

Debunking arguments have been very influential in the recent debate on retributive justifications of punishment and metaethics more generally (Bublitz 2020; Nichols 2014; Sauer 2018). Such arguments take issue with retributive justifications of punishment by essentially arguing that our retributive intuitions (and justifications) are epistemically unreliable. The debunking strategy is not completely new:

Nietzsche famously attacked retributivism with a similar methodology. He argued that retributive judgments are fundamentally based on or directly caused by *ressentiment*, and judgments which are based on ressentiment are unlikely to be true (Nietzsche 1968 [1887]). This short description of the Nietzschean argument already hints at the general structure of debunking arguments: They typically consist in an empirical premise (retributive judgments are caused by ressentiment) and an epistemic premise (judgments that are cause by ressentiment are unreliable and thus unlikely to be true).

As the debunking argument has a clear empirical premise, research from empirical sciences should obviously be welcomed—but philosophers have not always paid much attention to analyzing the empirical premise thoroughly. The brute retributivist's strategy that I will discuss in Chapter 3 builds on such an empirical premise and should thus be thoroughly analyzed in light of the available empirical data. More precisely, Michael S. Moore's and Shaun Nichols' arguments depend on whether or not feelings of guilt and moral outrage lead to retributive judgments, and whether laypeople uphold a retributive norm. Both arguments are not supported by the empirical data, as I want to suggest.

Fairness

Another prominent strategy to justify retributive punishment has been based on the fairness rationale. In short, the idea is that punishment is justified because crimes consist in the free riding of offenders, which can be accounted for by imposing burdens on them. The idea is very intuitive. If we conceive of society as a cooperative enterprise, then we have certain expectations regarding reciprocity of all people who participate in this endeavor. People who benefit from the cooperative practice without contributing anything (i.e., not adhering to the laws) deserve to be punished for that.

In recent decades, an abundance of studies using economic games have been conducted to strengthen the idea that laypeople generally have a strong urge to punish free riders—and to explain this urge with its evolutionary function of stabilizing cooperation (Axelrod and Hamilton 1981; Boyd et al. 2003; Fehr and Gächter 2002). The explanation is plausible enough. Participants punished free riders in one-off economic games. And in iterated economic games, the option to punish free riders had the effect that more people would cooperate with each other, which fits the retributivist's claim that respecting fairness is essential to uphold the cooperative endeavor (Dagger 2018).

Some philosophers used the results from economic studies and game theory more broadly to build an argument for the necessity (and thus justification) of criminal punishment (Gaus 1991). The huge literature on game theory, however, has in a very important sense been limited. It analyzed the effects of punishment in those cases where the only other option for participants was to do nothing. Even though it is interesting that the studies found a positive effect of punishment on cooperation, it excluded other reactions to the wrongdoing. Furthermore, the notion of punishment in such games is often very broad. Whenever participants chose not to cooperate with a partner again, that decision was counted as punishment in some of the studies. But for analyzing the impact of such research for the philosophical debate, we need to apply more precise conceptual distinctions than that. The collective benefits of not cooperating with free riders does not easily translate to whether the state is justified in deliberately imposing harm on free riders. For a comprehensive analysis of this strategy, we thus need to look at other reactions to free riding than mere punishment and use more precise understandings of the actions in question.

More recent empirical research included the possibility to compensate players who have been treated unfairly in economic games. In these studies, people were observers of an unfair distribution of goods, and had either the option to punish the unjust allocator or compensate the victim of the unjust allocation. The studies find evidence that participants prefer to compensate victims rather than punish offenders (Dhaliwal, Patil, and Cushman 2021; Doorn, Zeelenberg, and Breugelmans 2018; Doorn and Brouwers 2018; Heffner and FeldmanHall 2019; but see Prooijen 2010). These findings suggest a more complicated interpretation of the data for the philosophical theories. Taking the offender's unfair advantage away appears to be an important dimension of fairness—but the victim also ought to be compensated for the loss they unrightfully suffered. A proper analysis of all these results for the philosophical debate still needs to be done, and I will argue that it favors corrective to punitive approaches.

Penance and Censure

Communicative theories of punishment have become fashionable in the past, and in this chapter, I will take a look at three variations of said theory.

The first version of communicative theory of punishment is the penance approach. The idea is that punishment offers offenders a vehicle to undergo penance, which they deserve to do for their wrongdoing. But retributive penance theorists either have to show that penance is intrinsically valuable, which the theory fails to show; or the penance theory needs to provide empirical evidence that punishment is the best way to offer penance to offenders. I will argue that restorative processes and corrective sanctions do a better job at that than merely punitive sanctions.

The two other versions of communicative theories focus on censure. Censure-based theories come in two flavors: Retributive and consequentialist. The retributive theory, which I will discuss as the second approach, also fails along similar lines as does the penance approach. There simply is no convincing argument that it is intrinsically valuable for the offender to suffer the censure of society in the form of the infliction of punishment on them.

More promising, I will argue, is a consequentialist version of this approach. According to this version, communicating censure to offenders is not intrinsically valuable, but it has beneficial consequences that we should welcome in criminal law. Such a position, however, again depends on empirical research to make the case that punitive sanctions are the most promising and most beneficial means of communicating censure. I will argue that we do not have enough evidence to support this claim. Rather, corrective sanctions appear to be quite well-equipped to get this job done without intentionally imposing harm on offenders.

Victims' Interests

The role of the victim in criminal law theory experienced a resurgence in the recent debate on the justification of punishment. The central idea here is to argue for the justification of punishment based on the rights of the victim to have the offender punished by the state. As with the penance theory, there are genuine armchair arguments as well as those which are more directly linked to empirical research.

The more armchair-like arguments press for an intrinsic or objective connection between the victim's moral worth and the punishment of the offender. In such versions of the argument, only the infliction of punitive sanctions on the offender can restore the victim's moral worth. If we dismiss such arguments, as I think (and will argue that) we should, then a more contingent perspective opens up: What is the actual impact of crimes on victims—both physical as well as more abstract—and how can we alleviate these consequences of the wrongdoing?

This question requires robust empirical investigation. First, we need to take a more detailed look at the actual consequences of wrongdoing on victims. Besides the direct physical and emotional harm, philosophers were also interested in what we can call the expressive harm that is inflicted on victims. Such harm consists in detrimental effects of wrongdoing on the victim's perception of moral worth or feeling of justice. We then need a normative argument for why it should be the state's business to address all these dimensions of wrongdoing. And then even if we have such an argument, we still need to answer the empirical question by which means these dimensions of wrongdoing can adequately be addressed by the state.

As should be clear by now, there are a lot of empirical questions that need answers for a comprehensive analysis of victim-centered approaches to criminal law. I will argue that here, too, the empirical research points in the direction of corrective approaches and restorative justice rather than punitive approaches.

New Criminological Data

The relevance of criminological data for the debate on punishment is not new—and it probably thus does not need a whole lot of motivation to be included in principle. What I will take a look at in this book, however, is the criminological data with regards to punitive vs. corrective sanctions—that is, with a keen eye on the conceptual difference that I emphasized in this project. Most of the criminological research is of course not made with these conceptual distinctions in mind, and we will thus need to take a closer look at whether or not the data actually support punitive sanctions rather than corrective ones. I will argue that the data is not perfect for the conceptual distinctions made here, as much of the research would in principle favor both approaches. To mention just one example: If we want to analyze the effectiveness of certain monetary sanctions, then these findings would in principle support both punitive approaches as well as corrective approaches. As the only relevant difference between those two accounts is whether the money is paid to the state or to the victim, we should not expect the data to support one over the other approach without further argument.

I will argue that despite all these conceptual and methodological limitations, we have good reasons to suspect that corrective sanctions work just as effectively as punitive ones do—and in certain regards even better than punitive sanctions.

2.5 Conclusion

To recap: For all the rationales that have been brought forward in defense of criminal law, empirical research is directly or indirectly relevant to the normative debate. In some cases, it has already been used in order to strengthen the justification of punishment—but in most cases, the empirical literature has been somewhat neglected. In this book, I plan to work with the research in order to strengthen my main thesis that all the values that we should incorporate into criminal law are better realized with corrective sanctions rather than punitive ones.

Part II: **Backward-Looking Approaches**

Many authors now tell the same story about the history of retributivism (Davis 2008). Retributivism, historically, is most prominently attributed to Immanuel Kant and G.W.F. Hegel (but see Brooks 2003; 2004). Taking a rather big leap to the time after the Second World War, rehabilitative theories seemed ubiquitous in the debate on the justification of criminal law. But, with the frustration of the practical effects of rehabilitation (Martinson 1974), and its alleged ignorance of the autonomy of the criminal (Morris 1968), retributive theories rose again.

Two papers were spearheading the new retributive era, *Persons and Punishment* (1968) by Herbert Morris and *Marxism and Retribution* (1973) by Jeffrie G. Murphy. They defended what would later be called fair play theories of punishment, or fairness-based retributivism (FBR). FBR typically starts with a Rawlsian model of society as a cooperative venture for mutual advantage (Rawls 1999) and claims that a crime in such a venture should be conceptualized as a disruption of the just distribution of benefits and burdens. By committing a crime such as tax evasion, offenders gain an unfair benefit, given that all other law-abiding citizens pay their taxes. The unfair advantage does not consist in the monetary advantage of criminals by committing tax fraud, but in their having more freedom than the other citizens who do obey to the restrictions posed by the laws. Punishment's aim is to re-establish the just distribution of benefits and burdens by intentionally burdening offenders. This version of retributivism will be discussed in Chapter 4.

These early works concerning FBR inspired a general resurgence of retributivism. One version of retributivism that is as much debated as FBR in the recent literature is Antony Duff's (1986; 2001; 2003) communicative retributivism based on the penance rationale. Even though Duff does not take his approach to be purely retributive, he takes the retributivist commitment seriously, as only the deserved censure of the offender justifies that we have a criminal law in the first place. Duff's penance theory combines retributive, communicative, preventive, and rehabilitative elements for a comprehensive approach to criminal law. The penance theory and its retributive commitment will be discussed in Chapter 5.

Another variation of retributivism that people strongly discussed recently is victim-centered retributivism. Such accounts try to build the justification of criminal punishment on the rights of the victims of wrongdoing and their moral value. Wrongdoing violates the moral value of the victim (in a form that needs to be specified) and the punishment of the offender can rectify the violation of the moral value. Such approaches will be discussed in Chapter 6.

I will start however with a more direct motivation of retributive justice: Brute retributivism. Instead of pointing to a more general value such as fairness, penance, or victims' rights, brute retributivism takes our retributive judgements at face value and tries to build an argument on the observation that people uphold retributive norms.

My aim is not to simply criticize all these approaches and conclude that retributive punishment is unjustifiable. This task has been pursued by many scholars before me, and there would not be much to add except for taking issue with the newest arguments in the debate or finding some new angle that has been neglected to date. Even though I agree that the approaches ultimately fail to justify retributive punishment, I think that the approaches are up to something that is correct and valuable. Fairness, penance, and victims' rights really are values that need to be taken seriously in criminal law. But instead of pointing to retributive justice, I think these values are best captured within corrective approaches to criminal law.

Chapter 3
Brute Retributivism

> The paradox is that, on the one hand, a retributive principle of punishment cannot be explained or developed within a reasonable system of moral thought, while, on the other hand, such a principle cannot be eliminated from our moral thinking.
>
> John Leslie Mackie, *Morality and the Retributive Emotions* (1982, 3)

3.1 Introduction

As Douglas Husak (2016) rightly noted, there is no point in trying to aim for consensus on one understanding of retributive justice. Rather, we should take retributivism to encompass several ideas revolving around a similar theme: The moral worth of deserved punishment independent of future benefits. For such a broad account of retributivism, we can work with Michael Moore's often cited clarification:

> [Retributivism] is the view that punishment is justified by the desert of the offender. The good that is achieved by punishing, on this view, has nothing to do with future states of affairs, such as the prevention of crime or the maintenance of social cohesion. Rather, the good that punishment achieves is that someone who deserves it gets it. Punishment of the guilty is thus for the retributivist an intrinsic good, not merely the instrumental good that it may be to the utilitarian. (2010, 87–88)

Different philosophers have suggested different ways of specifying what the intrinsic worth—or the desert—precisely consists of. But in this chapter, we can discuss the brute retributivist's strategy sufficiently well without further specifying Moore's account of retributivism. The central task of the retributivist, of course, is to show how such a retributive principle can be justified. In general, two strategies to offer a justification can be distinguished (Boonin 2008, 86–87; Moore 2010, 106; Walen 2020; Westen 2016).

For the sake of clarification, we can refer to the first strategy as "derivative retributivism." The main aim of this strategy is to show that the retributive principle outlined above fits within or derives from a broader theory of justice or moral principle. Attempts to find such principles or theories of justice have led to a plethora of justifications for the retributive principle (Cottingham 1979; Walker 1999). I will be concerned with this first strategy in the three subsequent chapters (Chapters 4–6). There, I will discuss retribution as part of a fairness theory, a penance theory, and a victims' rights theory. But in this chapter, we will be discussing the second strategy to get at a justification for the retributive principle.

The second strategy can be called "brute retributivism." Brute retributivism takes an empirical observation as a starting point: Most, if not all, people under varying circumstances make the judgment that wrongdoers deserve to suffer for their wrongdoing. This empirical assumption alone, of course, does not do much normative work. For that, the brute retributivist can follow different strategies, two of which I will look at in this chapter.

The first version I want to take a closer look at was proposed by Michael Moore. According to him, the truth of the retributive principle is the best explanation for why people make retributive judgments. His argument sparked a thorough critical discussion of brute retributivism, albeit not necessarily under that name.

The second version of brute retributivism is based on sentimentalism in ethics more generally. According to that kind of sentimentalism, shared norms that are accompanied by emotions are at the fundament of our moral lives. Fundamentally shared norms—such as the norm to help people in distress—are as far as we can get with regards to a justification of moral norms. There is nothing more to add besides that. That is simply where ethical theorizing has to start—if it is to start anywhere—and the retributive norm is claimed to be one of such fundamental norms.

A defense of brute retributivism follows roughly three steps. I will structure this chapter accordingly.

The first step is to settle on a normative framework which allows bridging the is-ought gap. The brute fact that people make retributive judgments would only matter morally when we introduce a normative premise that makes such a move explicit. In Section 3.2, I will describe two such approaches briefly. For the purpose of this chapter, I will mostly stay agnostic on which of these normative frameworks is most promising—if any. My main point of critique will be the second and third step.

The second step concerns the empirical claim. Are the judgments people make when confronted with cases of wrongdoing essentially retributive? I will discuss this question in detail in Section 3.3.

In a third step, the brute retributivist needs to defend their account against epistemic worries. Such epistemic worries will be discussed in Section 3.4. The fact that people make retributive judgments is no help for the retributivist if there is something epistemically fishy about such judgments. The worries can be spelled out in different forms. Nietzsche (1968 [1887]) famously argued that retributive judgments stem from ressentiment, and judgments based on ressentiment are unreliable. A Freudian might object to Moore that judgments based on feelings of guilt are necessarily the product of unreliable unconscious processes. Furthermore, the recent debate has seen a surge of debunking arguments against retributive norms or judgments (Bublitz 2020 for an overview). According to contemporary debunking arguments, retributive judgments are seen as an evolutionary product that was selected for because of their beneficial consequences with regards to cooperation, not because of the truth of the retributive principle. A convincing version of brute retributivism needs to account for such epistemic worries.

My aim in this chapter is to discuss the second and third step of the brute retributivist's strategy in detail and show that brute retributivism fails in both respects to offer a promising justification of retributive justice.

3.2 The Normative Dimension

I will distinguish two types of normative frameworks that follow the general strategy mentioned above. This list is not meant to be exhaustive, but rather to help understand the brute retributivist's strategy. It will also help to clarify the empirical claims which the respective accounts make. This will be important to better examine the empirical and epistemic dimension of the argument.

Moore's Realism and Inference to the Best Explanation

Michael Moore is perhaps the most articulate and persistent retributivist in the current debate. What is more, he is a pure retributivist. Even though other considerations such as rehabilitation surely play a role for concrete policy proposals, only the retributive principle can ground the moral legitimacy of state punishment according to his view (Moore 2010). How does his justification of retributivism proceed?

The essence of his argument has been nicely captured by Sommers (based on Moore 2010, chap. 3):
1. If a particular moral judgment is motivated by a virtuous emotion, then it is likely (though not certain) that the judgment is true.
2. The emotions that motivate our retributive judgments are virtuous.
3. So, it is likely that our particular retributive judgments are true.
4. The retributive principle—offenders ought to suffer in proportion to their culpability—offers the best explanation for the truth of our particular retributive judgments.
5. So, it is likely that the retributivist principle is true. (2016, 6)

Clearly, the normative account in this argument is controversial. As the first premise states, moral judgments motivated by virtuous emotions are likely to be true. This step of the argument has been widely discussed—and it has often been dismissed as implausible (Rosebury 2011). In this chapter, however, I will not be concerned with the plausibility of the normative framework. I myself am not a fan of Moore's realism, but I will focus on the other aspects of the argument.

The two central aspects that will be relevant in this chapter are contained in the second premise of Moore's argument as described above. For the second premise to be true, it has to be the case that certain emotions indeed do motivate retributive judgments. As examples of virtuous emotions, Moore picks feelings of guilt and moral outrage. So first, we will have to ask whether these emotions really do elicit retributive judgments (3.3), and then, we need to ask whether the processes underlying these judgments are reliable (3.4).

The Retributive Norm and Sentimentalism

Shaun Nichols' brute retributivism builds on a pluralistic sentimentalist metaethics. According to this account, so-called entrenched norms are valid without further justification. If we want to justify certain moral norms, we cannot ground them in anything else besides the observation that they are entrenched. For a norm to be entrenched, it has to be widespread in the community, inferentially basic (i.e., not inferentially dependent on other norms or facts) and rooted in human emotion (Nichols 2015, 134).

With his account, Nichols also responds to worries concerning deontological ethics, best articulated by Joshua Greene and Peter Singer (Greene 2014; Singer 2005). Greene and Singer argue that characteristically deontological judgments are unjustified because they stem from emotions which cannot be rationally justified. In other words, they are merely an evolved disposition that might help to stabilize cooperation and rule-abidingness in humans. Nichols' counter to the charge that the deontological emotions or intuitions cannot be given a rational foundation is that there is no ultimate justification for the utilitarian norm that one ought to help suffering children as well (and neither the encompassing emotion of compassion). If it were not for our evolutionary history and our emotional make-up, we would not just rationally conclude that the norm to help people in need would be justified. Greene's and Singer's arguments prove too much. If we reject deontological morality because it relies on emotions, we are bound to reject utilitarian (and likely all other) norms as well. So, if we are to accept any moral norms at all (without subscribing to moral realism), we need to start somewhere—and Nichols suggests that we start with entrenched norms.

If we buy into this metaethical framework, we need to further investigate the same two questions as in Moore's account: Is the retributive norm really widespread? And if so, is it epistemically reliable?

3.3 The Empirical Dimension

First, I will take a look at whether the empirical dimension of the brute retributivist's strategy is convincing. My aim is to show that the support for retributive judgments and norms is limited—more so than retributivists themselves often assert. What is more, I will argue that many studies that were taken to show that we have retributive inclinations actually suggest a prevalence of corrective and compensatory judgments, inclinations, and norms.

Feelings of Guilt

Moore's argument that retributive justice is correct depends on the assumption that guilt is virtuous, and that guilt feelings lead to paradigmatically retributive judgments. He strengthens this empirical claim by using examples of severe wrongdoings. As one example, he uses the emotionally very powerful case of the murder of Bonnie Garland. She was brutally killed by her jilted boyfriend, Richard Herrin. Moore asks us:

> What would you feel like if it was you who had intentionally smashed open the skull of a 23-year-old woman with a claw hammer while she was asleep, a woman whose fatal defect was a desire to free herself from your clinging embrace? My own response, I hope, would be that I would feel guilty unto death. I could not imagine any suffering that could be imposed upon me that would be unfair because it exceeded what I deserved. (2010, 145)

What Moore wants us to take away from this cruel example is, first, that it would be morally required—or virtuous—to feel guilty in the aftermath of such a terrible wrongdoing. Furthermore, he thinks that experiencing guilt will lead to a retributive judgment with the content that we deserve to suffer whatever harm is deemed appropriate for committing such a heinous crime.

Moore's claim seems plausible on the face of it (for some problems with his reliance on the first-person perspective, see Husak 2016). It has an important drawback, however. The crucial problem is that Moore uses an extremely heinous (and statistically speaking, unusual) example to get at a very specific retributive judgment and then generalizes to the retributive norm based on that. Such a generalization is unsupported if we have reasons to suspect that feelings of guilt in the context of less heinous crimes will elicit different kinds of judgments. This criticism is also pressed by Sommers:

> Most crimes and offenses do not involve anything close to the evil brutality of Moore's examples. Moore's cases are also unusual in that there are few opportunities for restitution or reparation. Thieves can return their stolen goods. Vandals can work to repair the damage they've caused. But murderers cannot bring back their victims. This feature works to Moore's advantage because he wants to rule out what he calls 'corrective' theories of punishment that focus on restitution. Corrective theories pose a serious threat to Moore's defense of the standard retributivist model because the emotions that approve of restitution—making things right—are at least as virtuous as the ones that support retributivism. 'Non-neurotic feelings of guilt' do not only make us want to suffer. They make us want to make amends, to repair as best we can the damage we have done. (2016, 334)

Moore (2010, 184) himself thinks that non-retributive reactions to feelings of guilt put too nice a face on our emotional reactions. According to his intuition, describing experiences of guilt as solely eliciting corrective sentiments seems descriptively wrong. Unfortunately, he only relies on his introspection to make this point. I would like to suggest considering more systematic attempts to get a better understanding of what types of judgments and actions are elicited by feelings of guilt (and later moral outrage).

Here is what we need to keep in mind for the empirical investigation. First, Moore needs feelings of guilt to elicit retributive judgements in a broad range of cases. If feelings of guilt were to only elicit such judgments in very cruel cases of wrongdoing, he would not be able to directly generalize to the truth of the retributive principle in its broad version (i.e., that every criminal wrongdoing deserves punishment). Second, he needs it to be the case that feelings of guilt primarily output retributive judgments over other types of normative judgments. If Sommers for example were to be right, and feelings of guilt also (or mainly) elicit non-retributive reactions, then Moore also cannot generalize to the truth of the retributive principle in its broad sense.

A first line of research to shed light on this question comes from the investigation of self-punishment. Inbar and colleagues (2013) found that participants, who were tasked to remember an event which made them feel guilty, inflicted more suffering on themselves in the form of electric shocks than did a control group that was not made to remember events that made them feel guilty. Other studies also found a correlation between experiences of guilt and some form of self-punishment (Bastian, Jetten, and Fasoli 2011; Nelissen and Zeelenberg 2009b; Nelissen 2012)—and Bastian et al. (2011) explicitly mention retributive justice as one way of institutionalizing the preference for self-punishment in the face of experience of guilt and its guilt-relieving effects.

The problem for Moore's claim, however, is that self-punishment appears to be neither the preferred option to deal with feelings of guilt in such small-scale experiments, nor does the response appear to be strictly retributive in nature—rather, the crucial aspect of the response appears to be communicative, that is, people try to express remorse or communicate awareness of the wrong to the moral community.

With regards to the first point, the researchers investigating preferences for self-punishment that I have just mentioned suspected themselves that participants might prefer paying compensation to the victim to punishing themselves, if they were given the chance to decide. Indeed, Nelissen (2012) and Friehe et al. (2021) found evidence that when participants are given the option to inflict punishment on themselves or to compensate the victim in such scenarios, significantly more prefer to compensate victims. The earlier evidence in favor of the connection between feelings of guilt and self-punishment or even retributive justice might, in Nelissen's words, provide only evidence for the view that "[s]elf-punishment then, is only a measure of last resort" (2012, 142). If that is correct, we cannot generalize to the truth of the retributive principle based on such data.

With regards to the second point, the motivation for self-punishment might be less retributive than the brute retributivist would need it to be. If a preference for self-punishment is to count as a genuinely retributive motive, it needs to fit the retributive notion that the suffering is morally valuable in its own right. That is, strictly speaking, participants would need to be motivated by an at least implicit retributive notion that they deserve to suffer the self-punishment they inflict on themselves. Indeed, some evidence might count in that direction. As Bastian et al. (2011) mention, self-punishment leads to a decrease in feelings of guilt, potentially indicating that people think that they got what they deserve—thereby satisfying the retributive interpretation.

Though this is a plausible explanation, other evidence suggests that a communicative intent towards the victim or the broader moral community plays a more important role to participants when they chose to inflict punishment on themselves or compensate victims. Vel-Palumbo et al. (2019, 1082) for example argue that "self-punishment communicated a value consensus to third parties, and in doing so, redeemed the transgressor", hypothesizing that the function of such behavior is reconciliation. Nelissen (2012) argues that self-punishment is used to express remorse towards the victim, given that he finds that self-punishments are harsher when participants are in the presence of the people that they feel guilty towards. Similarly, Tanaka et al. (2015) emphasize the relevance of reputation-maintenance and relationship-maintenance in the context of participants who are prone to self-punishment.

All these data points do not exclude a retributive explanation, as most studies do not directly tap into the motivation of participants. But they do introduce a very important potential confound for our motivation to punish ourselves in a seemingly retributive fashion—namely to communicate remorse and foster reconciliation. And as far as I can see, there is no other direct evidence for the idea that people are motivated by a strictly retributive notion (even implicitly) when punishing themselves in the face of feelings of guilt.

The evidence in favor of the claim that guilt leads far more often to pro-social, that is, reparative, judgments than Moore suspects is corroborated by much research in the tradition of Roy Baumeister and colleagues. It is found that emotions of guilt are positively correlated with reparative actions (Baumeister, Stillwell, and Heatherton 1994; Schmader and Lickel 2006; June P. Tangney et al. 1996). Also, guilt leads to less externalization of blame and excusing oneself (Griffin et al. 2016; Stuewig et al. 2010) and increases other-oriented empathy (Leith and Baumeister 1998; June P. Tangney and Dearing 2002, chap. 2).

I am not familiar with any studies regarding feelings of guilt in cases of more severe wrongdoing than is typically analyzed in the lab. I agree with Moore's intuition that punitive reactions might be more prevalent in such cases. But if all I have argued above is correct, this is not enough to make the empirical case for the brute retributivist. In cases where we have data that is more systematic than a philosopher's introspection alone, we find that punishment is not the only reaction that feelings of guilt elicit—and maybe not even the most chosen one, at least in cases of minor wrongdoing. We also do not have any direct evidence to think that the motivation to self-punish is strictly retributive. In contrast, we have evidence to suspect that a communicative interest plays an important role when people choose to self-punish. That is not bad news for a generic punishment theory, but for a strict retributivist that is not the type of data that would allow them to make their case.

Moral Outrage

Moral outrage might be a more promising candidate for establishing the retributive norm within Moore's account. Regarding moral outrage, Moore writes:

> If it is morally odious not to care about others—either directly about others' suffering or indirectly through a concern for morality—then must it not be virtuous to feel such concern? And if the answer to this question is "yes", as I think it plainly is, then must it not also be virtuous to feel negative in some way towards flagrant moral violations that hurt others, virtuous to allow such negative feelings to cause retributive judgments? If so, we need to distinguish this virtuous emotion of outrage from the non–virtuous emotions of *ressentiment* (for

the very same emotion cannot both be virtuous and non–virtuous). [...] In my view, such revulsion is the only tolerable response of one who cares about other people and who cares about the morality that binds us together. (2010, 144)

Moore here addresses two points. First of all, the claim that moral outrage is virtuous, other than for example ressentiment. Other authors have suggested a similar argument to what Moore proposes here but with resentment rather than moral outrage (Jacobs 2016). For the purpose at hand, we can ignore these conceptual differences and grant Moore that moral outrage is a virtuous emotion. And indeed, whether we want to call it moral outrage or resentment, ignoring harm that has been inflicted on other people seems morally troublesome.[6] We want to express concern for victims and also acknowledge that a wrongdoing has been committed. But what kind of judgments specifically are elicited by moral outrage?

In Moore's view, it follows clearly from his introspection and experience that the answer has to be that moral outrage elicits retributive judgments regarding offenders. But again, this is not so clear when we take a more systematic look at the issue.

Moral outrage in the Moorean sense has been investigated by several researchers. To get at the judgments moral outrage elicits, the psychologists recorded the reaction of participants who observed or were confronted with unfair behavior. Oftentimes, psychologists manipulated the allocation of money in a way as to provoke a sense of moral outrage in participants, such as in the ultimatum game.

As was the case with the research on feelings of guilt, there is indeed initial evidence to back-up Moore's intuition that moral outrage elicits retributive-like judgments (Bougie, Pieters, and Zeelenberg 2003; Darley and Pittman 2003; Nelissen and Zeelenberg 2009a; Pillutla and Murnighan 1996). But the same problem as in the research on feelings of guilt applies. Some of the initial studies only focused on moral outrage's influence on retributive judgments and behavior. More recent studies investigated whether moral outrage has a similar effect on compensatory judgments in similar research settings.

Indeed, van Doorn et al. report that participants "who have been induced with anger kept less money for themselves than control participants, and spent more on compensating the victim rather than punishing the perpetrator" (2018, 591). Of those participants who chose to do something about the unfair behavior in ultimatum games (rather than simply not act at all), 84% opted for compensating the vic-

---

[6] That is not to say that we should make it our job to involve ourselves in every harmful action that we observe. Such behavior could itself have detrimental effects. The claim here is more parsimonious: It is good to care about the harm inflicted on others. And sometimes, caring involves expressing moral outrage.

tim in the anger condition rather than punishment of the offender (2018, 593). These findings have been replicated across three studies in their paper.

Vyver and Abrams (2015, Study 3) found that participants who were induced to feel moral outrage compensated victims of unfair allocations significantly more often than in a control group that was not induced to feel outrage, and a group that was induced to experience elevation. Moral outrage had no significant effect on punishment decisions in that study. Lotz et al. (2011), however, found that moral outrage had significant effects on both punishment and compensation decisions—with compensation being the preferred option over punishment.

At least in these low-stakes scenarios we find a similar result as we did with feelings of guilt. Moral outrage does indeed elicit punitive judgments at least in some scenarios, but so did it elicit compensatory judgments. I do not know of any data that analyzes moral outrage in higher-stakes scenarios, so it is hard to generalize on the basis of such studies. But for these low-stakes scenarios the retributive case is harder to make than Moore would like it to be.

We should also keep in mind that it is unclear whether the punishment decisions in these scenarios strictly speaking provide evidence for retributive desires. Most studies analyze the decision to punish generically, that is, they do not know which values motivated the punishment decision. It could very well be a retributive motivation, which would of course be crucial for making the brute retributivist's case. But it could also be the case that participants punish in order to protect their perceived moral value or honor (see Chapter 6 for such versions of retributivism), or for completely non-retributive reasons. This is important as there are not only different values why we punish, but also different articulated retributive values. Brute retributivism claims that offenders deserve to suffer for their wrongdoing. Moral outrage that motivates retributive-like punishment in order to restore the perception of self-worth of the victim would thus fall short of supporting the brute retributivist's strategy—at least strictly speaking. As most of the experimental designs do not capture these nuances that philosophers care about in the context of their debate, we simply cannot draw any clear conclusions from the research that we have to date.

What we can conclude with the data elaborated on above, however, is that the brute retributivists do not have enough data to make their case. The data certainly does not suggest that the retributivist is dead-wrong—I would rather interpret it as showing that our responses to wrongdoing are far more diverse than the brute retributivist might want them to be. And as I interpret things, the case for the brute retributivists based on feelings of guilt and moral outrage is certainly not strong enough to establish that the state should institutionalize the retributive norm as one of its guiding principles.

But maybe feelings of guilt and moral outrage are the wrong approach for brute retributivists. Next, I will go from judgments motivated by feelings of guilt and moral outrage to the more direct assessment of whether people hold retributive norms.

Retributive Intuitions and Norms

For better or worse, people seem to want offenders to suffer for their wrongdoing. There is a lot of initial introspective and observational evidence for this claim. Many people (me included) love good revenge stories, whether in books, TV shows, or in movies. It is enjoyable when the bad guy gets what he deserves at the end of the story. Maybe all of us felt these retributive urges after having been slighted in the past. Introspection and experience thus give the claim that we hold a retributive norm some initial strength—but what does the experimental evidence say?

Researchers find in surveys and experiments that people report that they care about several different values in criminal law: Retribution, deterrence, incapacitation, rehabilitation, and restoration (Carlsmith, Darley, and Robinson 2002; Carlsmith 2008; Crockett, Özdemir, and Fehr 2014; Gromet and Darley 2009). The details vary with the context of the wrongdoing, however. With regards to the death penalty, people regard deterrence motives as especially important (Ellsworth and Ross 1983), while they care more about victim- and community-centered motives with lower-level crimes (Gromet and Darley 2009).

The actual punishment decisions, however, seem to be mainly motivated by retributive concerns. Researchers have found evidence for the claim that the actual punishment decisions of laypeople are more strongly influenced by retributive concerns, even when participants were not aware of that influence (Aharoni and Fridlund 2012; Carlsmith 2006; 2008; Carlsmith, Darley, and Robinson 2002; Giacomantonio and Pierro 2014; Goodwin and Gromet 2014; Keller et al. 2010). To mention just one example, participants change their punishment decisions significantly more often when predominantly retributive factors are varied in the vignettes (i.e., intent, magnitude of harm, etc.) rather than when predominantly utilitarian factors are varied (i.e., likelihood of the crime occurring, and offenders being caught). Again, the details depend on the specific circumstances of the situation. If utilitarian punishment motives are made salient to participants before deciding on punishment, for example, participants tend to take these into consideration more strongly than when these considerations are not made salient (Twardawski, Tang, and Hilbig 2020).

These results lead to the provisionary conclusion that laypeople are pluralists on paper, but mainly retributivists in their actual decisions. The brute retributivist can use these results to defend their position. People mostly act in accordance with a retributive norm—though they also uphold other punishment norms. Pluralism on paper should not worry the brute retributivist too much. Their claim is not that people are solely retributivists, rather, they say that retributive justice is one of the fundamental norms of our moral psychology. This interpretation is initially corroborated by the evidence we have on how people form punitive judgments.

But things will get more complicated from here on. Carlsmith et al. (2008) themselves found—rather puzzling at the time—evidence that people who were given the chance to inflict retributive punishment in economic games did not feel more satisfied with their decision than people who were the victim of wrongdoing but did not have the opportunity to punish transgressors. This was surprising because the researchers expected that people who are given the chance to do the things which they want to do will be happier than those who do not have such a chance. If people really have a norm that wrongdoers deserve to suffer for their wrongdoing, we expect them to be satisfied after inflicting such deserved punishment. But that is not what they found.

Other researchers decided to try to solve this mystery. To do that, psychologists measured participant's justice satisfaction in economic games under varying circumstances (Funk, McGeer, and Gollwitzer 2014; Gollwitzer and Denzler 2009; Gollwitzer, Meder, and Schmitt 2011; McGeer and Funk 2017). In one study, the victim (the participant) had the chance to punish the offender but did not get any response from them (no-response condition). In the second scenario of that study, a response read: "I saw that you deduced money from me. I guess this was because of my unfair behavior" (acknowledgment condition). In the third scenario, the response read: "I understand why you deduced money from me. I shouldn't have been acting the way I did. I learned my lesson and won't do it again" (acknowledgment and change condition) (Funk, McGeer, and Gollwitzer 2014, Study 2a and 2b).

If punishing in accordance with the retributive norm were to be the main drive for people's punishment decision, we should expect satisfaction with the punishment decision in all conditions of the study. Whether or not the punished individual responds to being punished should not be directly relevant to the brute retributivist. After all, their thesis is about what people deserve, not how they should react. The researchers, however, found evidence that "an offender's change in moral attitude is ultimately what makes punishment satisfying" (Funk, McGeer, and Gollwitzer 2014, 995). What is more, not only did the researchers find a significantly higher satisfaction when offenders communicated acknowledgement of the wrongdoing and a promise to change their behavior than when there was no feedback, but the mean satisfaction with the pure retributive punishment was mostly around the mid-point.

In recent years, even more studies were conducted that suggest the communicative importance of punishment. Sarin et al. (2021) found evidence that people pursue punishment around principles of communicative intent more so than around the norm to inflict harm for its own sake, at least with day-to-day minor wrongdoings (also Cushman, Sarin, and Ho 2022). That does not mean that people never use punishment in the retributive manner (Nadelhoffer et al. 2013). Rather, these results suggest that people often are willing to sacrifice the retributive component in order to achieve a more communicative effect of the reaction to wrongdoing (Molnar, Chaudhry, and Loewenstein 2020). Aharoni et al. (2022) found that when the communicative dimension of punishment is satisfied, the suffering of the offender does not add to the overall satisfaction of participants with the sanction (though the suffering of the offender without the communicative dimensions is on its own right somewhat satisfying to participants).

All these results strongly suggest, I think, that it is not all about retribution for laypeople. Even though predominantly retributive aspects of wrongdoing drive punishment decisions, the communicative success of the sanction often is more important to people than the suffering itself. This is bad news for the brute retributivist. As Aharoni and Fridlund (2012) suggest, it might be more adequate to describe laypeople's punitive behavior as being driven by heuristics rather than holding a retributive norm. If that is correct, I think that the case for an entrenched norm cannot be made on the basis of this data. Similar caveats apply as in the case of Moore's retributivism: These studies mostly cover lab-situations, and more research should investigate whether the communicative dimension of sanctions overshadows the retributive dimension even in real-world situations. But with the evidence at hand, we have no good reason whatsoever to think that people are as invested into retributivism as the brute retributivists needs them to be in order for their argument to succeed.

And it gets even worse. Not only does the retributive norm appear not to be the main concern of laypeople when they punish wrongdoers, but past research also focused too much on retributive punishment as the only justice-restoring mechanism. As Lotz et al. put it, newer research (some of which I have already mentioned) "highlights the failure of the experimental game and altruistic punishment literatures to examine other types of justice interventions, in this case compensation" (2011, 479). In recent years, researchers attempted to correct for this bias and looked for other justice responses in economic games, especially compensation. The findings make the case for the brute retributivist even weaker.

Lotz and colleagues found that if participants in economic games were given the chance to impose fines on wrongdoers, or to give compensation to the victim of the wrongdoing, "participants actually used compensation more than they used punishment and the majority used both" (2011, 479). Van Doorn and colleagues—when reviewing the more recent literature on justice-restoring mechanisms—also argue that the preference for compensation in such economic games is larger than the preference for punishment across a wide range of conditions:

> By reviewing the current literature on punitive and compensatory motivations, it is asserted that people actually have a general preference for compensation to punishment. More specifically, it is argued that when people observe injustice (i.e. are not victim or perpetrator themselves), they would rather compensate a victim than punish a perpetrator when given the choice. Naturally, a preference for compensation to punishment does not mean that people believe punishment should not be applied at all—the preference for compensation merely signals that it should receive more weight. (Doorn and Brouwers 2018, 60; also Doorn, Zeelenberg, and Breugelmans 2018)

The same pattern of responses has also been found more recently by Dhaliwal et al. (2021) across 24 studies (N=21,296). It should be noted, however, that these studies do not necessarily give a good systematic overview of different types and severities of punishment, but rather focus on economic games as well.

The interpretation of the data with regards to more serious wrongdoing is complicated. Gromet and Darley (2006) found that people prefer restorative approaches to punitive ones when faced with minor wrongdoings, but prison as a punishment is more important than the restorative option to people when they are confronted with high-severity crimes. The study does not, however, offer any ways to investigate whether the results favor retributivism over consequentialism, for example, or maybe even safety concerns that have nothing at all to do with punitive inclinations (even though the authors suggest that the prison sentence is a retributive component). Maybe people simply think that more serious wrongdoers pose a higher threat to society and should thus be incapacitated for a longer time, which is corroborated by the finding that people gave more severe punishments (that is, higher prison sentences) when they though that the offender was likely to be dangerous (Gromet and Darley 2006, 408–9). The data we have on cases that go above economic games experiments thus does not speak in favor or against brute retributivism. The results are compatible with rationales that favor incapacitation of dangerous offenders, which need not be conceptualized under the punitive rationale. We simply cannot tell what the correct interpretation is with the available data here.

I think it is fair to say that the brute retributivists strategy fails along the empirical dimension for several reasons. Neither feelings of guilt nor moral outrage led to retributive judgment as robustly as the brute retributivists need it to be for their argument to succeed. What is more, the previously observed prevalence of retributive responses as a justice-restoring strategy might have largely been the result of a research bias that investigated retributive punishment as the only justice-restoring option. When compensation is added, for example, retributive judgments appear to hold less weight. Finally, even the evidence for retributive judgments that we do find might be better explained by their communicative intent. When people are given the opportunity to communicate censure without retributive punishment, such options are often preferred to the retributive strategy.

What I have argued here is not the final word on the matter. The empirical research still leaves a lot of questions open and did not reliably investigate different severities and different cultures. Also, it remains to be seen whether the studies reported here will stand the test of time. But still with this provisional data, we can, I think, confidently say that the brute retributivist's strategy fails to justify retribution as one of the central values the criminal law should pursue.

3.4 The Epistemic Dimension

Even though rejecting the empirical dimension might be enough to make a convincing case against the brute retributivist, I also want to take a closer look at the epistemic dimension. In this section, I will argue that retributive norms are all-things-considered not reliable enough to incorporate them into criminal law. A lot of economic and moral costs potentially come with the claim that we should put the retributive principle at the basis of our criminal justice institutions. The stakes should thus be high. If there are epistemic worries regarding retributive judgments, we should be extremely hesitant to accept them for the criminal law.

Quick, Dirty, and Unreliable

I will point to different arguments for why we should be hesitant to trust our retributive gut reactions or norms—especially given the grave potential costs of institutionalizing them within the criminal law. For reasons mentioned above, it will in some cases be difficult to differentiate the varying motivations of people to punish offenders because many studies research punitive judgments generically, without clearly having ways to experimentally distinguish between whether those judgments are retributive, utilitarian, communicative, etc. For our purposes in this section the problem is manageable, as even the skepticism towards generic punitive judgments should translate into skepticism towards putting retributive norms at the basis of our criminal law institutions. So here are some of the reasons why we should be at least cognizant of the epistemic worries regarding punitive or retributive judgments.

First, punitive judgments seem to be most salient when people make default judgments or have little information about the criminal case. Gromet and Darley (2009, Exp. 3), for example, suggest that sanctions which are focused on the offender are the default choice of participants, but change when the victim or community is made salient. If the victim is made salient, for example, sanctions that restore the victim become as important as does punishing the offender.

This finding itself does not tell us much about the reliability of retributive judgments for the moment. For that, we would need to make a couple more assumptions. One of these is that the criminal law should consider more information before coming up with justified sentencing recommendation than just what the offender did. Some retributivists will agree with that assumption, especially those who think that the victim's harm should also be taken into consideration when making a sanctioning judgment (Hampton 1991; 1992; Duff 2001; 2002). If we find that taking into account the victim's perspective actually leads to less punitive and more corrective sanctions, then implementing retributive norms might not be our best choice.

Further reasons to be skeptical of the reliability of punitive or retributive judgments can be derived from findings suggesting that having more information about the offender and the broader context of the wrongdoing makes punitive judgments more lenient. Balvig et al. for example write that "with a greater insight into the negative effects of imprisonment and with greater proximity to the offender, reactions become less punitive" (2015, 352). More generally, they say:

> In line with the point of departure employed in the project, this finding has been interpreted as showing that the propensity for punitiveness, and particularly for the use of imprisonment, declines as the amount of information provided about the case and the proximity to the individuals involved increase. (Balvig et al. 2015, 354)

Their study involved Scandinavian participants, and only a preference for non-custodial sentences over prison sentences. But similar observations have been made with regards to information about the criminal procedure and guidelines. In a study in Britain, researchers found that giving participants such information made their punitive judgments more lenient (Roberts et al. 2012). There is also some evidence suggesting that punitiveness is mitigated, though by no means absent, when participants are given more concrete sentencing options rather than simply being asked whether punishment should be harsher. And participants are significantly more lenient and open to alternative sanctions when such alternatives are made salient as options (Cullen, Fisher, and Applegate 2000, 7). People also vastly overestimate the costs of punishment and almost treat it as an unlimited resource (Aharoni et al. 2019; 2020).

So there seems to be good evidence to think that punitiveness is especially prominent in cases where participants have little information. That certainly does not speak in favor of the quality of harsh punitive judgments. But the results of course do not suggest that people are not punitive at all when they are given time to think about wrongdoing and are presented with many different facets of the wrongdoing.

Then there is a plethora of evidence suggesting that both laypeople and experts are biased in many different ways when making punitive judgments (Hoffman 2021). Laypeople and also in part experts are significantly influenced by the attractiveness of the offender (Sigall and Ostrove 1975) and the victim (Aharoni and Fridlund 2013) when making punishment decisions. The punishment decisions of participants that were based on intuitive thinking where more revenge-approving than more reflected judgments (Gollwitzer et al. 2016; Oswald and Stucki 2009). Judges' punishment decisions are harsher when mortality is made salient (Koppel and Fondacaro 2017) and are subject to the Knobe-effect—that is, judges significantly tend to rate otherwise identical cases of action to be intentional when the outcome of the action is morally bad rather than good, which by some is interpreted to be a bias or at least to be at odds with the notion of intentionality used in criminal law (Kneer and Bourgeois-Gironde 2017). All these bits of evidence suggest that punitive and retributive judgments are strongest under circumstances where our epistemic confidence in them should be low.

There is another line of research in social and evolutionary psychology that should make us hesitant to accept brute retributivism. As many researchers now agree, there is a plausible evolutionary story to be told about our preferences for third-party punishment and specifically regarding retributive urges (Fehr and Fischbacher 2004; Price, Cosmides, and Tooby 2002; Trivers 1971). This story has little to do with the intrinsic worth of the retributive principle, and much with the beneficial effects of having retributive norms at place for societies (Aharoni and Hoffman 2021; Cushman 2015).

Why should the fact that there is an evolutionary story to our punitive and especially retributive motives make us hesitant to accept retributive punishment? It should not, at least as such. As some philosophers and psychologists have argued, the benefits of retributive punishment might even be used to give a better justification of the retributive principle than intrinsic accounts (Aharoni 2021; Dagger 2011). The problem here is that such a move gives up the supposed bruteness of retributivism. If the retributive norm is potentially justified because it was selected for in virtue of its beneficial consequences, then the principle is not inferentially basic, as for example Nichols wanted it to be. According to this move, it is not the fact that retributivism is a fundamental norm of our moral make-up that gives it its moral value. Rather, it is the benefit to society of this norm that does the work. This might be plausible, but it will not help the brute retributivist.

So, what to make of the epistemic reliability of punitive and retributive judgments? I think that the evidence provided in this section favors a strong hesitance of putting the retributive principle at the fundament of our criminal law. The retributivist could counter and argue that biases are pervasive in all of our ethical judgments, and that we therefore should not be especially critical of retributive judgments. But such a response will not do. First, if the retributivist's response is correct, maybe we should indeed be hesitant of moral judgments generically, especially when it comes to implementing them at the very center of important institutions (Sauer 2021).

But the brute retributivist has a different problem. Of course, we can try to nudge our punitive judgments as to better reflect the retributive principle. But that would amount to putting the cart before the horse. The very point of the brute retributivist's strategy is to justify the retributive principle by pointing to the virtuousness or pervasiveness of retributive judgments. But if in all reality the day-to-day punitive and retributive judgments are epistemically unreliable and do not even amount to what the normative principle would want them to be—then there is no way we can get from the judgments to the principle. We would need an independent argument for the principle, which would amount to abandoning the brute retributivist strategy. So maybe abandoning it is the right thing to conclude for the time being.

Turning the Table on the Retributivist?

When I initially researched this chapter, my strategy was to turn the tables on the brute retributivists—show them that by their own standards, the corrective principle comes out on top. That is: Virtuous emotions evoke corrective judgments more often than retributive judgments. Also: Corrective judgments are far less epistemically flawed than retributive judgments. By the brute retributivists very own standards, we could then make a case for "brute restitutionism."

However, I do not think that this part of the arguments succeeds, at least for now. I still think that the corrective principle is the better justice-restoring principle when compared to the retributive norm—and the arguments presented in this chapter should speak to that. But a comparatively better justice principle might still not be good enough to establish the "brute" strategy followed in this chapter. We still know too little about whether corrective norms would be supported in the context of grave wrongdoings, and I do not think that we know much about whether similar epistemic worries apply to corrective judgments. This is simply because punishment has been the more researched topic. But if I had to guess, I would expect corrective judgments to also be susceptible to all sorts of biases. Furthermore, I also do not think that corrective norms are inferentially basic any more than retributive principles are. If the evolutionary account applies to the retributive norm—and if the retributive norm likely needs to be supplemented by forward-looking considerations to get off the ground—then so probably will the corrective norm. Because of that, the tables cannot be turned on the retributivists, as I have thought before.

3.5 Conclusion

The brute retributivist claims to justify the retributive principle without deriving it from a broader normative principle. Rather, they state that retributive judgments and norms are a fundamental part of our moral psychology and argue that because of that we should give it at least *pro tanto* moral consideration.

I have said nothing about the plausibility of this normative step in this chapter. Rather, I have looked at the empirical and epistemic dimension of the brute retributivist's strategy. The argument fails to convince on both of these dimensions. Retributivists overestimated the extent to which virtuous emotions such as feelings of guilt and resentment produce retributive judgments. And where people do make retributive judgments or hold retributive norms, a communicative intent seems to be lurking in the background of their motivation to punish. Furthermore, there are many reasons to think that retributive judgments are epistemically flawed—or at least flawed enough to doubt that they should serve as a ground for the criminal law.

If all this is correct, we should reject the brute retributivists' strategy. The retributivists need a broader moral principle to make the case for their theory. I will look at three such principles in the next three chapters, respectively.

Chapter 4
Fairness

> Justice is the first virtue of social institutions, as truth is of systems of thought. [...] [L]aws and institutions no matter how efficient and well-arranged must be reformed or abolished if they are unjust.
>
> John Rawls, *A Theory of Justice. Revised Edition* (1999, 3)

4.1 Introduction

Fairness-based retributivism (FBR) is rooted in the attempts to revive retributivism in the second half of the 20th century (Finnis 1972; Morris 1968; Murphy 1973). One of its central assumptions is that society is a cooperative venture for mutual advantage, which is best known from Hart's and Rawls' work in political and legal philosophy (Hart 1955; Rawls 1964; 1999). For such successful cooperative ventures to be possible, all people within a certain society need to agree to restrict their freedom to a degree. By accepting some burdens in the form of the restriction of their freedom, all participants are said to gain the benefits of the protection of their rights. Crimes in societies thus understood are then said to be best conceptualized as disruptions of the just distribution of benefits and burdens: When offenders break the law, they disregard the burdens they ought to be faced with, while still enjoying the benefits of the cooperative venture. By committing tax fraud, for example, offenders gain an unfair benefit, given that all other law-abiding citizens limit their economic freedom by paying their taxes. The unfairness of such crimes does not simply consist in the monetary benefit the offender gains (many crimes have no such benefits), rather it consists in the additional freedom offenders enjoy by committing an act that others are refraining from committing for the sake of the cooperative venture. The aim of legal punishment is to re-establish the just distribution of benefits and burdens by intentionally inflicting additional restrictions of freedom on the offender. According to another well-known formulation of FBR, people are said to owe a debt to society when they benefit from the cooperative enterprise, i.e., the debt of adhering to the law (Morris 1968). And they should be punished if that debt is not paid properly by adhering to the laws of society.

My first claim in this chapter is that FBR fails as a plausible justification of legal punishment. FBR has been subject to thorough criticism in the recent decades, to the point that Antony Duff claimed that the criticism of FBR is "complete"

(2001, 22). Newer defendants of FBR tried to respond to these critics—but, as I will argue in this chapter, without definitive success.

Nonetheless, and this is my second claim, we need not completely dismiss the fairness rationale when theorizing about criminal law. FBR fails to justify punishment, but the fairness rationale can help to illuminate why we should opt for corrective approaches in criminal law. Or to be more precise and modest, I will argue that fairness plays an important role in a pluralistic approach to criminal law. Even though I think that a corrective fairness approach is the most plausible version of FBR, it still cannot address all objections sufficiently. Nonetheless, rather than disregarding fairness approaches because of that shortcoming, I want to suggest that we should see them as an important part in a pluralistic approach to criminal law. Fairness matters to people, and social institutions with fairness norms incorporated into them are useful for our society. Because of that, we should not discard it completely.

Corrective versions of FBR as I envision them in this chapter have not been very much debated in the literature, barring some notable exceptions: Boonin's (2008, chap. 3.3.) central argument against FBR is that it fails to clarify why intentional harm (i.e., punishment), rather than merely foreseeable harm (i.e., corrective sanctions) are needed to balance the benefits and burdens disrupted by the crime. But instead of exploring this argument for a defense of a corrective fairness approach, Boonin is content with simply rejecting FBR's justification of punishment. Duus-Otterström (2017) mentions in the conclusion of his paper that his defense of FBR remains agnostic on whether punitive or corrective approaches best do justice to the fairness rationale. I think agnosticism is uncalled for, and I want to argue that the fairness rationale grounds corrective approaches convincingly. Sayre-McCord (2001; 2002) mentions only in passing that corrective sanctions can restore the balance of burdens and benefits that resulted from crimes, without going into any elaborations. It thus remains to be shown that the fairness rationale favors corrective approaches to criminal law.

I will start by giving a short overview of the four central problems FBR faces (4.2). I will then turn to new responses to these problems and offer a nuanced defense of fairness approaches. If FBR is to be plausible at all, it needs to be understood as a corrective approach. But even such a fairness account fails as a comprehensive justification of criminal law, as I will argue (4.3). Finally, I will motivate why such a limited fairness approach should nonetheless play a role in theorizing about criminal law and defend it against the recently emphasized objection in the literature that corrective sanctions are insufficiently condemnatory (4.4).

4.2 FBR: The Central Problems

I will discuss four central problems for FBR that have been raised in the literature and which newer accounts try to accommodate: First, FBR is said to fail as a comprehensive theory of criminalization as it does not capture all types of actions that we deem punishable as acts of unfairness. Second, FBR fails to capture the nature of the wrong that some crimes pose. We do not abhor rape and murder because those acts consist in a surplus of freedom for offenders (assuming that they do), but because these acts are simply morally abhorrent. Third, FBR fails to justify proportionality of punishment. Fourth, FBR fails to apply in real-world societies, as in most (or all) societies benefits and burdens are not distributed fairly in the first place (which FBR appears to presuppose).

Problem 1: FBR Is Not Comprehensive

FBR captures a certain range of crimes well. Take the example of tax fraud. Most citizens within a state pay taxes, which, among other things, are used to provide for public goods almost all citizens enjoy: Roads, hospitals, police, education, etc. But we can safely assume that many people would rather enjoy these benefits as free riders—meaning that they would love to have the freedom not to pay taxes while others do not have this freedom. There is a wide range of experimental evidence suggesting that people will cheat and free ride if given the chance to—at least as long as they think that their free riding will not be discovered (Mazar, Amir, and Ariely 2008). But interestingly, most people only cheat a little, possibly indicating that they do care about the laws governing the cooperative practice. This would suggest that tax frauds really do have an unfair benefit that others do not—both in the material benefit which results from not paying taxes, but more importantly for FBR in the benefit of enjoying less restrictions of their freedom while everyone else's freedom is restricted in that regard.

But the same does not seem to hold true for many other crimes, especially those that rest on *mala in se* wrongs (Boonin 2008, 122–24; Duff 2001, 22). Mala in se wrongs are such that their wrongness does not depend on them being forbidden by law—they simply are wrong according to the standards of a society's (or virtually everyone's) moral code, and therefore should be criminalized. Paradigmatic examples of such crimes are assault, rape, and murder.

According to the critic, FBR is committed to the view that people who assault, rape, or murder others are thereby gaining an unfair advantage over other citizens —a surplus in freedom which other citizens would like to also have. This seems to be an appalling consequence of the theory, as it implies that most citizens would rather go around and assault, rape, and murder their fellow citizens. It simply does not seem to be true that most people are burdened by laws restricting much of such behavior. Also, some crimes are not even possible to commit for many people. I am not able to hack into someone's bank account (without training to do so, anyway), and I therefore do not feel burdened by any laws prohibiting hacking (Boonin 2008, 124). Nonetheless, we want to criminalize such actions, even if they do not constitute unfair advantages for offenders. FBR thus fails as a comprehensive account of criminalization that explains why especially mala in se wrongs should be criminalized.

Problem 2: FBR Does Not Capture the Nature of (All) Wrongdoing

A closely related problem to the one mentioned above is that FBR fails to capture what we take to be wrong about mala in se wrongs. Even if it was true that people gain an unfair advantage by assaulting others (because we all would prefer to have the freedom to assault others, or because we benefit from having laws in the first place), unfairness does not capture all there is to the wrongness of such crimes—not even what is most important about them. Assault, rape, and murder are wrong not because they pose unfair advantages to offenders, but simply because they are awful things to do to another person. And as the framework of FBR fails to capture the correct reason why we are abhorred by such crimes, or at least all relevant reasons, it fails as a plausible theory of criminal law.

Problem 3: FBR Disregards Proportionality of Punishment

Proportionality of punishment is typically taken to be a cornerstone of good theories of punishment (Hirsch 1993). A theory that is committed to disproportionate punishment is seen to be at the very least in the need of explanation—at worst it has to be dismissed as implausible. The problem of disproportionate punishment can come in two related forms. First, if the sentence the theory recommends is disproportionate to the severity of the wrongdoing, and second, if the sentence is disproportionate to the sentence given to someone else who committed a similar offense.

Why would FBR be committed to disproportionate punishment? To better understand the objection, we need to distinguish between the *particular compliance* version of FBR, and the *general compliance* version (Dagger 2018). The particular compliance version takes crimes to be unfair because the other citizens refrain from committing the same kinds of acts. Tax fraud is unfair as other people pay their taxes. The general compliance version argues that crimes are unfair because of the compliance to a system of laws in general. The fact that any law is broken is unfair given that all citizens agree on burdens that are necessary for having a productive cooperation in society.

The objection regarding the particular compliance version of FBR states that because the severity of the wrongdoing is a function of its unfairness, crimes such as tax fraud might warrant harsher punishment than murder because many more people feel more burdened by having to pay taxes than by not being allowed to murder other citizens. According to the specific compliance approach we would thus have to punish crimes we consider to be less grave very severely, whilst punishing grave crimes leniently. Thereby, FBR violates an important dimension of the proportionality of punishment and needs to be dismissed on these grounds (Anderson 1999, 17).

The objection regarding the general compliance approach to FBR states that it is committed to the view that all crimes have to be punished equally, thereby violating another dimension of the proportionality requirement. If the claim of the general compliance approach is that crimes are unfair because they violate the general compliance with laws, thereby disrupting the fair balance of burdens, it seems that every crime equally violates the general compliance with the law (Boonin 2008, 124–26). FBR would then not be able to distinguish any crimes in terms of how much punishment they warrant, and the account should be dismissed on these grounds.

Problem 4: FBR Does Not Apply in the Real World

Murphy (1973) famously argued that while FBR provides the best theory of punishment, it is inapplicable in the real world (also Anderson 1997; Duff 2007; Heffernan and Kleinig 2000; Holroyd 2010; Tadros 2009). Murphy (1973, 231) correctly notes that there is at least one important empirical assumption in FBR which we need to take a closer look at: FBR seems to presuppose that the benefits and burdens in the society are distributed fairly in the first place. Duus-Otterström refers to this as the *Social-Injustice-Objection:*

> In order for us to say that a crime is a source of unfairness, the status quo ante must itself be fair. Therefore, in any society in which the status quo ante is unfair, some crimes will not be sources of unfairness. Since they are not sources of unfairness, then as far as FBR is concerned they should not be punished. (2017, 12)

Recall that FBR starts with the assumption of society as a cooperative venture for mutual advantage. Only when there indeed is *mutual* advantage, FBR applies, as it concerns the disruption of fair benefits and burdens. The theory would thus have no grounds to punish poor or otherwise disadvantaged offenders who would not be worse off without being part of the society. And however many crimes may be committed by members of disadvantaged social groups, the theory fails to apply to a wide range of crimes (for an overview of social and health determinants of criminality, see Caruso (2017)).

4.3 Corrective FBR to the Rescue

I have presented four problems for FBR. Proponents of the theory have reacted to these problems and tried to either dismiss them or show that their theory does not fall prey to the objections. The responses generally come from two different directions. The first is to focus on the general compliance version of FBR and try to respond to the objections within that framework (Dagger 2018). The second is to introduce a new perspective that understands some or all crimes as unfair disadvantages for victims, not unfair advantages for offenders (Duus-Otterström 2017). Both perspectives promise to solve the problems facing FBR.

In this section, I will argue that especially the victim-centered perspective helps to solve some of the problems facing FBR, but that it only does so when we adopt a corrective framework.

Revisiting FBR's Lack of Comprehensiveness

According to Duus-Otterström, shifting the focus of FBR to the unfair disadvantage for victims that result from wrongdoing will help to address the challenge of offering a comprehensive account of criminalization. In his version of FBR, some crimes are best understood as unfairly disadvantaging victims, rather than advantaging offenders. In the cooperative venture, every member is said to have certain rights granted in exchange for the limitation of their freedom. With this assumption of the fairness approach, we can explain why crimes unfairly disadvantage victims: Crimes take something away from them that they rightfully should have due to fairness considerations. With the help of this adjustment, we can begin our response to the problem of comprehensiveness.

Given the strategy outlined above, the proponent of FBR would now have to show that all crimes either unfairly advantage offenders or unfairly disadvantage victims (or even both). According to the lack-of-comprehensiveness-objection, FBR was especially struggling to capture mala in se wrongs as acts of unfairness. To see how the victim-centered approach improves the theory, Duus-Otterström asks us to imagine a situation where Adam assaults Bob. In such a situation,

> [the crime] could just as well be characterized as one where Bob has *lost* something which Adam has not lost since Bob, unlike Adam, does not enjoy the physical security that the legal order should provide. This is unfair, because it is unfair when someone contributes to the maintenance of the legal order without enjoying its fruits (and more unfair still, of course, if others are enjoying the fruits without contributing). (Duus-Otterström 2017, 8)

The response seems convincing on the face of it. As mala in se crimes often do not come with any advantages for the offender, but disadvantages for victims of wrongdoing, the adjusted version of FBR can now capture such crimes within the framework. The critic of FBR now would have to show that there are crimes which neither consist in advantages in freedom for offenders, nor unfair disadvantages of victims. If there are none, the response by the fairness theorist appears convincing (for a more detailed discussion of the possibility of victimless crimes, however, see Chapter 9).

This adjustment to FBR seems to solve the problem of comprehensiveness, but does it also justify punishment? I think that the main problem of the victim-centered perspective for the retributivist is that it is unclear how punishment helps in this picture. Duus-Otterström writes with regards to the example quoted above: "When Adam assaults Bob, he invades Bob's legally protected interests, and punishment can 'restore the equilibrium' by invading Adam's interests in turn—that, too, is a way to ensure that the benefit and burdens are equitably distributed" (2017, 9). He immediately mentions that a reviewer of his article raised the question how punishment helps with unfair disadvantages of the victim. More specifically, one could argue that punishment in such cases would merely be a levelling down response. The victim is made worse off, and as this constitutes an unfair disadvantage, the offender has to be made worse off as well, as to equalize the standings of both. This seems blatantly irrational—or does it? Duus-Otterström writes:

> The response is that punishment is arguably always about levelling down on a retributive account. Indeed, even when we are dealing with punishment that seeks to remove benefits, there is no point to punishment beyond the fact that it makes the offender worse off, thus restoring fairness. So there is nothing special about punishment of merely harmful crime, and to the extent we find it pointless it is because we assume that punishment must produce instrumental benefits such as crime prevention in order to be justified. (2017, 11)

Duus-Otterström is correct in pointing out that we have to be careful not to reject retributivism simply because we find levelling down to be unappealing in principle. The sole purpose of retributive punishment is to level the offender down because it is morally valuable to do so regardless of future consequences. But this response by Duus-Otterström misses the heart of the objection, I think. The problem does not simply consist in the immorality of levelling down the offender, it consists in the punishment's inability to address the victim's unfair disadvantage—which is what justifies the criminalization in the first place. Even after the punishment is carried out, the distribution of benefits and burdens will be mismatched, as the victim is below the line they ought rightfully to be on. If we take the victim's rights to be what we should care about in the first place, then focusing on the punishment of offenders appears to be an odd decision, as this does nothing to rectify the unfair distribution of burdens with regards to the victim. Punishment only helps to put both the victim and the offender equally below the just distribution of benefits and burdens. But it remains unclear why we should be more concerned about such a levelling down response rather than with lifting the victim up.

Corrective approaches to FBR have a better response at hand. If the wrong consists in the unfair disadvantage of the victim, then coercing the offender to correct the wrong done to the victim might be a viable strategy to re-balance the just distribution of benefits and burdens. So, punishment proponents need another argument if they want to make use of the victim-centered approach but still defend punishment rather than corrective approaches.

Indeed, punishment proponents do have another argument up their sleeves. As mentioned above, Dagger tried to account for several problems of FBR with the general compliance response. For the current discussion, the response states that the unfairness not only consists in the unfair disadvantage of the victim, but also in the unfair advantage of offenders who benefit from participating in a cooperative endeavor without themselves restricting their freedom in the same way as law-abiding citizens do. The victim-centered approach can thus be combined with the general compliance version and make the following argument in defense of punishment.

With the victim-centered perspective, we can show why mala in se crimes are unfair. By doing that, we illuminate why the unfair disadvantage of the victim needs to be corrected. But beyond that—the retributivist now argues—offenders also deserve to be made additionally worse-off as they took advantage of the general system of cooperation. The correct response to the wrongdoing should thus be the punishment of the offender and additional compensation for the victim. By doing that, we raise victims to their rightful standing, and lower offenders to theirs. The retributivist can thus explain both the necessity of punishment and defend FBR against the comprehensiveness objection.

This response by the retributivist, however, is not compelling. The general compliance view does not take a stand on how much the offender should be punished. Every crime similarly takes advantage of the general systems of laws (we will discuss that in more detail below when addressing the proportionality objection). Can we pinpoint the amount of punishment with reference to how much the victim has been disadvantaged? No, that will not work. In the framework just laid out, the severity of the victim's disadvantage is used to explain how much restitution they are owed, not how much punishment offenders deserve. We simply cannot extrapolate the one from the other.

The corrective approach, however, can do so. It can do so, because it understands the corrective action to be determined by how much the victim has been disadvantaged. The graver the disadvantage for the victim, the graver the corrective action has to be in order to restore victims to the level they should rightfully enjoy.

But if that is my argument, why should offenders be involved in the first place? Why not simply compensate victims via state taxes, an insurance, or donations (Barnett 1977)? If offenders do not gain an unfair advantage, why make them responsible for repairing the harm within the fairness rationale?

The answer to that question depends on what we take the unfairness to consist in precisely. Someone might propose that the crime simply is the violation of the property right (broadly understood) which can be compensated from a fund or a tax. If that is your understanding of what is unfair about wrongdoing, then there really is no issue with compensation. But my guess is that most people will have a more nuanced account of wrongdoing. Wrongdoing is not like a hurricane that damages your house and after which you simply turn to your insurance company for reimbursement of the loss. Rather, to understand wrongdoing properly, it is crucial to bring the offender into the picture (Radzik 2009, 46–50). A response to a wrongdoing that simply ignores the role of the offender does not seem to be what we expect from an adequate response to wrongdoing. And if that is indeed a more adequate understanding of wrongdoing, corrective fairness approaches can explain why we should involve the offender rather than go for compensation alone. We need restitution or reparation (not compensation) because only such sanctions adequately acknowledge the unfair disadvantage as a wrong done to the victim.

Revisiting FBR's Mischaracterization of What Is Wrong about *Mala in Se* Crimes

I have just argued that the comprehensiveness objection can be accounted for if we adopt a victim-centered perspective within FBR and corrective approaches to address the wrongdoing. But can the same strategy address the second objection? It states that FBR gets the nature of crimes wrong. In short: FBR mischaracterizes the wrongness of mala in se crimes. Assault, rape, and murder are not primarily wrong because they involve unfairness, but because they are simply horrible things to do to another human being.

Dagger refers to this problem as the *irrelevance objection*. He offers two solutions. The first tries to paint a different picture of unfair crimes than the critic does. Assault is not simply unfair, but it can even impair a victim's ability to continue enjoying the fruits of the cooperative practice:

> The tax evader takes unfair advantage of many people, but her offense typically does not make it difficult for them to continue doing their part in the cooperative practice. With the rapist, the murderer, and the batterer, however, the offender has done something that makes it difficult or even impossible for his victim to contribute further to the ongoing cooperative endeavor. (2018, 192)

Dagger here attempts to address the mischaracterization objection by suggesting that FBR can acknowledge the wrongfulness of mala in se crimes as they not only disadvantage the victim unfairly, but also burden them in their ability to further participate in the cooperative endeavor.

I think that it is the right move to acknowledge the victim-centered perspective, but Dagger's description still seems off in two regards. First, it does not seem to be true in all cases that mala in se crimes result in the victim's inability to "contribut[e] further to the ongoing cooperative endeavor" (2018, 192). Even though Dagger might be right in many instances, victims of battery could still be perfectly fine to continue in the cooperative effort directly after the wrongdoing without the wrong being less severe because of that. The severity of the wrongdoing and the ability to contribute to the cooperative effort might overlap, but the severity does not seem to be a function of the ability to contribute to the cooperative endeavor.

More importantly, and this is the second worry, the response might not help to solve the problem at all. The critic can still press that FBR mischaracterizes what makes certain wrongs so heinous. It is certainly not, the critic might say, the fact that victims are not able to continue doing their part in the cooperative practice. We do not solely care that victims can continue to do their part (even though that certainly is important)—we also (and maybe more importantly) care about the fact that their moral integrity was gruesomely violated. Even if we phrase the understanding of the wrong in terms of the ability to continue in the cooperative endeavor, the response seems misplaced.

Dagger anticipates that his "direct response" will not fully satisfy critics. He presents a second way to respond to what he calls the irrelevance objection:

> [W]e should expect that the lawmakers and the people alike will insist that offenses must be graded according to the public's view of their gravity. If all offenses are treated in the identical way—with a fine of 100 Euros for the murderer and the traffic offender alike, for example, or lifetime imprisonment for both of them—then those subject to the law are likely to lose their regard for the law and for the cooperative practice it underpins. Indirectly, then, the desire to maintain a cooperative practice grounded in fair play requires that some crimes be treated as much more grave than others, even if their offensiveness is not entirely or even mainly a matter of their unfairness. (2018, 194)

Dagger uses this consideration to address the mischaracterization objection, but it rather sounds like a defense against the proportionality objection (to which we will return below). Nonetheless, let us take the response seriously as one against the mischaracterization objection.

The argument Dagger presents here presses the point that for the cooperative endeavor to work—and especially for public policy to work—we need to take into account the intuitive demands of the members of the cooperative enterprise. The characterization of mala in se crimes as especially heinous is thus not directly a function of their unfairness, but rather a function of people's intuitive reactions to wrongdoing. People would be appalled if shoplifters were to be punished to the same extent that murderers are. And because taking into account the intuitive demands of people in a cooperative venture matters for its success, the fairness rationale can characterize why mala in se crimes are especially gruesome.

But this response does not help after all. As Dagger himself agrees, this strategy only gives indirect support to FBR. Even worse, what FBR was tasked to do is to answer to the objection that we intuitively do not think that mala in se crimes are wrong in virtue of them being unfair. His response that we should conceive of such crimes as especially heinous because people do so is not a response to the problem at all. He still does not have a theory to describe what the heinousness consists in, at least as long as we think that they are not only a function of people thinking that they are heinous.

Dagger seems to acknowledge this, after all. He writes that his response "may not be enough to give us a complete explanation of why some crimes are more heinous than others, but it provides a significant part of the explanation" (2018, 193). As argued above, I disagree that the response entails a significant part of the explanation. Nonetheless, I think that it is the correct move to accept that the fairness rationale simply is not the full story about the wrongfulness of mala in se crimes. But as I will argue later, this need not be a reason to dismiss FBR completely.

Revisiting FBR's Disregard for the Proportionality of Punishment

As mentioned above, both the particular and the general compliance approach appear to disregard proportionality of punishment. In the particular compliance version, unfairness is a function of how much the law restrains other individuals, and thus tax fraud turns out to be a graver wrong than murder. In the general compliance version, all crimes are unfair because they violate the system of cooperation that consists in the acceptance of the general burden to refrain from certain actions. In that version, all crimes are equally violations of the general restriction to respect the benefits and burdens and would thus warrant the same amount of punishment for all crimes (whatever universally applied punishment this would entail).

Dagger offers two responses to this problem from the view of the general compliance version (2018, 189–90)—as nobody defends the particular compliance version, we can ignore it in the following. I will go through them in turn.

The first strategy to defend FBR points to the well-known distinction between the definition of punishment, the aim of punishment, and the question whom and how much to punish (Hart 2008, 4). Dagger writes:

> It is, after all, not uncommon to face a situation in which we are convinced that someone did wrong and deserves punishment, yet we are not at all sure of what his punishment should be. Even when there are reasonably clear guidelines for the punishment this kind of offense typically warrants, there may well be special or individual circumstances that call into question the fairness of such "typical" treatment. In such cases, the desire to play fair does not lead directly to a certain sentence. (2018, 190)

Even though it remains a bit unclear how this response helps in detail, a charitable interpretation in my view is that he claims that it is okay for approaches to punishment not to tell the whole story regarding the offender's sentence. That seems to be true. But the objection was that FBR does take a stand on the matter and that the stand involves punishing offenders equally for different crimes. A reasonable way in which Dagger's response helps FBR would be to read it as saying that FBR sometimes does not take a stand on proportionality. But that response would simply ignore the objection. Dagger does not motivate why the critic is wrong about FBR's commitment to amounts of punishment. It is true that we can conceive of FBR as a hybrid theory that only answers the question whom we should punish, but not how much. But if that is the answer, Dagger would have to spell such an account out. As the previous discussion has shown, he does seem to think that FBR has something to say about proportionality. His second response hints at such a move, so let us take a look at whether it helps.

The second response is to point to the pluralistic nature of fair-play theories in general. I have mostly talked about fairness-based retributivism (FBR), but the theory need not be restricted to the retributive principle—consequentialist concerns might also matter for the fairness theory. Dagger even argues that consequentialist concerns are crucial for fairness theories of punishment. After all, the perpetuation of the cooperative venture is valuable because people benefit from living in such a system—which clearly introduces consequentialist concerns. Dagger goes on to argue that "[p]unishing fairly thus requires us to punish with an eye to maintaining fair play under the rule of law, which in turn requires us to consider how serious a threat a particular offense poses to the rule" (2018, 190).

The problem with this response is that Dagger stops short of showing that the types of punishment that guarantee the successful continuation of the cooperative venture completely overlap with the proportionality demands that should be met. Maybe the consequentialist concerns give us initial reasons to respond to graver crimes with severer punishment, as those crimes typically are very dangerous to the cooperative endeavor as such. But this response replaces the initial problem with another. It could also be beneficial for the continuation of society from a consequentialist perspective to punish minor wrongs disproportionally harshly. If theft is rampant, for example, there might be a consequentialist case to be made for harsh punishment of property offenses. By introducing the consequentialist perspective, Dagger only replaces the proportionality worry from the perspective of FBR with the proportionality worry from the perspective of consequentialism. As long as he does not show that consequentialist concerns guarantee proportional punishment, which is questionable to say the least, the general objection still stands.

Can we save FBR from the proportionality objection from the perspective of the corrective approach? Only partly, I think. The victim-centered approach indeed helps to explain why some crimes are worse than others. Victims of graver wrongdoings are more heavily disadvantaged with regards to the rights which should be protected. For this argument to convince, we have to accept that an attack on the bodily integrity of a person (assault or battery) is more disadvantageous within the fairness rationale than a simple attack on property rights (theft). There may be two ways to motivate this claim.

First, robbery—in comparison to theft—violates several rights that should be protected *qua* being member of the cooperative practice. Whereas theft only violates material property rights, robbery also violates the right to bodily integrity. As more rights are violated, the unfair disadvantage for the victim is graver and thus a severer corrective sentence is necessary. The second strategy is to argue that certain violations of rights are worse than others. To show this within the fairness rationale, one would have to argue that some crimes are worse disadvantages than others. Dagger proposed a similar strategy in response to the irrelevance objection. Some crimes seem to undermine our ability to enjoy the benefits of the cooperative endeavor, especially those crimes that have lasting physical and psychological consequences for people, and as such require severer corrective sentences.

But this response runs into a similar objection I introduced in the discussion concerning the irrelevance objection. It does not seem to be true that the wrongness of an actions is solely a function of its unfairness, e. g., the capacity to continue in the cooperative venture. Fairness can thus broadly explain why severer crimes indeed often warrant severer sanctions—but it is questionable that such an account will nicely overlap with a retributive proportionality principle. There will likely be cases in which victims are fine to continue in the cooperative endeavor after crimes such as assault, and the fairness theorist would then lack the tools to describe why such crimes nonetheless warrant severer sentences. To arrive at a corrective account that satisfies proportionality demands, we thus cannot solely rely on the fairness rationale.

FBR in an Unjust World

Not many will find it hard to belief that the benefits and burdens in most of the currently existing societies are not distributed fairly (Credit Suisse Research Institute 2021). Murphy took this concern to undermine FBR, even though, in his view, it is the strongest justification of punishment that has been offered in the literature. Why does it undermine FBR? If the benefits and burdens are not distributed fairly in the first place, then the offender may not gain an unfair advantage by committing a crime. In the worst case, offenders might be better off without the society in its current state, which would make their crime not advantageous with regards to a society where the benefits and burdens would be distributed fairly. Phrasing it in terms of the debt-to-society view: As offenders do not benefit from society, they do not owe other participants anything in terms of law-abidingness.

One could object that the fairness account is supposed to work as an ideal theory and should thus ignore these empirical conundrums. But we do not need to join the critique of ideal theory to find this unappealing (Mills 2005; O'Neill 1996; Simmons 2010). As Murphy emphasizes, FBR typically does make empirical assumptions and it thus cannot ignore those. If it assumes the just distribution of benefits and burdens, it either is not applicable to most societies (which is not good for any ethical theory), or the empirical facts need to be addressed by the theory.

But the proponent of FBR has several responses to the objection at their disposal. Dagger for example emphasizes that

> [t]here must be, of course, some degree of cooperation among people, some cooperative threshold they must have crossed—before we can properly deem them to be engaged in a cooperative practice, but it need not be complete and unfailing cooperation. Indeed, if such a level of unanimous cooperation were ever attained, there would be little need for the principle of fair play. Between the cooperative threshold at one end, however, and complete cooperation at the other, there will be ample room for the principle of fair play to do its critical and aspirational work, with much more to be done in some times and places than in others. (2018, 198)

His point has appeal. It is true that we cannot describe something as a cooperative venture in the relevant sense if some people are simply exploited. Exploited people, in this picture, do not owe anything to their exploiters in the name of fairness. But practices can be cooperative even if they are not completely fair.

What Dagger does not tell us, though, is whether diminished fairness also impacts the wrongfulness of the crime. He could take either of two directions. First, he could argue that starting from a certain threshold of fairness, people have full obligations to obey the law, which would justify punishment in every case of wrongdoing committed by a person above that threshold. Or he could say that the obligation to obey the law is weaker or stronger depending on how just the cooperation is. Both options have their problems.

The first response seems to underestimate the power of the social injustice objection. If some (potentially low) threshold of just cooperation suffices to justify the imposition of punishment, then many of today's Western criminal law institutions might be sufficiently just (for most people), as to justify punishment. This seems to disregard the criminological facts that many offenders come from socially underprivileged classes (Caruso 2017). There really seems to be an important problem with that fact. Arguing that the status of socially disadvantaged citizens in the cooperative scheme is sufficiently fair thus appears to disregard the very point of the criticism. The fairness theorist would then need a compelling argument for a threshold that takes the objection seriously while still being applicable to the real world.

The second response implies practical problems: Would the punishment have to be diminished in cases of unjust (but not too unjust) distributions of benefits and burden—and if so, do we need to take this into account for every single crime? Things would get complicated (and costly) if for every crime, judges would have to determine the social circumstances of the offender. They would then have to adjust the length and type of the sentence to the injustice of the offender's circumstances. This might not pose a principled problem, but certainly a practical one that needs to be taken seriously.

Another response to the problem of unjust societies points to the fact that offenders who commit crimes against equally disadvantaged victims might still take an unfair advantage (Dagger 2018, 200; Matravers 2014). Even if offenders do not owe those who are better off anything, they might still owe other disadvantaged people their law-abidingness. But this defense against the objection seems to be off. The fact that offenders do not owe society anything is not a function of their victims being advantaged or not. Rather, the fact that offenders do not owe anything to other people in their society is a function of the unjust distribution of benefits and burdens with regards to the offender. If that is true, the response fails because the social injustice objection does not state that people do not owe anything to those in society who are well-off, but that they do not owe anyone anything in terms of law-abidingness, as they do not benefit from the cooperative venture.

A third response is offered by Duus-Otterström. He focuses on what he calls the narrow distributive view of benefits and burdens and argues that people generally enjoy some benefits, while they lack others. Whenever they commit crimes against laws whose protection they enjoy, they are liable to punishment or corrective sanctions according to FBR:

> Punishing thieves, for instance, is seen necessary to ensure that the benefits and burdens specifically *of the laws regulating property offenses* are fairly distributed. Since this view does not require that the benefits and burdens of social cooperation in general are fairly distributed, it is not vulnerable to the objection that an offender might be unfairly disadvantaged all things considered. Thieves who enjoy the safety of their own possessions without respecting other's in turn, this view holds, are unfairly advantaged *with respect to the law against theft* even though their income and wealth are lower than they should be. In stealing, they have the benefits of the system in this particular regard without accepting the burdens, and punishment ensures that those benefits and burdens are distributed equitably. (Duus-Otterström 2017: 13 f.)

This response has some initial plausibility. A person can have their right to protection of their property violated while their right to bodily integrity is still properly guaranteed. If that is the case, said person would still be liable for crimes against the bodily integrity of another person because they themselves enjoy the benefit of the practice that ensures that right.

There are, however, two problems with this response. First of all, there will still be ample cases in which punishment will not be justified even though crimes have been committed. It is unclear how much the supposed shortcoming of the theory should bother us here. Maybe it is simply true that we are not morally justified in punishing disadvantaged members of the community, or at least not as much as we do others. But that does not seem to be completely convincing. Even in cases where the property rights of the offender are not respected, many will still think that it is wrong for the offender to steal from others—or, at least, to assault, rape, and murder others. In order to be able to capture the wrongness in such cases, FBR then needs to be supplemented by other approaches to explain the wrongness of such actions despite social disadvantages of the wrongdoer.

The second problem of the response is that the disadvantages in many cases cannot be as neatly separated as Duus-Otterström would like them to be for the narrow distributive view to work. If a certain neighborhood is not protected by the police, then this entails that several of their rights are not protected. They are more likely to be the direct victim of assault, but also of non-violent theft or other crimes. We thus cannot neatly categorize disadvantaged people into which laws they have a duty to obey and which they do not have to obey—which would render the response useless for its application.

So, what to do with the social injustice objection? The most plausible response is, I think, to accept it to a certain degree. FBR really fails to explain why people ought to be punished if benefits and burdens are distributed unfairly. It is unclear, though, whether this is a vice or a virtue. It would be implausible, too, if the theory were completely insensitive to the injustices in the society and also the criminological observation that socially disadvantaged people are relatively more likely to commit offenses.

Nonetheless, we still want to be able to say that even someone who comes from such a disadvantaged social background did something wrong when they assaulted another person. The fairness theory, however, does not offer the adequate tools to describe the wrongness of offenses committed by disadvantaged offenders adequately, as the theory does not give a full account of what makes some wrongs so heinous.

* * *

I have argued that the new responses to the problems for FBR are only partly convincing. FBR still mischaracterizes what is wrong about many mala in se crimes. Furthermore, it cannot guarantee proportionality of punishment in all cases—even though the victim-centered perspective has been an improvement in that regard. Also, it is questionable whether the theory is applicable to real-world scenarios where benefits and burdens are not distributed fairly in the first place. Lastly, I have argued that—where plausible—the fairness rationale is better conceived of as a corrective theory, not a punitive one.

What conclusion should we draw from these mixed results regarding the plausibility of the fairness theory? My suggestion is that the best way to conclude this discussion is to accept fairness as an important dimension of criminal law, one that favors corrective justice, but at the same time one that has to be supplemented by other moral considerations that ground criminalization. The other chapters will offer defenses of these other motives that plausibly also play an important role in theorizing about criminal law besides fairness considerations.

In the last section, I want to address two concerns regarding what I have argued until now. The first one addresses the role of fairness in criminal law. If, as I have just argued, fairness cannot give us a full account of criminal law, why should it not be simply dismissed? Here, I will argue that even though fairness is not the whole picture, it is an important part of a comprehensive approach to wrongdoing. Then, I will address a concern that has been voiced against corrective fairness approaches as defended in this chapter. The criticism states that corrective fairness accounts are insufficient in their expressive dimension (an objection which, as noted in Chapter 2, will be a steadfast companion throughout this book).

4.4 The Benefits of Fairness Norms and the Condemnation Objection

In this section, I want to motivate why we should care about fairness norms even if the fairness rationale on its own does not offer a comprehensive approach to criminal law. Also, I want to respond to an objection by fairness theorists themselves which was raised against corrective fairness theories as I defended them here.

Why Care about Fairness If It Fails as a Comprehensive Theory?

I have argued that even with the victim-centered and corrective approach to fairness, the success of the theory is limited. It can plausibly explain why all crimes are crimes of unfairness, but it does not give the full picture of wrongness because especially mala in se wrongs are more than just unfair. It does a decent job accounting for proportionality of sentences but cannot guarantee it in all cases.

Why not simply dismiss the fairness rationale for theorizing in criminal law if that is the best the theory can do? If you are looking for a single rationale (be it backward- or forward-looking) to justify punishment, then you should indeed reject the fairness rationale as it fails to provide such an account. Such monistic attempts to justify punishment, however, are not promising as I will argue in Chapter 8 of this book.

The alternative is to show that fairness should at least be part of a pluralistic theory of criminal law. For that, we need to motivate why the state should be concerned with promoting fairness at all. It might seem intuitive to say that the state has the duty to promote fairness, but without further argument as to why this should be the case, critics cannot be persuaded by the claim. There might be viable arguments that fairness is intrinsically valuable—but in this section I want to give a more functional argument as to why the state should promote and defend fairness norms.

In a nutshell, my argument is that fairness norms are useful for societies such as ours, and the state thus has prudential reasons to protect fairness norms by not letting them go unsanctioned. Why should fairness norms be so important in our society? Fairness norms stabilize cooperation within market societies such as ours that are very large, often have one-off interactions, and consists of many people that do not know each other well. Fairness norms here can mean a variety of things. On the one hand, they concern upholding reciprocity. That is, people should not be free riders and benefit from cooperation without doing their own part. But fairness also concerns the distribution of resources. In economic games, offering just 1 dollar out of 10 is considered to be unfair—and the same generalize to other situations where the distribution of resources is concerned. The empirical part of this argument claims that fairness norms aimed at preventing free riders and allocating resources in a specific manner are beneficial to market societies.

The empirical dimension of this argument can be split in two separate claims. First, market societies are associated with a stronger adherence to fairness norms as described above than non-market societies. That is not to say that fairness norm only exists in market societies. On the one hand, market societies come in degrees, and the adherence to fairness norms appears to correlate with the degree to which markets are prevalent in societies, as we will see below. On the other hand, almost all societies about which we have some information show at least some adherence to fairness norms, as anthropologists and economists suggest (Curry, Mullins, and Whitehouse 2019; Fehr and Fischbacher 2004; Henrich 2009; Henrich et al. 2006; Henrich 2016; Seip, Dijk, and Rotteveel 2014; Marlowe et al. 2008)—at least in the minimal sense that free riders ought to be punished, or sometimes that victims of unfair behavior should be compensated (Chavez and Bicchieri 2013; Doorn, Zeelenberg, and Breugelmans 2018; FeldmanHall et al. 2014; Heffner and FeldmanHall 2019; Lotz et al. 2011; Doorn et al. 2018). Another caveat is that we have some evidence to believe that preferences for fairness can be seen early in human development (McAuliffe, Jordan, and Warneken 2015; McAuliffe et al. 2017; Li et al. 2016; Starmans, Sheskin, and Bloom 2017), potentially suggesting a non-cultural factor. The only claim I want to make here is that the stronger the market integration is, the stronger adherence to, and protection of, fairness norms becomes.

The second empirical claim is that these fairness norms help facilitate cooperation in such societies—which is likely why such norms have persevered.

As for the first empirical claim, Joseph Henrich reports data from a study investigating the adherence to conditional cooperation, that is, investment of own resources in group projects depending on the money partners are willing to give. He finds that people from communities which are closer to markets have significantly higher conditional cooperation behavior (Henrich 2020, chap. 9; Rustagi, Engel, and Kosfeld 2010). These differences come in degree, of course. Researchers found that among people who are integrated into market societies, as opposed to those who are not integrated into market societies, the adherence to impersonal fairness norms is significantly higher. Impersonal fairness norms were measured with how much money was offered by participants in economic games such as the Ultimatum Game or Dictator Game. While people who did not come from market integrated societies offered around 25 % of their available money, and almost never rejected offers even when these were unjust according to the current Western standard of fairness, people from market societies offered closer to half of their money in ultimatum games and rejected unfair offers more often (Henrich 2020, chap. 9).

Such norms have tangible benefits. In the cooperation study just mentioned, researchers observed that people from market communities and thus higher conditional cooperation norms have a higher success rate in the forming of associations to regulate, for example, timber extractions. Long term, these individuals were more successful in protecting a designated forest area than individuals from non-market communities (Henrich 2020, chap. 9).

On a more abstract level, we should expect fairness norms to be beneficial to cooperation as they reduce uncertainty and costs such as checking whether a specific person one interacts with is actually trustworthy (Anomaly 2017). The more trust we can have in the adherence to specific fairness norms, the less resources we have to spend on making sure that cooperation succeeds. Adherence to such norms is of course always limited and might need additional extrinsic motivation as is provided by criminal sanctions. But the more such norms are respected independent of intervention, the better cooperation works (see also the game theoretic motivation why such norms might help with cooperation and productivity, Axelrod and Hamilton 1981). Fairness norms in the broadest sense have been described as a central catalyst for cooperation in non-kin-based communities by several authors (Curry 2016; Henrich 2016; 2020; Tomasello 2016).

As for the normative claim, I am not sure how much resistance there will be to the thesis that it is good for the state to promote fairness norms given that these will stabilize cooperation and further productivity. The plausibility of this claim will of course depend on the costs of enforcing these norms, but as I am not defending punishment in order to protect fairness norms, but instead I am defending corrective sanctions, I think that the costs are relatively low and thus all-things-considered justified. Also, I do not want to say that there is no intrinsic justification for defending fairness norms. I am not sure whether I find such arguments convincing, but if they were, they would only add further strength to the claim that the state has good reasons to protect fairness norms by imposing corrective sanctions on those who break these norms.

Fairness and Condemnation

Richard Dagger (2018) has stressed the objection that purely corrective approaches fail to communicate the adequate censure which the criminal law should communicate. As described in Chapter 2, one of the crucial characteristics of punishment is that it expresses condemnation of the wrongdoing. For communicative theories of punishment, as we will see in the next chapter, communicating censure through punishment is even a crucial part of its justification.

I doubt that the critic wants to say that making someone repair the harm done to a victim after a wrongful action is completely morally neutral (Boonin 2008, 267–68). Coercing someone to repair harm typically expresses that the offender should not have done what they did. But according to Dagger, this is not the type of censure that the criminal law ought to aim for:

> There is, after all, a significant difference between *disapproval*, on the one hand, and *censure* or *condemnation*, on the other. You may disapprove of the way I dress or of my taste in music or my attempts at humor without condemning or censuring me—you may simply shake your head and walk away, for example. In similar fashion, society may express its disapproval of my conduct by requiring me to make restitution to those I have injured without condemning that conduct or censuring me when it does so. To convey such condemnation or censure—the terms Duff uses in connection with the communicative aspect of punishment—is to move beyond pure restitution to some form of punishment. (2018, 242–43)

Let us assume for the sake of the discussion that the state's response to criminal wrongdoing indeed should be condemnatory—Dagger is in good company in thinking so, and I happen to agree with this claim. To assess whether corrective theories have a problem here, we need to ask whether it is true that punitive sanctions express something that is categorically different from what corrective sanctions express.

Let us first try to better grasp the proposed distinction. Dagger's first assumption seems to be on point: We disapprove of certain things without condemning them. I disapprove of certain music genres while I in no way condemn people who produce the music or listen to it. Such differences have practical importance. I do not blame people who engage in actions that I disapprove of—but I likely blame those who do something that I condemn. These distinctions will not always be clear-cut. We can observe many people who clearly condemn certain music genres and people who produce the respective music.[7] With regards to some actions, I might be somewhere between disapproval and condemnation. But as long as there is an interesting difference to be captured, Dagger's argument can proceed.

We granted that the state ought to condemn offenders, and that there is a difference between condemning someone and disapproving of something or someone. The crucial point that remains to be analyzed, then, is whether Dagger is right in saying that, first, enforced restitution only expresses disapproval, and second, that only state punishment expresses condemnation in response to criminal wrongdoing. I will argue that both claims are wrong.

What does Dagger say in favor of the first claim? Not much, I think. He mainly relies on his intuition that restitution does not express condemnation. He writes that "society may express its disapproval of my conduct by requiring me to make restitution to those I have injured without condemning that conduct or censuring me when it does so" (Dagger 2018, 242) and in response to Boonin's defense of restitution-as-condemnation he writes that we "can either hold that the expression of mere disapproval is sufficient, [which we rejected above], or he will have to abandon pure restitution in favor of a form of restitution with an openly punitive aspect" (Dagger 2018, 243).

So, according to Dagger, pure restitution is not condemnatory, and when we make restitution condemnatory, we need to make it punitive. Unfortunately, Dagger simply goes on to another objection against purely corrective approaches without elaborating on this central point of his. Furthermore, Boonin does not use the distinction between disapproval and condemnation. He simply writes about "reprobation" (Boonin 2008, 68). There is thus no reason to think that Dagger's argument is convincing—at least independent of his intuition that restitution only seems to express disapproval. To me, and probably also to other corrective theorists, coerced restitution seems to express exactly what the critic is after. Without further explicit argument by the critic, there is no reason to think that there is a problem for corrective theories to solve.

To clarify this point of conflicting intuitions, we can take a look at an example by Boonin. He asks us to imagine a case where a child steals a toy from another child, and the father makes the first child give back the toy. Broadly speaking, this is coercion compatible with the corrective rationale. What is more, the coer-

---

7 Thanks to Eddy Nahmias for the pointer.

cion expresses that the child ought not have stolen the toy—it expresses that it was not their right to do so. Boonin writes:

> And just as clearly, it seems to me, [the father's] son would recognize that in forcing him to return the toy, his father was telling him that he had no right to take the toy in the first place. After all, if [the father's] son was entitled to take the toy in the first place, wouldn't it follow that [the father] was not entitled to force him to return it? (Boonin 2008, 268)

If it is true that coercing someone to give something back expresses that the person had no right to act in such ways in the first place, corrective sanctions seem to be condemning rather than disapproving. When we tell the child that they should give back the toy, we do not express a (mere) preference as in the example of music which we disapprove of. The critic's intuition here is that such an explanation does not capture our experience properly. But by coercing someone to adhere to a corrective sanction, we deny that the wrongdoer had the right to act in such a way in the first place. It thus seems far more fitting to see a corrective sanction as expressing condemnation rather than disapproval. The father might not need to express blame or threats of punishment for pedagogical reasons, but this does not make the demand to give back the toy mere disapproval. Coercing to give the toy back is not like saying "your taste in music is bad." It expresses something far stronger: Condemnation. If Boonin's description of the expressive dimension is correct, it thus satisfies Dagger's condemnation requirement.

You might wonder whether I am missing something, though. It seems obvious that coerced restitution expresses something different than punishment, at least in degree. This leads us to Dagger's second claim. Even if we grant the critic that corrective sanctions also express condemnation, only punishment expresses adequate condemnation. We thus still need punishment even though corrective sanctions are able to express some form of condemnation.

This response runs into the conventionality-of-punishment objection (Hanna 2008). The objection states that people only think that the way they express condemnation is adequate because they have a convention in society to do so. But there is no objective fact that would make this correct.

The conventionality of how we express condemnation can be clarified when we take a historical or cross-cultural perspective. Many states in the past condemned murder by brutally torturing offenders to death, and some do so even today. But even disregarding these very brutal punishments, we can observe a vast difference in how states express condemnation for murder. While many of the U.S. states allow for capital punishment, Norway sentences murderers to around 20 years in prison; these prisons, compared to other countries, are fairly comfortable. Still, both countries will likely claim that the way they express condemnation for the offenses is adequate.

These examples suggest that condemnation is at least to a degree conventional. This then offers grounds to reject Dagger's second claim. If our perception of adequate condemnation is dependent on cultural circumstances, then there is no reason to think that it is impossible to have a convention of adequate condemnation with corrective sanctions; except if Dagger has an argument for the objectivity of condemnation. But such an argument cannot be found in his account.

The objection against corrective approaches can also take a more practical turn. The critic might admit that it is possible to have a convention which expresses adequate condemnation with corrective sanctions, but that is not our society, and there is no reason to think that we can get there.

But this does not seem convincing from a moral perspective. At best, I think, this would give us reasons to try to adopt corrective condemnation in small steps with incremental policy changes. But even that objection does not seem completely convincing. As I argue in Chapter 6 in more detail, victims seem more concerned with acknowledgment, empowerment in the criminal process, and adequate reparations rather than pure punishment. From a policy perspective, advertising with "no more punishment" likely will not make many people, especially conservatives, happy, but this seems more of a marketing issue rather than a moral one. We can sell the corrective condemnatory approach as taking victim's rights seriously and thus as superior to purely punitive condemnation. Such a strategy might be conducive to achieving more acceptance of corrective approaches among the public.[8]

Either way, it seems that the objection based on the claim that corrective sanctions are not condemnatory enough fails. There is no convincing reason to think that corrective sanctions do not express condemnation, and there is also no good reason to think that punitive condemnation is objectively more adequate than corrective condemnation. Also, practical concerns with corrective condemnation can be accounted for.

4.5 Conclusion

I have argued that FBR fails to plausibly justify punishment, but that a victim-centered corrective fairness approach can account for many of the problems that FBR

---

[8] See Chapter 9 for a more detailed discussion of the objection that corrective theories clash with the public's demand for punishment.

faced. Nonetheless, not all of the problems can be accounted for successfully because there is more to wrongdoing than merely its unfairness, even on the victim-centered approach. Nonetheless, we should include a corrective and victim-centered fairness approach into a pluralistic approach to criminal law, as it captures something that almost all people take to be important when confronting criminal wrongdoing.

Chapter 5
Penance and Censure

> It's not about money. It's about sending a message.
>
> Joker, *The Dark Knight* (2008)

5.1 Introduction

Communicative theories of punishment have been on the rise in the recent debate (Bennett 2008; Duff 2001; 2003; Günther 2014; Lee 2016; Primoratz 1989; Wringe 2016). Not only in philosophy has this approach received more attention, but recent empirical research also supports the idea that punishment, apologies, and reparation all have an important communicative function (Cushman, Sarin, and Ho 2022; Bilz 2016; Funk, McGeer, and Gollwitzer 2014; Gollwitzer and Denzler 2009; Gollwitzer, Meder, and Schmitt 2011; Nahmias and Aharoni 2017; Ohtsubo et al. 2018; Sarin et al. 2021). The theory does seem to strike a very important chord in people's intuitions that offenders should be censured for their wrongdoing—and that we as a society need to communicate condemnation of their actions.

In this chapter, I want to take a closer look at three variations of communicative theories. The first has been dubbed the "penance approach" and is mostly associated with some of the arguments that Antony Duff (2001; 2003) presented, but which other authors also picked up or developed independent of Duff's approach (Garvey 1999; 2003; Radzik 2009; Lee 2016). The central idea for the penance approach is to argue that offenders ought to undergo some form of secular penance, and that a punitive sanction offers the most adequate way of doing so.

The second version of communicative theories lays aside the idea of penance and merely argues that censuring offenders is intrinsically valuable and should therefore be done in the form of punishment by the state. Call this communicative retributivism. According to this version of communicative theories, offenders deserve to be censured for their wrongdoing—closely following the retributive rationale here—and the state should punish offenders in order to express the intrinsically valuable condemnation towards the offender.

For a third variation, I will look at consequentialist and epistemic arguments for the communicative theory. Here, the idea is that offenders should be censured, and that censure should be punitive because of its beneficial consequences or because it gives us reliable epistemic indicators that the censure was successfully communicated.

There are of course also theories that combine these different approaches. But for this chapter, it will be useful to analytically distinguish between the different claims and see for each one individually whether they succeed in justifying criminal punishment.

I will go through these three versions in turn. In the next section (5.2.), I discuss the basic idea of the penance approach and offer three reasons why we should be hesitant to embrace it. First, it is unclear whether aiming at the penance of the offender is a legitimate aim of criminal law. Critics have objected that such a value should not be the concern of liberal states. Second, if penance is the aim of criminal law, we cannot guarantee the proportionality of punishment. To undergo adequate penance, some offenders might require harsher sanctions than others for the same wrongdoings. This, however, is unacceptable according to the objection.

I will argue that both objections raise important worries, but do not necessarily show that we should completely disregard penance as a value for criminal law. The more important problem is a different one. Penance theorists need to convince us that penance requires punishment. Here lies the problem. A retributive account of penance would elegantly explain why punishment is necessary for penance, but it fails on independent grounds. A consequentialist penance account needs to give evidence that punishment best serves this aim, which is also doubtful, as I will argue.

In the next section (5.3.), I will argue that communicative retributivism needs to show two things: First, that censure is deserved—or in other words, that it is intrinsically valuable. And second, that censure can only be adequately communicated with punishment. I will argue that the first claim is somewhat doubtful, while the second one has no good argument to offer at all. We should thus discard communicative retributivism.

In the last section (5.4.) I will discuss consequentialist and epistemic communicative theories of punishment and argue that they are more promising in offering a plausible justification for sanctions in criminal law. Such theories need, however, to give us an empirically informed argument for the epistemic and consequentialist benefits of punishment. After reviewing the evidence that we have to date, I will argue that no such argument is convincing.

I will conclude by arguing that we have reasons to communicate censure in the form of corrective sanctions and by offering stakeholders of a conflict restorative justice processes in order to incentivize the experience of guilt on part of the offender. But neither censure nor penance justifies punitive sanctions.

5.2 Penance

The idea that penance should play a role in criminal law might sound surprising to some. After all, the debate on the justification of punishment typically concerns Western liberal states—and relying on a contested religious notion such as "penance" appears to run counter to the values of liberal states. Defendants of penance approaches are well aware of this problem and thus try to offer secular penance accounts that are supposed to work without any contested commitments to religion.

Stephen Garvey, for example, asks us to imagine a (near-)ideal community and how such a community would respond to wrongdoings performed by people within the group. His own answer is that "[p]unishment in such a community would [...] be a form of secular penance aimed at the expiation of the wrongdoer's guilt and his reconciliation with the victim and the community" (1999, 1802).

Antony Duff, similarly, argues that the aim of punishment with regards to the community should be understood along these lines:

> I have argued [...] that we should understand criminal punishment as, ideally, a kind of secular penance. The culpable commission of a crime involves wrongdoing that violates the central values of the political community, as expressed in its criminal law; the crime thus damages or threatens the offender's normative relationships not only with the direct victim, but also with her fellow citizens. (2003, 300)

Linda Radzik also reasons that the perpetrator-victim and perpetrator-community relationships are paramount; she asks what "morality demands of wrongdoers themselves" (2009, 4) and how they can make amends with their victims and the broader community in order to atone.

As a first approximation, we can thus say that, according to all of these theories, punishment is justified because criminal wrongdoing violates the central values of the community and the rights of the victim, and morality demands that the offender somehow account for said violation. The state's job, in this context, is to enforce the offender's compliance with that expectation. The specifics may vary regarding how penance should be understood and defined within each of these different penance approaches, but all of these approaches share some common aspects that will guide our discussion, which I want to highlight now:

Radzik (2009, 85) argues that the appropriate response of an offender to their own wrongdoing consists of reconciliation with the victim and the community. Reconciliation requires that the offender: 1) make moral improvements, 2) express that the victim holds value (this response also entails that the offender feel guilty, remorseful, or ashamed), and 3) take reparative actions towards the victim.

For Garvey (1999, 1813), two stages of penance are important: expiation and reconciliation. Expiation, in particular, consists of repentance, including feelings of guilt, apology, reparation, and some measure of intentional hard treatment of the wrongdoer.

For Duff (2001, 107), wrongdoing deserves censure, and punishment-as-penance is a way to communicate this censure, in addition to being a way for offenders to restore their moral standing within the community by accepting the punishment and expressing remorse.

The commonalities across these three perspectives consist, first, of the role of recognition and feelings of guilt.[9] In each of them, it is important that offenders show a certain emotional response that not only acknowledges their wrongdoing but also signals that: 1) the gravity of the action has been understood and 2) they will not violate the victim's right or the community's values in the future. The three authors also agree that the offender must provide reparation for the victim.

Two of the three authors also agree that penance requires that the offender be punished. For Garvey, punishment constitutes the penance stage of atonement (here is where he deviates from my suggested terminology); as penance must be burdensome, punishment is needed. Similarly, Duff argues that punishment is the only adequate means of expressing censure for the offender's act, and accepting a sentence offers a way for an offender to signal their assent to undergoing some form of penance and their desire to reconcile themselves with their communities. Radzik, by contrast, does not agree that penance requires punishment.

However, all three do agree that one of the aims of penance is reconciliation between the stakeholders in the conflict. It is thus important to stress that the penance rationale can aim to offer a justification for punitive treatment, as in Duff's and Garvey's accounts, but that it can also aim to justify non-punitive treatment of people in accordance with other penance demands, such as reparation, feelings of guilt, and reconciliation, as in Radzik's account.

In short, all three authors emphasize the role of recognition and experience of guilt, punishment or reparation, and reconciliation. Moreover, these elements are valuable intrinsically and by virtue of their beneficial consequences. On the one hand, "[w]hat justifies the claim that [an offender] ought to repent, and the attempt to bring him to repent, is the very fact that he has done wrong" (Duff 2001, 107). In other words, a wrongdoing itself is enough to justify that penance be exacted. Simultaneously, there are also forward-looking considerations that

---

9 For the sake of simplicity, I will not differentiate between feelings of guilt and remorse; I will only talk about feelings of guilt.

speak in favor of applying the penance rationale; penance is meant to foster reconciliation between the stakeholders of the conflict (for the sake of the future of these relationships) and—by making offenders understand the wrongness of their actions—to reduce future wrongdoing. I will come back to these different motivations of penance when discussing the third objection.

The Liberal Objection

This first objection aims at one of the central assumptions that has just been mentioned: Namely, that the justification for punishment-as-penance can be built on the relationship between the offender and the victim, as well as between the offender and the broader community. The liberal objection will go on to argue that such a justification of punishment grants the state too much authority over the "inner feelings" of offenders.

Andrew von Hirsch and his colleagues have raised versions of the liberal objection several times in debates over Duff's penance account, but these objections can be applied to Garvey's and Radzik's accounts as well. The criticism concerns Duff's (alleged) overestimation of "how deeply the censurer may properly involve himself in the feelings and attitudes of the offender, in order to bring about a morally appropriate response" (Hirsch and Ashworth 2005, 95). I shall use the term "inner feelings" henceforth to refer to the aspect of penance that involves feelings of guilt, along with core moral commitments and values—all, arguably, deeply personal, internal experiences and perspectives. The pull of the objection comes from the intuition that a state that concerns itself with such inner feelings oversteps its legitimate boundaries towards its citizens.

As "inner feelings" is quite vague, it is worth elaborating on this notion a bit. What the critics cannot mean is that penance theories account for the intentions of the offender and should therefore be dismissed. Typically, it is taken to be uncontroversial that the criminal law has a stake in the intentions—*mens rea* (guilty mind)—of the offender in order to determine an adequate sanction. For deciding on an adequate sanction, we need to know whether the offender acted intentionally, planned the crime in advance, etc. As this is typically not questioned to be a proper concern of the criminal law, a charitable reading of the objection against penance accounts cannot refer to this with "inner feelings." Where, then, does the problem lie exactly?

For the objection to have some pull, penance accounts have to be committed to caring not only about such aspects of mens rea as intentionality, but also with other attitudes and emotional states of the offender. And as summarized above, the penance accounts talk about bringing about a repentant recognition of the wrongdoing on part of the offender, and the need for the experience of feelings of guilt. With this reading of the objection, it becomes more apparent why there might be a problem. The argument would then be that it is none of the liberal state's business to try to bring about feelings of guilt or repentant attitudes in the offender. Or at the very least, it is illegitimate to impose intentional harsh treatment, i.e., punishment, with this aim in mind. Penance theories thus understood resemble strongly rehabilitative theories of punishment, which also focus on bringing about a change in the offender's attitudes and values or press the experience of emotions such as guilt or shame. As such, penance accounts face similar worries as rehabilitative accounts—one of these worries being that the state lacks the moral authority to use punishment in order to bring about a change in character and inner feelings (Morris 1968).

What is the precise argument that such an aim is problematic? To illustrate their argument that the liberal state lacks a right to be concerned with the inner feelings of offenders, von Hirsch and Ashworth (2005, 95) start by highlighting examples of parties who (they believe) are indeed justified in demanding penance thus understood because of their close and intimate relationship to each other. It might very well be morally appropriate, for instance, that a religious leader demand (and enforce) penance from their followers whenever these commit sins, because the religious leader stands in the appropriate relationship to make this legitimacy claim. To add another example: When a family member or a close friend wrong me, I might be entitled to expect (among other things) that they show remorse in response to the wrongdoing. In cases like the aforementioned, an insistence on regret, feelings of guilt, and penance more broadly would be justified, because the stakeholders in the conflict stand in the appropriate relation to each other for making such demands. In the case of the state and its citizens, however, von Hirsch and Ashworth insist that the relationship is of a very different kind (ibid.)—one that lacks the closeness and intimacy that intrusions upon the inner feelings arguably require.

So far, von Hirsch and Ashworth only try to pump the intuition that the respective relationships are different in kind, without offering a clear-cut argument. The success of the argument hinges on several intuitions that are at least not explicitly argued for. First, the analogy assumes that we are justified in demanding penance in cases of close relationships. This might be intuitive, but the claim is not uncontroversial. Even in cases of wrongdoing concerning family members I can retort that while it is appropriate for me to apologize for my misbehavior, my family does not have any right or legitimate claim to my feeling guilty or repentant. Without a more convincing argument, this intuition stands somewhat unsupported—which is unfortunate given that it has to do a lot of work for the argument to succeed.

But for the discussion at hand, we can accept the first intuition that there are at least some cases where it is morally justified to demand feelings of guilt and repentance, and maybe even pursue this with the imposition of punishment. Let us focus on the second intuition that the argument is pumping. Von Hirsch and Ashworth press that the relationship between family members is different than the relationship citizens have with each other. And that is certainly true for most cases—but is the relationship different in a way that explains why penance is appropriate in one case and not the other?

Here, we are also left without a clear answer as to why this should be the case. Certainly, there is a difference, but what are the criteria that make the difference morally relevant in this case? As it seems to me, we are left alone with the intuition—there does not seem to be a more detailed account of the appropriateness of demanding feelings of guilt and penance. But maybe the intuition pump is enough in this context, as at least Duff does seem to take examples such as these seriously. In his publications he feels the need to respond to the claim that citizens do not have the right kind of relationship to each other or the state for demands of penance to be legitimate.

Duff's strategy is to argue that we are mistaken in viewing citizens as complete strangers with no relevant ties to each other. At the very least, they share "central liberal values [such] as freedom, autonomy, privacy, and pluralism, and [...] a mutual regard that reflects those values" (2001, 47). But even if that is correct, we should press Duff to tell us more about why such a connection justifies demanding penance from offenders. The simple observation that there are some such shared values, assuming that there are, does not in itself say anything about the adequacy of demanding penance. The penance theorists need a further justification for this claim.

To defend the state's concern with the inner feelings of offenders, Duff attacks the liberal conception of freedom held by such critics of penance theories, along with their understanding of harms and wrongs. The harm suffered by the victims of central *mala in se* crimes (such as murder, rape, theft, violent assault) consists not just in the physically, materially, or psychologically damaging effects of such crimes but in the fact that they are victims of an attack on their legitimate interests—on their selves. The harmfulness and wrongfulness of such attacks lie in the malicious, contemptuous, or disrespectful intentions and attitudes that they manifest, as well as in their effects. The agent's intentions and practical attitudes (those directly manifest in their conduct) are thus relevant as conditions of liability—that is, as conditions for holding them liable for conduct that causes or threatens to cause harm (Duff 2001, 128).

Duff, in other words, argues that the inner feelings and moral commitments of an offender do concern the state after all, as the state should be concerned with wrongs—and wrongs, in turn, can only be adequately understood when we take a look at the offender's attitudes. Thus, the state should be concerned with an offender's inner feelings, if it hopes to address (adequately) the wrongs as wrongs.

There are at least two problems with this response. First, as Duff mentions, his description concerns mala in se crimes—not all crimes in general. If that is true, his account would be plausible for a good range of criminal wrongdoings but not as a comprehensive approach to justify punishment for all wrongdoings, as not everything that the state criminalizes relies on mala in se wrongs.

Second, Duff's justification might not even be plausible in cases of mala in se crimes. It is true that we need to pay attention to the disrespectful intentions of an offender in order to be sure that we capture all dimensions of their wrongdoing—but even then, one could argue that the inner feelings of the offender (or anyone else) are beyond the state's jurisdiction. As argued above, there is a difference between taking into account the malicious intentions in order to determine an adequate amount of punishment from a retributive or consequentialist perspective versus doing so with the goal of changing these attitudes through the imposition of punishment. Duff's attempt to counter the liberal objection by pointing to the necessity of taking the offender's intentions into account, thus, fails to show that the state ought to be concerned with bringing about certain feelings in offenders, and making it the aim of a sanction to make offenders repent their actions and intentions.[10]

I think that the discussion remains imprecise because of a lack of a definite account of when concerns with penance are justified—if ever. We have not really encountered a convincing argument as to why even close friends or family members have a right to someone's experience of feelings of guilt or penance more broadly. We also do not know what the characteristics are that a relationship needs to have in order for such a right to be morally justified.

And even if we are justified in accounting for intentions, this in itself does not give a sufficient reason for the state to have a legitimate interest in trying to change these attitudes with sanctions. After all, Duff appears to want more than a theory that accounts for intentions of the offender:

---

10 Maybe the argument should not be that we need punitive penance to address wrongs as wrongs but to make the offender see that what they did is wrong and change their future behavior. This response, though, first presupposes that punishment will reliably bring about penitent recognition in the offender and change in future behavior. That is an empirical question. More importantly, if behavioral change is the main justification, we run into proportionality worries: If what justifies penance is that the offender will change future behavior, hard-headed offenders might require disproportionate punishment. More on that in the next section.

> Penances, and penitential punishments as I have portrayed them, address not just offenders' conduct, but their moral attitudes, dispositions and feelings. They seek not just to dissuade, or to condemn, criminal conduct, but to bring the offender to repent it; and what he must repent is, it seems, not just the conduct itself, but the motives, attitudes and moral dispositions from which it flowed. (2003, 301)

In such formulations, the penance account has clear commitments to changing the attitudes of the offender and bringing about repentant recognition of the wrongdoing. We are still missing a definite argument whether or not pursuing this with the imposition of punishment is legitimate for a liberal Western criminal law institution, given their commitment to be value neutral. The liberal objection should thus at the very least caution us against embracing penance theories of punishment.

The Proportionality Objection

Another objection is that the penance rationale alone cannot guarantee the proportionality of punishment, in either of two senses: First, it cannot guarantee that the punishment is proportional to the gravity of the wrongdoing, and second, it cannot guarantee that similar crimes would receive similar punishments. But both of these proportionality concerns are often seen as foundational to justice in criminal law.

According to the penance approach, a hard-headed offender might, for example, receive a punishment that is disproportionate to the gravity of the wrong, as the amount of punishment is determined by what is necessary to evoke penance. In other words, a particularly hard-headed person might "need" a fairly harsh punishment for a relatively minor offense, simply by virtue of their stubbornness. Not only this, but furthermore (and by extension), if two different offenders were to commit a similar wrong (in kind, gravity, and culpability) but were hard-headed to unequal degrees, this would mean that each of them would require different amounts and maybe even different types of punishment in order to understand that what they did was wrong. Of course, given that every account of criminal law should respect the principle of proportional and equal punishment (so the argument goes), we have to dismiss justifications of punishment which are based on the penance rationale.

Duff explicitly addresses the proportionality objection in his work. He argues that what justifies the imposition of punishment upon offenders is the deserved censure, which takes the form of penance. When the deserved censure is the primary focus, then the proportionality worry can be addressed. Censure must be proportional to the gravity of the wrong; therefore, similar actions must always receive similar types and amounts of censure.

So, the proportionality of the punishment stems not from the penance demand directly, but from the retributive commitment that offenders deserve to be censured. Penance then only comes into play as the most adequate way to express censure towards the offender. This is a fair response, but the plausibility of it entirely depends on the plausibility of the retributive commitment, and on the idea that there is no tension between the strictly retributive commitment and the aim of penance.

Is there a different response to the objection? At least in the literature mentioned in this section, not explicitly. But this is not surprising, as for many authors the principle of proportionality simply is an extension of the retributive principle. There is thus no way around looking at this retributive motivation for the penance approach. We should thus lastly take a look at whether penance theorists have a convincing argument to explain why we should be concerned with penance in the first place. If the retributive dimensions fail, then, as an extension, the response to the proportionality objections falls along with it.

The Value of Penance

I have argued until now that we should be careful to fully embrace a penance approach to criminal law because such a value as the foundation of our criminal law might overstep the boundaries of a liberal state, and it cannot explain the proportionality of punishment by itself. But a crucial question has nonetheless not yet been answered: Why should the state care about penance in the first place?

It might be odd to end with this question in this section. It would seem more obvious that penance theorists should start with a good answer to this from the very beginning. But asking this question now will provide a good transition to the next sections. Because as I want to argue now, the penance approach runs into a problem here if it aims to justify punitive sanctions. It can either follow a retributive strategy or a consequentialist one. The retributive strategy fails, I will argue, to motivate why penance is intrinsically morally valuable. The consequentialist perspective is problematic for the punitive penance theorist because they need to show us empirical data suggesting that punishment is the most adequate way of bringing about penance in offenders and that penance induced by punishment, in turn, has good consequences for the offender, the victim, or the broader community. This is not the case, as I will argue later.

As mentioned in the beginning of this section, penance theories typically take a pluralist or hybrid stance towards why the state should be concerned with penance. On the one hand, penance is taken to be the intrinsically valuable response to wrongdoing, or to put it in more retributive terms: The offender deserves to undergo penance for their wrongdoing. On the other hand, penance is meant to serve as a pathway for the offender to reintegration into the community and change of behavior in the future.

What is the argument for the retributive part of the penance account—namely that offenders deserve to undergo some form of penance? Duff (2003, 300; 2001, 30), for example, argues that offenders deserve to be censured for their wrongdoing, and that penance is the most adequate form of censure. This argument will not do for a retributive grounding of penance, however. Because in this version of the argument, only censure has the retributive commitment, not penance. So, the answer to the question whether penance is intrinsically valuable is "no." It is valuable insofar as it is conducive to communicating censure to the offender. We will look at this more parsimonious version of a communicative retributivism in the next section.

Garvey gives us an argument that aims to show more directly why penance is intrinsically morally valuable. This argument has several steps. Garvey first begins with the observation that guilt—both as an emotion and as a moral status—is the basis of the moral justification of punishment: "Guilt is good. [...] If guilt's virtue isn't obvious, consider the alternatives. One could respond to one's wrongdoing with no feeling. That, however, would be a moral failure, not a moral virtue" (1999, 1811). Let us assume that guilt is indeed a morally required response to wrongdoing. How does this translate to punishment? In the next step, Garvey argues that "of course, making amends is the *ideal* response to one's guilt" (1999, 1812). So, the guilty person should make amends. But why is punishment needed for making amends? Garvey continues the argument by using the difference between harms and wrongs. Reparation only serves to alleviate the harm done to the victim, not to expiate the wrong: "To make amends for the wrong, the wrongdoer must submit to penance [i.e., punishment]" (1999, 1818).

So here is the argument as I understand it: Guilt is the morally appropriate reaction to wrongdoing. Guilt ideally leads to making amends. Making amends for harms requires offenders to offer reparation. Making amends for wrongs requires offenders to submit to punishment (penance). Therefore, the offender should undergo some form of punishment. As philosophers like to say: There is a lot to unpack here—but the two most important assumptions, I think, are that guilt plays the role Garvey wants it to, and that the harm vs. wrong distinction works in his favor.

First, guilt. Garvey pumps the intuition that guilt's virtue is obvious because a reaction to wrongdoing without feelings of guilt seems unvirtuous. But contrary to Garvey's and maybe others' intuition, feelings of guilt have had their fair share of bad reputation in philosophy and psychology, famously described by Nietzsche and Freud respectively. Also, even assuming that guilt is virtuous, it is unclear what makes it so. Is it intrinsically valuable—as Garvey appears to think—or does its value depend on whether victims get satisfaction or offender change their behavior? A clear argument is needed here—especially given that this argument leads to the justification of a fundamental institution such as the criminal law. I will investigate the value of feelings of guilt in more detail in the last section of this chapter.

What about the difference between harms and wrongs? This difference is often used in the debate on corrective versus punitive sanctions, as does Garvey in this case. Corrective sanctions or reparations are said to address the harm, but punitive sanctions are required for the wrong. But why is this the case? Why do corrective sanctions not adequately address the wrongfulness of crimes?

Here, Garvey takes an expressivist position, which we will take a closer look at in the next chapter. The idea here is that punishment is necessary to adequately vindicate the victim's moral worth: "We need penance too, because insofar as the wrongdoer identifies with the victim and insofar as punishment is necessary (albeit conventionally so) to vindicate the victim's moral worth, so too is penance a necessary part of the process of expiation and atonement" (1999, 1823).

But again, why is the punishment necessary to vindicate the victim's moral worth? Garvey's argument begins with the observation that the victim's reaction to wrongdoing is to strike back at the offender in order to defend their moral status: "The victim's impulse to punish represents, among other things, a legitimate urge to strike back, not vindictively, but as a way of reaffirming his own moral worth. The retributive instinct is to that extent a healthy sign of self-respect" (1999, 1822). The argument then turns to punishment by observing that under ideal circumstances, the offender "*identifies* with the victim" (1999, 1822) and the victim's anger to strike back for preserving their moral worth. This identification leads to the offender's realization that they deserve to be punished.

Two crucial assumptions in this argument are that victims want to strike back at the offender in order to restore their moral worth, and that this urge is legitimate. Unfortunately, Garvey argues for neither of the two claims in more detail. As I will argue in detail in the next chapter on victim-centered theories of criminal law, we have some empirical evidence to think that the interests of victims in the aftermath of wrongdoing are far more complex than merely an urge to strike back. Garvey is right that victims benefit from having their perceived moral worth restored by a state response to the wrongdoing. But contrary to his intuition, there is more systematic evidence suggesting that corrective sanctions, restorative justice or granting the victim procedural rights during the trial do a far better job of reaching this aim than merely punitive sanctions. I will argue for this claim in detail in the next chapter, so for this discussion I will not spell out the details of the research on that matter.

Without any evidence supporting Garvey's intuitions, I do not see a convincing argument as to why penance should be intrinsically valuable—and even if it were, why punishment is needed to realize it. One of the crucial problems I see is that authors argue with the help of intuition pumps in such cases—but these are not very well equipped to show the intrinsic value of actions, let alone their retributive character. That is not to deny that people care—maybe even deeply—about feelings of guilt, repentance, or related things. But this observation alone does not say anything about their status as retributive, consequentialist, virtuous, utilitarian, deontological, etc.

I do not presume to have shown that it is impossible to show that penance is intrinsically valuable, but only note that penance theorists such as Duff and Garvey have not yet provided us with the necessary arguments for drawing such a conclusion. Also, the methodology probably has to go beyond mere intuition pumping to make a convincing case for such an argument. But maybe a more parsimonious approach has more success. Maybe penance is not intrinsically valuable, but expressing censure at least is. This is what I will look at in the next section.

Before that, I should quickly mention the consequentialist perspective. The penance theorists I mentioned generally agreed that forward-looking considerations certainly feed into the justification as to why the state should be concerned with penance. Penance is supposed to help with reconciliation, change of heart in the offender, and defending the values of the community, among other things.

Crucially, however, only empirical investigation can answer whether this is true, and which parts specifically about the penance approach are conducive to the mentioned effects. In Section 5.4., I will take a look at the empirical evidence to date that I could find and argue that some aspects of penance, especially feelings of guilt, do seem to promote these consequences. We have less evidence, however, to take a confident stance on whether punitive sanctions promote these benefits.

5.3 Communicative Retributivism

I have argued that it remains unclear why penance should be seen as intrinsically morally valuable, and that it is very questionable that penance is necessarily linked with punishment. So, a retributive theory of penance fails. But what about a more parsimonious communicative theory, that solely focuses on the censure that offenders deserve, without any mention of penance? Again, the retributivists need to convince us of two things here. First, they need to show us that it is intrinsically morally valuable to express censure towards the offender—or in other words, that offenders deserve to be censured. But secondly, for the retributive strategy to be successful, they also need to argue that there is an intrinsic connection between censure and punishment. I will argue that the first claim is at least questionable, and that the second one remains unconvincing.

The Intrinsic Worth of Censure

Censure in the broadest sense is no doubt a central part of our moral lives. By censure I mean the act of communicating disapproval towards a person for their moral behavior. This is often done by expressing reactive attitudes such as blame or condemnation. Censure is not a neutral stance, as in the mere descriptive statement that someone has acted against a legal or moral rule. It is the communication or expression of a disapproving attitude that makes censure, condemnation, or blame, what it is. Censure thus understood is typically seen as a communicative enterprise (Macnamara 2015 for an overview), and recently much research has surfaced showing that the same is also true for punishment (Bilz 2016; Cushman, Sarin, and Ho 2022; Funk, McGeer, and Gollwitzer 2014; Gollwitzer and Denzler 2009; Gollwitzer, Meder, and Schmitt 2011) and corrective sanctions (Dhaliwal, Patil, and Cushman 2021). But this important role of censure for our moral lives and communication with wrongdoers alone does not show that it is intrinsically valuable to express censure. So what arguments are there in favor of this claim?

Bennett (2019), when discussing von Hirsch's (1993) censure theory, says that most censure theorists stand in the tradition of retributive theories. What such theories share is that there is something intrinsically morally valuable about expressing some form of censure, and many censure theorists take it that it has something to do with respecting wrongdoers as moral agents (Morris 1968 for the retributivist argument). Bennett writes:

> The corollary of this in the censure theory would be the view that wrongdoers should get their 'just censure' – and it is this view that I propose to consider here. On this view, there would be something lacking in a state that did not have an institution of censure, whether or not it was also an institution of punishment. (2019, 73)

We start here without the idea that censure necessarily has to be communicated by using punitive sanctions. Before we get to this part of the retributive position, we have to explain the intrinsic value of communicating censure first.

As mentioned, taking the wrongdoer seriously as a moral agent is of key importance here:

> And although sometimes we criticise people only when there is some further end we seek to achieve by doing so, sometimes the faults are such that their deservingness of censure itself, or the need to mark or acknowledge the gravity of the wrong, is sufficient reason to give expression to the criticism. Therefore it can sometimes be neglectful of the seriousness of wrongdoing, and of the perpetrator's identity as an agent competent to respond to moral reasons, if we do not subject them to moral criticism. (Bennett 2019, 73–74)

Here, Bennett presents what he takes to be von Hirsch's position, which argues for deserved censure by claiming that merely communicating prudential reasons, i.e., threats of punishment, would fail to respect people as moral agents who are capable of grasping the appropriate reasons for sticking to rules. A purely deterrent approach would treat wrongdoers as "tigers" or "beasts" (Hirsch and Ashworth 2005, 26), that is, solely as potential dangers and disregard their capacity of moral agency.

I will have more to say about this negative argument against a deterrent approach in Chapter 7, where I discuss deterrence theories in more detail. The upshot in that chapter is—and Bennett agrees with that—that communicating prudential reasons does not always lead to treating people as mere dangers, thus denying their moral agency. I will argue for this in more detail later, but for now it suffices to say that this response assumes what it needs to show: That only a theory that incorporates desert treats people as moral agents. We thus still need a positive argument as to why this should be the case.

Bennett also sees the need for a positive argument, and he offers the following in defense of the assumption:

> My thought is that it must be a wrong that involves a failure to stand in the right relation to the offence and to the offender: that sometimes when we fail to censure wrongdoing, we are effectively consenting to it, acquiescing in it, condoning it, and hence becoming complicit in it. The central thought on this aspect of the retributive tradition is that it is wrong to allow the original offence to persist, unanswered. When it does, we are implicated in the wrongdoing unless we do something to dissociate ourselves from it; and it is the act of censure that does the dissociating. (2019, 78)

Bennett's argument here essentially works by observing something about our practice of taking other people seriously as moral agents. His observation is that when we are a bystander of wrongdoing and do not intervene in any shape or form, we communicate an implicit consent, and in a way become implicated in the wrongdoing.

That is of course quite a controversial claim. Bennett mentions that his observation is not right for every wrongdoing. While writing his paper, as he admits, a lot of wrongdoings are committed, and he does not do anything about them—neither could he. Why, then, should we be implicated in cases where we are bystanders? There is of course something to Bennett's intuition. A victim could say to us "Why did you not say anything in my defense, why did you let his actions go unanswered?"—and we might feel that the victim is justified in challenging us in such a way. But even if we grant this kind of case, things are more complicated.

First, being a bystander does not seem to be sufficient for being implicated in the wrongdoing. If I walk around in the city, and a person is insulted, should I also communicate censure if five other people already condemned the wrongdoer? At least on social media, such behavior does not really seem to benefit the community. Or is my implication somehow covered if others already accounted for the communicative dimension of wrongdoing? If yes, then the argument only applies to cases where no one yet communicated censure.

But even in the paradigmatic case Bennett describes, it is not so clear that censure, blame, or condemnation is necessary for respecting the moral status of the victim. Remember that in order to get a retributive position off the ground, there needs to be some form of intrinsic connection between censure and respecting people. Bennett—and many others in the discussion on the intrinsic worth of censure—likely follow the tradition of appealing to our reactive attitudes (Strawson 1962) that has become very popular in the last decades. The idea is that reactive attitudes are fundamental to how we treat each other as moral agents, and a failure to express reactive attitudes simply is a failure to express the kind of respect that we should communicate. It might be a contingent feature of human nature that we happened to be a species that expresses moral respect with censure—but this is where we are at, and this is what we have to work with. Censure simply is intrinsic to how we take both offenders and victims seriously as moral agents.

This argument in defense of reactive attitudes is questionable. It is true that most people express concern for moral agents by communicating censure, but it is unclear whether this is intrinsic to the practice of moral agency. There have been several traditions that pressed against using blame, condemnation, and other forms of reactive attitudes while still wanting to account for moral agency. Some versions of Stoicism, Buddhism, and free will skepticism (Caruso 2019; 2020) argue that we should not blame agents—and by extension not censure them. But that does not necessarily entail that we should not communicate respect towards the victim or even the offender, while still judging that what the offender did was not a good thing to do.

Shoemaker (2015, 35) suggests that we can differentiate at least three types of responsibility: Attributability, answerability, and accountability, which evaluate character, judgment, and regard respectively. Accountability concerns what intrinsic censure theorists are typically interested in: Resentment towards others or guilt towards oneself. But if Shoemaker's account is on the right track, there is more to responsibility than that. We can still evaluate a person's character and disapprove of it (attributability) or disapprove of their judgment (answerability) without resorting to blame. If that is correct, the argument presented by Bennett faces a challenge. Censure is certainly part of the moral practice of most people, but we can imagine a slightly different practice that still claims to account for the moral agency of persons without resorting to blame or censure in the strict sense of the term. If that is correct, the case of the retributivist is somewhat dampened.

If the criticism I alluded to is correct, then we need an additional argument as to why we should resort to censure in order to express concern for victims or concern for the moral agency of the offender, given that alternatives are available. It might of course not be easy to switch to the alternatives—after all, Strawson was right in describing reactive attitudes as very important to our typical conception of morality. But at the very least Bennett and others need to argue more substantially for the intrinsic connection between censure and respecting moral agency—or other ways of explaining deserved censure. Though nothing I argued here is a definite case against the intrinsic censure theory, it should be clear that the case is harder to make than expected.

But for the second part of the discussion, we can grant the communicative retributivist this part of their argument. Even if censure is not intrinsically valuable, it certainly has a strong case going for it. The next challenge already awaits the communicative retributivist. Even if we assume that censure is intrinsically valuable, or at least an almost inevitable part of our moral practice—why should we express it with punitive sanctions?

Censure and Punishment

Even if we assume that expressing censure or blame is morally valuable in itself, we need an answer to the question how best to communicate censure to the offender. According to a retributive theory of communicative punishment, there needs to be an intrinsic connection between punishing offenders and expressing adequate censure. We are thus looking for an argument in defense of that.

But finding an explicit argument for this part of the retributive argument is not an easy feat. In the early version of censure theories, von Hirsch (1985, chap. 5) began by noting that censure itself is not intrinsically linked to punishment. Censure could be expressed verbally or in other symbolic ways; the hard treatment, however, can only be justified with the deterrent effects it supposedly achieves. Such an argument would of course not help the retributivist's case.

A different strategy that is also sometimes appealed to similarly fails to establish the retributive argument (Günther 2014, 134–35 for an overview). The central idea of this strategy is to argue that the hard treatment has an important epistemic function for the offender, the victim, and the society as a whole. As Duff says, humans are fallible beings, and we might be tempted to misjudge whether we have repented our wrong adequately. A formal sanction helps to avoid such mistakes (Duff 2001, 108). But it is also important that punishment "constitute[s] a forceful and weighty kind of apology" (Duff 2001, 109), one that is easier to believe for the victim and the community when it is accompanied with some form of hardship.

These passages also nicely explain why Duff and others take a broader perspective on what counts as punishment than I do in this book. Duff (2001, 104–5; 2003) explicitly accepts community service and other forms of reparation as punishment because they involve some form of hardship that serves as an epistemic indicator for successful censure. This argument looks promising as a justification of the hard treatment of the offender—be it punitive or corrective—but it does not support a retributive position. The retributivist has to show that there is something intrinsically fitting about hardship—that it is something that offenders deserve to undergo for their wrongdoing. But according to the epistemic argument, it is not the case that offenders deserve the hardship. If we had a perfect futuristic device in order to detect successful communication of censure, hardship might be unnecessary in such cases, given that the pure verbal or symbolic communication both expresses censure towards the offender and respect towards the victim. If that is so, then there is no intrinsic connection between censure and hardship. The epistemic argument thus fails to ground a retributive position.

The most promising argument for the retributive element in censure, I think, draws from the principle of proportionality. That is von Hirsch's more recent attempt to ground the necessity of hard treatment in censure. What retributivism supposedly explains well is why we need to scale censure depending on the magnitude of the wrong. Von Hirsch and Ashworth write:

> The requirement of proportionate punishment is, instead, derived directly from the censuring implications of the criminal sanction. Once one has created an institution with the condemnatory implications that punishment has, then it is a requirement of justice, not merely of efficient crime prevention, to punish offenders according to the degree of reprehensibleness of their conduct. Disproportionate punishments are unjust not because they possibly may be ineffective or counterproductive, but because they purport to condemn the actor for his conduct and yet visit more or less censure on him than the degree of blameworthiness of that conduct would warrant. (2005, 134)

The strategy here is to start with the observation that it is intrinsic to the function of blame that it is proportional. Even if this assumption is correct, why should we scale the blameworthiness with the amount of punishment inflicted on offenders? As Günther (2014) notes, we can scale the severity along many different dimensions. We can simply express that the action was worse than other actions, or we can have a more elaborate symbolic response to graver wrongdoings than less grave ones. Why hard treatment? In the newer version of von Hirsch's censure theory, deterrence is not independent of censure, as it was in his earlier work. But it still would not work without the assumption that there is some deterrent effect to punitive sanctions. So, there are actually two problems here. First, there is still the assumption that punishment deters, which is not defended by von Hirsch and Ashworth. Furthermore, the scaling argument for retribution requires an independent justification for punishment, for example deterrence, as von Hirsch and Ashworth admit. Once we punish, we should punish proportionally. That might be true, but that still does not offer us a retributive defense of censure. The argument first requires deterrent effects of punishment, which are unclear as I will argue in Chapter 7, and the argument requires that we cannot scale censure on other dimensions than punishment. Both parts of the argument remain undefended for the moment.

In sum, the most prominent accounts of supposedly retributive or intrinsic communicative theories have turned out to be either epistemic or consequentialist. We have not encountered an argument for why there is an intrinsic connection between expressing censure and imposing punishment on offenders. But the epistemic and consequentialist candidates are still interesting. Of course, in order to properly analyze them, we need data—data which philosophers typically do not provide. So, we need to ask: Is there any data that speaks to the necessity of hard treatment for the epistemic or deterrent benefits of communicating censure? We will investigate this question in the next section.

5.4 Consequentialist and Epistemic Communicative Theories

The retributive positions on penance and censure remained unconvincing. The discussion led to interesting non-retributive communicative theories, however. Maybe harsh treatment is necessary in order to reliably communicate with the offender, victim, and community (the epistemic argument), and in order to realize beneficial consequences for the community (the consequentialist argument). What remains to be done in this section is to try to take a closer look at both these arguments.

I will take a look at two lines of research here. First, I want to discuss whether we have any data to support the claim that punitive sanctions are necessary in order to reliably communicate censure to stakeholders of the conflict. The honest answer, I think, is that we simply do not know for certain with the available data to date. We are thus likely better off for the moment to reserve judgment on that point, maybe even be a bit skeptical towards purely punitive sanctions as I understand them.

For the last subsection I want to revisit a point from the penance section. We rejected the retributive account but remained with a consequentialist version of penance. I will argue that we indeed have good reasons to pay attention at least to some part of the penance approach, namely feelings of guilt, for the beneficial consequences it brings. But given the objections we encountered to penance theories in the first section, I suggest we best realize these benefits by implementing restorative justice procedures.

The Problems of Estimating the Epistemic Argument

A lot of behavior is communicative: Blaming offenders, helping victims, corrective sanctions, punitive sanctions, etc. The question we need to answer here is whether punitive sanctions are particularly suited to communicate censure to the offender, or respect towards the victim.

The idea that punishment is a good way of doing so is certainly suggestive. In general, pain, harsh treatment, and accepting burdens have these communicative functions. This is suggested by research on hazing and religious rituals in various contexts. There, the hypothesis is that costly initiation rituals or other costly rituals were so successful because they communicate commitment to the respective causes (Cimino 2012; Henrich 2009; Sosis and Bressler 2003). Should not the same hold for punishment in criminal law? The more burdensome we make the sanction for the offender, the more certain can we be that the censure has been understood and accepted. So far, so good. The initial case for the epistemic argument in defense of communicative punishment is certainly strong.

The problems, however, start with differentiating between punitive and corrective sanctions. After all, for a genuine theory of punishment, the argument has to be that we need intentional infliction of harm on the offender, i.e., punishment, in order to communicate censure adequately. But a lot of things are burdensome for the offender in criminal law, without the burden being the point of the action. The fact that the offender is confronted with an official legal accusation, has to spend time and resources to attend legal proceedings, has to face uncomfortable situations, might be the object of social disapproval when perceived as a criminal, might have to pay compensation to the victim, participate in restorative settings that make the offender feel uncomfortable and maybe pained with facing the consequences of their actions, and ultimately has to undergo some form of punishment—all of these experiences are burdensome, but only the last has been defined as intentionally burdensome in the context of my project.

For the epistemic argument in defense of punitive sanctions to succeed, we would need to show that the punitiveness of the sanction itself is what drives

5.4 Consequentialist and Epistemic Communicative Theories

the success of communicating censure. That is, the punitive theorists have to claim that whatever we communicate via the official legal procedure, potential corrective sanctions, and restorative processes, is not enough and needs to be supplemented by additional burdens.

I am not aware of anyone who has presented evidence in defense of this claim specifically. After all, many communicative theorists use a broader understanding of punishment than I do in this book. Duff, as already mentioned, sees corrective sanctions as alternative forms of punishment, not alternatives to punishment. Garvey (2003, 309), whom we discussed in the penance section of this chapter, also claims that corrective sanctions are merely a form of punitive sanctions. Lastly, Nahmias and Aharoni (2017, 147), when outlining their communicative theory, also argue that reparation and apology count towards the communicative function of punishment.

But these conceptual disagreements are irrelevant for the content of what we are concerned with. No matter what conceptual framework we use, the question still arises: Is there need for punitiveness over and above restorative processes and corrective sanctions? If not, then the corrective approach I outline in this book does not face any problems with regards to the epistemic argument. If you want to call these corrective sanctions "punishments," there is no substantial disagreement—only a conceptual one. But if there is no epistemic need beyond corrective sanctions and restorative processes, this is a substantial new insight that stands contrary to most theories of criminal law in the current debate on the justification of punishment. We should thus not downplay this insight by merely noting that corrective sanctions are also burdensome in that regard. We thus need to ask whether there is evidence that the epistemic argument justifies imposition of hardship beyond corrective sanctions.

There is some data that the punitive theorists could use to try to defend their position. But we first need to start with the question what criteria need to be met in order to assess whether or not censure has been adequately communicated. I am not sure whether there is an objective criterion that we can find in order to measure adequate censure—so we probably need to work with somewhat subjective criteria. One candidate would be to measure the behavior of people or their satisfaction with the punishment decisions that they make. Here is one way of putting the argument: If people who are made aware that the offender has some form of understanding of the wrongdoing still opt for punitive sanctions, then we might hypothesize that the punitive sanction is still doing some epistemic work in order to make sure that the communication was successful.

There is however little direct data to investigate this question. One study on the communicative dimension of punishment finds that people lower the recommended sanction length when they are told that some form of communicative aim has been achieved, for example when the offender has apologized (Nahmias and Aharoni 2017). A possible argument the punitive theorists could make is to emphasize the observation that achieving a certain communicative dimension only lowers the suggested punitive sanction but does not make it superfluous to participants in these studies. This might indicate that there is something unique about the punitive sanction itself that other parts of the criminal process cannot cover. Thus, we should also use punitive sanctions.

Not only have we insufficient data to date to give a confident assessment of this argument, but the argument would also require a different experimental setup than is often used in research on punishment decisions. The problem with this argument, and the research more generally as it is typically conducted, is that we mostly cannot tap into the motivation that people have for their punishment decision. As in the study just mentioned, the demand for punishment even in the face of successful communication could simply be due to a status quo bias driving people to think that there has to be some form of punishment in cases of criminal wrongdoing. Or participants might have a partial interest in retribution that is not covered by other communicative means (Nadelhoffer et al. 2013). Or they might be concerned with deterrence over and above the communicative aspect of punishment. We simply do not know. And as long as we do not know, the epistemic argument in defense of punitive sanctions does not get off the ground. We thus need more research before we can analyze this argument in more detail.

Do we have any evidence in the opposite direction—suggesting that corrective sanctions and restorative justice are sufficient to communicate censure? That depends on what part of censure we focus on. As mentioned above, communicative theories concern the offender, the victim, but also the broader community. In the next chapter, we will focus in detail on the victim's interests in criminal law. But as already mentioned in the discussion of Garvey's defense of penance, victims appear more satisfied with the criminal justice system, and seem to better restore their moral self-worth, when they receive restitution from the offender and are respected during the criminal trial rather than only see the offender punished by the state (Laxminarayan 2013).

There is also one set of studies that looked into low-stakes informal punishment behavior. Sarin et al. (2021) found that at least under some circumstances, people prefer non-punitive punishments to punitive ones with the aim of communicating to the offender. In economic games—again with very low stakes—Molnar et al. (2020) found that participants were willing to choose a less severe punishment in order to be able to communicate a message to the offender. Funk et al. (2014) found that participants were only satisfied with their decision to punish when the offender responded with a message acknowledging the communicative success of the punishment and a promise to change their behavior in the future. If punishment were to be seen as an epistemic heuristic to reach communicative aims, we would expect participants to be satisfied even without explicit acknowledgment that the communicative intent was successful.

How much can we draw from these studies? I think the honest answer is: Not much. There is no evidence that I know of that specifically helps the punitive theorists. But even the evidence that helps the corrective theorists is extremely limited. It mostly concerns very low-stakes scenarios and were not conducted with the specific question in mind that I think we should ask with the epistemic argument in mind. So, our conclusion in this chapter must be limited.

Given that we are concerned with the justification of punishment, a convincing case needs to be made—and in this discussion, the case requires good data speaking to the necessity of punitive sanctions. To date, I do not think that we have such data, and we should thus not endorse the argument at this point. But that is not to say that we successfully dismissed the epistemic argument. Communicative theorists emphasize the importance of corrective sanctions and restorative justice, and at least a bit of evidence speaks to the sufficiency of these means for successful communication of censure. But again, we should tread carefully here, given that we are concerned with the justification of an important institution. There is a lot more interesting research that needs to be conducted in this area, but currently we can only suggest that there is no case for punitive sanctions over corrective sanctions from a communicative perspective.

The Importance of Feelings of Guilt for Various Aims of Criminal Law

In the first section of this chapter, I left the option open that there is a consequentialist argument for penance to be made. In this section, now, I want to specifically make the claim that at least a part of penance approaches can be motivated within a consequentialist perspective: Feelings of guilt. I will not talk about punishment specifically in this section. Whether or not punishment has any beneficial consequences will be analyzed in Chapter 7—and the outlook is quite bleak. There, I will argue that we do not really have evidence to be confident in the effectiveness of punishment—be it for penance or independent of it. But things are different with feelings of guilt, as I want to argue in this subsection.

Feelings of guilt and remorse play an important role in all of the penance accounts discussed in the first section of this chapter. For Garvey, remorse and guilt constitute one of the stages of complete penance; for Duff, remorse and guilt are what result when a penitent understands their wrong; and for Radzik, guilt, in particular, plays a major role in re-establishing the relationship between the stakeholders in a conflict.

As we move forward, I wish to argue that feelings of guilt are typically valuable from a consequentialist perspective, and that restorative justice is the best way to incorporate the role of feelings of guilt into the criminal law. Such an argument of course presupposes that there is some *other* justification for punishment or corrective sanctions than penance. Restorative justice is only a procedure to address criminal wrongdoing—in this context it does not say anything about why there should be a criminal law in the first place.

When talking about guilt, I want to refer to the definition used in social psychology, in the tradition of Roy Baumeister and colleagues:

> By guilt we refer to an individual's unpleasant emotional state associated with possible objections to his or her actions, inaction, circumstances, or intentions. Guilt is an aroused form of emotional distress that is distinct from fear and anger and based on the possibility that one may be in the wrong or that others may have such a perception. [...] Guilt can be distinguished from shame on the basis of specificity. Guilt concerns one particular action, in contrast to shame, which pertains to the entire self. (1994, 245)

Why should guilt, thus understood, be valuable for criminal law? The argument works by showing that guilt facilitates the achievement of goals in criminal law that are widely considered justifiable, and independently argued for in the rest of this book.

To make this argument, we must examine some of the research on guilt from social psychology. First, "[g]uilt often motivates reparative action (e.g., confession, apology, efforts to undo the harm)" (Tangney, Stuewig, and Hafez 2011, 710; also Ketelaar and Au 2003; Lindsay-Hartz 1984; Tangney 1996; Wallbott and Scherer 1995; Wicker, Payne, and Morgan 1983). Second, "[f]eelings of guilt go hand in hand with other-oriented empathy" (Tangney, Stuewig, and Hafez 2011, 710; also Leith and Baumeister 1998; Stuewig et al. 2010; Tangney 1991). If offenders start to empathize with their victims, we can hypothesize that the former are also more likely to acknowledge the wrong that was done. Third, "guilt-prone individuals are inclined to take responsibility for their transgressions and errors" (Tangney, Stuewig, and Hafez 2011, 710; also Tangney, Stuewig, and Mashek 2007). Furthermore, guilt proneness "negatively predicted arrests and convictions" (Tangney, Stuewig, and Hafez 2011, 712) in a long-term study of children.

Direct research on inmates themselves with respect to the relation between guilt and pro-social behavior is still scarce. Bagaric and Amarasekara (2001) argue that the few studies that have been conducted favor the claim that there is no correlation between remorse and change in behavior. More specifically, they base their argument on a study by Romanowski (1988) in which no significant effects of remorse on recidivism were found. However, Romanowski's study only examined a few inmates, who were very high in remorse (Proeve, Smith, and Niblo 1999); a definite conclusion from Romanowski's work, thus, cannot be drawn. In 2001, when Bagaric and Amarasekara published their paper, it was plausible to argue that, as no good evidence exists for the claim that remorse correlates with lower recidivism, the burden of proof thus lies on anyone who claims that there is a correlation.

Indeed, a newer and more comprehensive study by June Tangney and her colleagues did find that guilt proneness correlated with recidivism;[11] specifically, guilt proneness reliably predicted lower rates of recidivism within the first year of release among inmates (Tangney, Stuewig, and Martinez 2014). Although Tangney et al.'s study relies on guilt proneness among offenders, not actual incidences of guilt feelings, its results nonetheless suggest that the beneficial consequences of guilt are empirically plausible. An earlier study by Hosser et al. (2008) analyzed reported feelings of guilt in young offenders and found a negative impact of experiences of guilt on their recidivism rate—though instances of feelings of guilt were not very prevalent in that population.

If the research mentioned above drew accurate conclusions, then we are justified in believing that feelings of guilt are likely positively correlated with an array of benefits, such as reparative actions, the taking of responsibility, behavioral changes, and potentially even reconciliation with the transgressed parties. As mentioned above, these are the positive effects which the consequentialist argument relies on.

On the face of it, many theorists of criminal law should welcome these benefits; reliable behavioral change on the part of the offender is, in principle, valued in almost all accounts of criminal law. Various consequentialists should welcome the potential impacts that feelings of guilt might have, if these theories value lower recidivism rates and the prospect of reconciliation between a conflict's stakeholders. Again, feelings of guilt need not justify having criminal law, in principle, but as long as there is (in this case) an independent consequentialist justification—and if feelings of guilt contribute to socially-valued effects—then integrating these into our approaches to criminal law is justified.

Even retributivists can allow for guilt to play a role, because of its beneficial consequences; retributivism does not allow such consequences to play into the justifications for punishment, but once we have a retributive justification, we can at

---

[11] Guilt proneness was measured with the Test of Self-Conscious Affect-Socially Deviant Version (TOSCA-SD), which asks participants how they would react and feel in a series of everyday life situations.

least allow the knowledge of guilt's correlation with beneficial outcomes to influence how we address wrongdoing.

In the following subsection, I shall argue that the benefits of guilt, and hence penance, can be best captured by using restorative justice methods. With the benefits of conveying censure through either punishment or corrective sanctions, I stay a bit more agnostic. It seems that censure is indeed valuable, and that corrective sanctions do a fine job in communicating censure, so that we can adopt such a consequentialist communicative account without resorting to punishment. The evidence, however, is still scarce and the conclusions should accordingly be drawn carefully and with the appropriate amount of modesty.

The Case for Restorative Justice

Now that we have established that guilt is likely to be valuable in virtue of its beneficial consequences, we need to ask how to best bring about feelings of guilt in offenders. I want to argue here that we have good reasons to expect restorative justice to be successful to bring about this aim.[12] June Tangney and her colleagues who research feelings of guilt agree with this connection:

> Although not always explicitly addressed, the philosophy inherent in restorative justice interventions seems to us at heart a "guilt-inducing and shame-reducing" philosophy. Restorative justice approaches emphasize the need to acknowledge and take responsibility for one's wrongdoings and act to make amends for the negative consequences of one's behavior. But the restorative justice approaches eschew practices aimed at shaming offenders, ascribing bad behaviors to a bad defective self. Restorative justice interventions are consistent with [the reintegrative shaming theory] (Braithwaite, 1989) and with psychologists' self vs. behavior distinction [...] but they often do not refer to the emotions of shame and guilt explicitly. Such interventions may be enhanced by the addition of components aimed explicitly at transforming problematic feelings of shame about the self into adaptive feelings of guilt about behaviors and their negative consequences for others [...]. (2011, 717–18)

While people in the debate still disagree about the details of what restorative justice entails, they agree roughly on some central themes. First, a wrongdoing is not understood as an offense against the state or the rule of law, but as an offense

---

[12] Punitive theorists could also use this argument to make a case for punishment. For that it would have to be the case that punitive sanctions promote feelings of guilt, and that doing so is morally legitimate. I will not follow this argument here because I already argued that we should be careful to use criminal punishment with the explicit aim of provoking feelings of guilt. I also do not know of any research showing that punitive sanctions rather than any other aspect of the criminal trial correlate with feelings of guilt in the offender.

against an individual (or a community), which creates a conflict (Christie 1977). According to restorative justice, then, the aim of the criminal justice system should be to resolve the conflict that has emerged from the wrongdoing, and for this, it is crucial that the conflict remain in the hands of the stakeholders (i.e., the offender, victim, respective friends and family members, broader community, etc.). The central idea of restorative justice is that the stakeholders enter a dialogue about the conflict. In this dialogue, the victim's voice is heard, and in the best case, the offender apologizes to the victim. In some versions of restorative justice, the stakeholders can also make sentencing recommendations.

Research offers promising, albeit only tentative, data for the relationship between restorative approaches and the evocation of guilt in the offender. As John Braithwaite argues, it is to be expected that guilt might arise naturally in face-to-face communication with the victim(s) and the other stakeholder(s).[13] Evidence shows that "74 per cent of victims get an apology from the offender in [restorative] conferences compared to 11 per cent with cases randomly assigned to court" (Braithwaite 2000, 123). If we take apology to be a proxy for guilt, then these figures support our expectations that restorative justice holds promise as a guilt-evoking method for addressing criminal wrongdoing. (For a more comprehensive account of the benefits of restorative justice, see Latimer, Dowden, and Muise 2005; Saulnier and Sivasubramaniam 2018).

I have argued here that promoting feelings of guilt in criminal law is valuable for the beneficial consequences feelings of guilt are correlated with. Now, I provided some evidence that restorative processes are well-suited to bring about feelings of guilt—or at least pick those people out in the judicial system that are guilt prone. But should we worry about the objections from the first section, given that we implement the role of feelings of guilt in criminal law?

The first worry over penance rationales was expressed by the liberal objection: Namely, given that the state is not a close-knit community with shared values that go beyond minimal liberal principles, the state has no right to intervene in the inner feelings of the offender. The restorative justice approach mentioned above is untouched by this worry, as restorative justice does not directly aim to make the offender feel guilty in the first place. It offers them an opportunity to express these feelings and puts them under circumstances where such feelings will more likely occur. But whether or not the feelings of guilt actually occur is indeed none of the state's business in the context of this argument. There is an argument,

---

[13] Braithwaite uses the term "reintegrative shaming" but means what Baumeister et al. call "guilt."

as we have seen, to structure our criminal law in a way that makes this more likely, but none to enforce feelings of guilt.

Solving the liberal challenge by resorting to a procedural claim alone, rather than to a justification of punishment or corrective sanction, might seem like a cheap trick: The idea that, instead of aiming *directly* at feelings of guilt and making these the justification for criminal law, we propose a strategy that aims only *indirectly* at such feelings and thereby believe that we have solved the problem.[14] In fact, on the contrary, this shift toward the concept of restorative justice is more than a mere rephrasing; it has important implications for the state's role in the matter, specifically with respect to whether the state is justified in imposing its will on offenders. For this reason, the liberal worry does not apply here.

Up until now, my suggestion has been merely a procedural one. Because of this, such a limited defense of penance, of course, presupposes that there is a plausible justification for punishment or corrective sanctions in the first place; otherwise, the thesis concerning how to approach criminal law would be vacuous. The suggestion is to give the offender the opportunity to express remorse or experience feelings of guilt within the personal setting of restorative justice, but not to force them to do so. Furthermore, the state need not be involved in the restorative setting at all; thus, we also bypass the worry that the state will intrude into the offender's inner feelings. In sentencing, the state needs to have the last word, but the victim-offender mediation—and even a suggestion for an adequate sentence—can come from the conflict's stakeholders themselves. The worry that the state might intrude into the inner feelings of offenders within the procedural suggestion is therefore unjustified.

What about the worry concerning proportionality? Let us assume here that proportionality of punishment is something that every approach to criminal law must guarantee. As explained above, the risk that is run by making penance a direct aim of criminal law is that two people who commit equal crimes but are unequally "hard-headed" might be sentenced to different kinds and degrees of punishment. But this worry does not apply to the limited account of penance; because such an account does not aim to offer a justification for punishment, the proportionality worry becomes irrelevant. Rather, if implementing restorative justice fails at any point to evoke feelings of guilt, then no justification remains for pushing the offender further. Unlike the account of penance that tries to justify punishment, the procedural thesis thus does not trigger worries about proportionality. On the

---

[14] Radzik also argues that the difference should be understood as one between pursuing a goal and guaranteeing it. Restorative justice approaches are not justified because we aim to make offenders feel guilty, but rather because we have reasons to think that such an outcome will more likely occur during restorative processes than traditional court procedures.

other hand, if we still have good reason to expect feelings of guilt to occur generally—as I have argued that we do—then the social psychology literature can be used to argue for restorative justice as an approach to criminal law.

5.5 Conclusion

The conclusion in this chapter is arguably somewhat messy, given that we do not have the type of data that I think we need in order to satisfyingly answer the most important parts of the arguments in this debate. But here is where I see communicative and penance theories:

Penance approaches fail to provide convincing arguments as to why penance should be the aim of criminal law. There is no convincing argument why penance is intrinsically valuable, and I have foreshadowed that punishment will likely not have the beneficial consequences it would need to bring for a good justification in the context of the penance rationale. Also, when we impose punishment with the aim of penance, several moral objections need to be addressed: Why should a liberal state be concerned with bringing about penance, rather than merely deter offenders or prevent crimes with other means? And how can the penance rationale guarantee proportionality of sanctions if penance is the aim of the criminal law? After all, different offenders likely need different punishments for the same actions in order to come to repent their wrongdoing.

Next, I turned to communicative theories that focus on censure rather than penance. There, I have argued that retributive versions of these theories fail along the same line as retributive penance theories. It is questionable whether censure is intrinsically valuable, and even if it is, there is no convincing argument that it necessarily has to be expressed through punishment.

From this discussion, a more plausible candidate emerged: Assuming that we should communicate censure, punishment is needed for epistemic and consequentialist reasons. We want to really make sure that the offender understood the message the sanctions aim for, and that the community is certain that their values have been defended. The problem with this argument turned out to be that there is no clear data speaking in defense of this claim. To the contrary, I argued that there is at least some evidence suggesting that corrective sanctions and restorative justice can fulfill both the communicative function of punishment and promote feelings of guilt in criminal law, which we should value for their beneficial consequences.

In sum, I think that with the currently available data a communicative approach to criminal law favors corrective sanctions and restorative justice over punitive sanctions.

Chapter 6
Victims' Rights

> The victim is a particularly heavy loser in this situation. Not only has he suffered, lost materially or become hurt, physically or otherwise. And not only does the state take the compensation. But above all he has lost participation in his own case. It is the Crown that comes into the spotlight, not the victim. It is the Crown that describes the losses, not the victim. It is the Crown that appears in the newspaper, very seldom the victim. It is the Crown that gets a chance to talk to the offender, and neither the Crown nor the offender are particularly interested in carrying on that conversation. The prosecutor is fed-up long since. The victim would not have been. He might have been scared to death, panic-stricken, or furious. But he would not have been uninvolved. It would have been one of the important days in his life. Something that belonged to him has been taken away from that victim.
>
> Nils Christie, *Conflicts as Property* (1977, 7–8)

6.1 Introduction

In the previous three chapters I discussed backward-looking justifications of punishment which mainly focus on what offenders deserve for their wrongdoings. Such an offender-focused perspective is very intuitive when thinking about punishment. However, the focus on the offender often comes at the cost of missing another important perspective, one which I have been trying to emphasize throughout this book: The perspective of the victim.

Victims of crimes had many different roles and rights in criminal law throughout the recorded history of legal systems, both with regards to actual practices and the philosophical approaches to criminal law (for a historical and systematic overview, see Braun 2019). In the Middle Ages in Europe, victims of crimes were mostly on their own—they had to initiate the criminal proceedings themselves (if there were any institutionalized ways to do so in the first place) in order to receive compensation for the harm they suffered, or in order to have the right granted to take revenge on the offender. And even if judges were in place, victims in many instances throughout Europe had to literally fight for their right to compensation. In so-called "trials by battle," the victim and the accused party were tasked to fight (sometimes until death) to figure out whose case was justified (the result of the battle was then often seen as a divine judgment) (Braun 2019, 32–35; Rubin 2003). Of course, such a regulation was not about victim empowerment, as is often the motivation in today's debate concerning the role of the victim in criminal law. Rather, the trial by battle was one of the pragmatic mechanisms to solve civil disputes.

The role of the victim became more and more limited once most crimes were also—or rather mainly—understood as crimes against the crown or the sovereign, rather than simply against the direct victim (Braun 2019, 32–35). From that point onward, compensation or revenge for the victim were possible demands in some cases, but the most important aspect of the response to wrongdoing became the punishment of offenders in order to maintain social order and the respect for the sovereign.

Only in the 70's and 80's of the last century has the victim been rediscovered as an important agent in criminal law—both in practice and in the Western literature on criminal law (Braun 2019, 44–51). The return of the victim was especially brought about by feminist movements which conceptualized the lack of victims' rights in the criminal procedure—and thus the ignorance of the impact of wrongdoing on their wellbeing—as *secondary victimization*, particularly with regards to sexual assault (Ash 1972; Braun 2019, chap. 2; Dignan 2005, 15; McDonald 1976). The demands to take the interests of victims seriously and also to prevent secondary victimization has since lead to many policy changes granting victims more rights before the trial, during the trial, and after the trial (Braun 2019).

Parallel to the debate motivated by worries concerning victims' interests and secondary victimization, Nils Christie wrote one of the influential papers for the philosophical debate on the role of the victim in criminal law. In "Conflicts as Property" (1977), he argued—figuratively speaking—that lawyers and judges took the conflict that crimes constitute away from the victim, the offender, and other people who are impacted by the crime (the so-called "stakeholders" of the conflict). Christie sees the lack of autonomy over the conflict as a central problem of most criminal justice systems, because letting the stakeholders resolve the conflict on their own—or at least giving the stakeholders more autonomy when resolving their conflict—will empower the victim, it will do a better job at taking the offender's responsibility seriously, and it helps facilitate reconciliation between the stakeholders; at least that is what Christie tried to convince us of.

Since these groundworks in the 70's and 80's, the literature on the role of the victim in criminal law has been steadily growing. The central question in this chapter will be whether taking the victim's perspective seriously requires and thus justifies the imposition of punishment on offenders. I will argue that this is not the case. Instead, what the victim's interests and rights can justify are claims to restitution from the offender and procedural rights.

I will begin in the next section by motivating why the victim's interests should be taken seriously in criminal law in the first place (Section 6.2). Then, I will turn to the claim that punishment of the offender is necessary to adequately address the victim's interests (Section 6.3).

6.2 Why Care about Victims?

Putting the question this bluntly might seem ignorant. We should obviously care about victims of crimes. But as I mentioned above, for most of the recent centuries, victims were practically irrelevant in criminal law. The state was seen as the primary victim and thus stakeholder of crimes, not the individuals that have been directly harmed by the wrongdoing. Only more recently has the role of the individual victim been discussed, both in politics and philosophy. And that begs the question: Why exactly should the criminal law care about victims of crimes, instead of, for example, simply focusing on the offender or the community?

I will build on an expressivist account of why we should care about victims in criminal law. Expressivist accounts focus on the expressive dimensions of wrongdoing, that is, a certain dimension of harm that goes beyond the purely physical harm victims suffer. I will reject, however, an objectivist and a revenge-based reading of the expressive harm done to victims. The objectivist states that there is intrinsic worth in accounting for expressive wrongs, while the revenge-based strategy understands the expressive harm as a mere desire for revenge that results from the wrongdoing. I will argue that even though the latter is at least on the right track, it misrepresents the actual dimensions of the expressive harms. Instead, expressive harms are best understood as damages to the perceived self-worth of the victims and their perception of justice as well as fairness of the system. The state has good reasons to address both these aspects of the expressive harm.

Objective Expressivism

Victim-centered expressive retributivism is often attributed to Jean Hampton's (1991; 1992) latest work. Unfortunately, the secondary literature does not agree on how exactly to pinpoint the details of her account—whether it is strictly retributive, corrective, based on an objective notion of expressive harms, or a conventional one. Her writings allow for different characterizations depending on where one thinks the emphasis lies (Farnham 2008; Gert, Radzik, and Hand 2004). Objectivists say that the victim's moral worth is intrinsic, based on their rights, dignity, or a similar property, and that a wrongdoing expresses disregard for such an objective value. Conventionalists, on the other hand, focus more on the contingent (though not entirely subjective) expressive effects of wrongdoing on victims, such as a loss of moral self-worth and feeling of justice. There is evidence for both views in her work—but as what I want to call the objectivist version of the argument has been more clearly presented by Farnham (2008), I will discuss his version of the argument here first.

Farnham (2008, 609) agrees that there is an objectivist (metaphysical, in his words) and a conventionalist (epistemic, in his words) reading of Hampton's argument. On the epistemic reading, wrongdoing is taken to give evidence of the violation of the victim's moral value, whereas on the metaphysical reading, there is a concrete realization of the violation of the victim's value. Farnham thinks that the epistemic reading of the argument is unpromising, and thus rejects it—I will return to the reasons why later. For now, we need to get a better understanding of Farnham's version of Hampton's objectivist or metaphysical argument:

> This interpretation focuses on Hampton's concept of *moral injury* and its related notions of *realization* and *acknowledgment* of a person's value. These elements of Hampton's view are Hegelian, recalling his philosophy of giving the concept of abstract right a concrete realization in the world. On this understanding of Hampton's view, some expressive acts do not just *say* something, they *make something the case*. By distinguishing this element of the theory and the kinds of expressive acts that are relevant, we uncover a compelling version of retributivism. (2008, 608)

Farnham embeds this argument into a wider Hegelian metaphysics of sociality, which we need not look at in detail for the purpose of the critique that I want to defend. The central idea, however, is that instead of simply expressing something about the victim's value, wrongdoing actually fails to realize the victim's moral value (2008, 610). Wrongdoing thus creates a relationship between the victim and offender in which the offender has mastered the victim because the offender did not acknowledge the victim's moral value. And it is that failed acknowledgement that matters mostly for objective expressivism:

> There is of course the physical harm to the body or the loss of resources involved, but more importantly there is the objective meaning of this direct interference with a person as an embodied agent. This sort of direct interference involves a personal relationship of master to mastered between two (or more) people. (2008, 613)

Farnham goes on to accept that it is to some degree a matter of convention how societies conceptualize the relationship between offender and victim even within the Hegelian picture he proposes. Because of that there is naturally some margin in which people have responded to different kinds of wrongs historically and cross-culturally. Nonetheless, he thinks that the epistemic reading of the argument overestimates the conventionality of certain responses to wrongdoing:

> One might worry about diminishment being a function of conventions. If the problem is that some convention conveys inferiority, then perhaps the solution is to teach people to overcome the convention. But I think this would be to underestimate the depth of the conventions involved in wrongdoing and the moral injury it involves. Here are some examples of wrongful behavior. Is their wrongness due to their nature, or is it merely a conventional matter? A man rapes a woman. A man kills a convenience store clerk in the course of a robbery. A terrorist kidnaps several people and holds them hostage in order to gain a bargaining advantage. A policeman tortures a member of a group opposed to the current government's policies in order to get more information. (2008, 615)

The immediate problem with this response to a conventionalist reading of expressivism is that it does not really answer the challenge that has been raised. Even though his assessment of the wrongness of such grave wrongdoings is likely correct for the Western audience, that alone does not show that the harms are objective in the relevant sense. Furthermore, not all instances of murder are considered as morally wrong, and rape has for a long time been considered to be morally justifiable at least for some groups (Smith 2011; 2020). Also, another problem is that the argument against conventionalism is somewhat unfair. Even if rape, torture, and murder will never cease to be seen as extremely gruesome acts, our reactions to other wrongdoings might be more malleable. After all, rape and murder are luckily only a fraction of crimes committed. A generalization from most extreme cases simply does not hold—at least not without substantial further argument (see also the objection against Moore's defense of retributivism in Chapter 3 for this point).

Farnham also turns to the topic of our responses to expressive harms to nail down the point that those harms are objective in an important sense:

> Where no public action is taken against a wrongdoer, it doubles the threat his action projects: First, the wrongdoer conveys and realizes his disregard for his victim's will, then the public does so also through knowing inaction. A lack of retributive action both conveys and realizes indifference in a case where acknowledgment requires an active response. [...] Publicly excoriating the wrongdoer and exalting the victim will not do this. It would be like saying, "Well, you've mastered that person, and that person has been mastered by you, and we just want to say that we think it's bad and your victim deserves better." That's taking the unengaged perspective of a spectator who has no direct responsibilities to the people concerned. [...] In the same way that wrongful action is not just an expression of the victim's lesser value, but also a realization of it as lower relative to the wrongdoer who effects this realization, punishment should be a realization by a moral authority of the victim's value as equal to the wrongdoer, correcting the relation of inequality that has been established. (2008, 618)

Farnham wants to pump the intuition that merely saying that one cares about victims will not adequately express respect for them. Even though I think that there is something to this intuition, his characterization of the state's verbal response seems somewhat unfair. Phrasing the response in the way he did clearly symbolizes a disinterested state, but that need not be the wording the state takes when expressing respect for the victim, or even making a parade for her, as Hampton (1992, 15) argued is also possible.

But let us accept that purely verbal or symbolic expression will not suffice to adequately express respect for the victim. Still, the question that needs to be answered is why we should understand the expressive harm in an objective way that can only be addressed with retributive action. After all, other tools such as corrective sanctions are conventionally seen as taking the offender's responsibility seriously by coercing them to provide proportional restitution or reparation to the victim.

There is no explicit argument against the corrective alternative, but I suspect that Farnham's response would be similar to what others have said in the debate: Restitution and reparation simply do not seem to be cut from the same cloth as retributive sanctions (Hampton 1991; 1992; Kleinig 1991, 418; Wringe 2016, 85–87). Corrective sanctions do not realize the victim's value in the same way retributive sanctions would.[15] There are two problems with this response, however.

The first problem I see is that the objectivist's responses seem to push the account dangerously close to what I envision for conventionalist accounts. If the fundamental argument in favor of punitive sanctions rather than corrective sanctions is that corrective sanctions will not find adequate acceptance among the community (rather than being intrinsically inadequate), then such a position is barely distinguishable from what I have in mind with conventional accounts.

The second problem is that Farnham's intuition pump stands unsupported. Whether or not corrective sanctions will be understood within a certain society as acknowledging the victim's moral value needs to be answered with hard data, not just educated guesses from the armchair. Also, whether the victims themselves will consider their moral worth as acknowledged needs to be analyzed in more detail.

In short: Even if the advocates of objective accounts are correct in that punitive sanctions seem on an intuitive level better capable of satisfying the victim's and the public's expectations—the fact that these philosophers resort to what they think would be acceptable for the community warrants that we take a more systematic look at the issue. And if we have to resort to systematic empirical

---

15 The nuances of the critique differ with the accounts. Wringe emphasizes that purely verbal condemnation is insufficient, Kleinig argues that restitution will (realistically speaking) not express the same form of moral seriousness for the offense as punitive treatment.

evidence to answer this question, we basically adopt what I take to be a conventionalist view.

Conventional Expressivism

To get a better understanding of the conventional dimension of expressivism, we need to get back to the question of what expressive wrongs are in more detail. To attempt an answer, Hampton writes:

> Sometimes wrongdoers go out of their way to be deliberately disparaging of their victim's worth; sometimes they intend their actions to be demeaning or degrading. But often they do not *intend* their immoral actions as insults. And yet they are insulting; people who believe their purposes warrant them in taking another's wallet, or another's savings, or another's life, are people who believe their victims are not worth enough to require better treatment. Indeed, they are convinced enough about the importance of their own purposes—and thus of their own importance—to regard their behavior as permissible with respect to these others. (1992, 6)

It is important to note that Hampton wants to evade the conclusion that wrongdoing can literally degrade the moral worth of a person. If that were the case, our actual moral worth would be dependent on how other people treat us. Those who are treated with disrespect would then be less morally valuable than those who are treated with respect—a rather unappealing consequence for an ethical theory (Gert, Radzik, and Hand 2004).

Furthermore, other than the objectivist approach, the wrongfulness does not consist in an objective violation of the victim's moral worth here. Rather, the wrongfulness has to do with the victim experiencing diminishment of her moral self-worth or perception of justice. As Farnham already mentioned above, such a response is often a consequence of being wronged, though the specifics can vary from culture to culture and throughout time.

A conventionalist approach that focuses on such consequences and impacts of the expressive dimension of wrongdoing comes with some problems. First of all, it introduces a measure of subjectivity. Not all people experience loss of value similarly, and some might be wronged without feeling diminished at all. Furthermore, the wrongness cannot literally correlate to the psychological diminishment because some people are wronged without knowing about it (the wrongness of sexual abuse is real even if the victim was drugged beforehand).

This objection stems from a general problem of giving a plausible theory of criminalization. Harm is a prime candidate, but not all criminal wrongdoings result in harms (some can even by accident benefit the victim). I think the most plausible answer to that challenge for the context of this discussion is to emphasize that we typically generalize norms from our experiences. We have a general sense of the typical impact of wrongdoing on people's self-worth and sense of justice—although our shared sense of that should remain open to change. That is to say, when people overreact to certain wrongdoings, we respond by saying something like "it is not really that bad." When someone is pushed after a verbal dispute, and the person experiences extreme loss of self-worth and demands severe punishment, we would correct that person in their assessment of the severity of the wrong. (Sometimes, however, such responses can also be used to trivialize the experience of victims—imagine a sexist wrongdoer responding to allegations of sexual assault with "it is not that bad"). The same happens for the reverse cases, too. Sometimes, we expect people to take the things done to them more seriously, and not let others treat them as they typically do (we say things like "you deserve better than this").

These examples go to show, I think, that we have lively debates about the norms governing the impact of wrongdoing on victims. Such an interpretation allows for the conventionality of such norms to play a role—but at the same time does not resolve to pure arbitrariness.

Another limitation that is worth mentioning here is that this version of the expressive theory does not offer a comprehensive approach to criminal law (see also Hörnle 2019 for this point). Crimes such as tax fraud also have victims in a more abstract sense in that all tax-paying citizens are being cheated in a certain way. But it would seem somewhat off to say that the victims will likely experience some form of diminished self-worth. Tax frauds likely do express a certain disregard for norms of fairness, but that is not quite what the victim-centered perspective is aiming for. This is not too big of a problem, however, as the victim-centered approach need not make claims to offer a comprehensive theory of criminal law (see Chapter 8).

With these limitations in mind, we should take a closer look at the actual effects of wrongdoing on victims. As a first approximation, we can look at the revenge-based motivation that is discussed by Hörnle (2019). I will argue that such an account goes in the right direction but is too narrowly focused on revenge as the central aspect of what victims want after being criminalized.

Hörnle starts with the observation that people will often respond to being victimized with retributive (or vengeful) responses. These vengeful reactions, she hypothesizes, might be important to people's perception of self-worth and justice (Hörnle 2019, 215). It is true that some victims crave revenge after being wronged (Deutchman et al. 2021; Eder, Mitschke, and Gollwitzer 2020; Sjöström, Magraw-Mickelson, and Gollwitzer 2017), but that observation alone does not adequately represent the expressive harm inflicted on them. Understanding expressive effects of wrongdoing on the victim is complicated by the fact that there is no single category of effects on victims where all individuals can be subsumed under. Nils Christie once tried to capture what he thinks is the ideal victim, that is, the type of person most likely to be given the label "victim." The stereotypical or "ideal" victim as described by Christie is female and weak (compared to the offender) and blameless, whereas the offender is depictured as bad and big and anonymous (Christie 1986, 19).

The realistic picture is more complicated, and that has important implications for how we understand the expressive dimension of wrongdoing. But for general terms, it appears to be fair to say that wrongdoing impacts victims' self-esteem and can even lead to self-blame (Dignan 2005). But it can also result in a loss of feeling of justice, that is, a feeling that the state is not doing a good job in upholding the norms of the society, which can lead to distrust of institutions, which, in turn, can have the consequence that victims will report crimes less frequently in the future. This is especially troublesome as many victims come from socially disadvantaged backgrounds (Dijk 2000; Genn 1988; Trickett et al. 1995).

Uli Orth summarizes the effects on the victim in the following way:

> Feelings of revenge among crime victims have another quality compared to empathic feelings of revenge among observers. Important motives for feelings of revenge among victims are re-equilibration of power in relation to the offender, restoration of self-esteem, and escape from psychological pain. (2003, 175)

Two things are important from the research Orth mentions. Firstly, the material harm cannot be completely separated from the expressive harm and failing to take the victim seriously in the criminal procedures can inflict additional expressive harms on the victim. Secondly, the vengeful desires of the victim are not narrowly retributive. Rather, as Hampton suspected, they are primarily focused on re-establishing the person's own self-worth, especially in relation to the offender. But that interest alone does not say anything about which mechanism best re-establishes the victim's perception of justice and feeling of self-worth. I will focus on this question in the next subsection. For now, we can summarize that the expressive harms are indeed best understood as harms to the perceived self-worth of victims and their general feeling of justice, fairness, and trust in the institutions.

Why Should the State Care about Expressive Harms?

With this empirically more adequate picture of expressive wrongs, we still need to motivate "why the state ought to address victims' emotions and why an institution such as criminal punishment with its high monetary and non-monetary costs could be justified on this basis" (Hörnle 2019, 215). After all, the mere fact that victims will suffer expressive harms in addition to material harm does not show that the state needs to intervene. We need a further argument why it should be the state's business to address these harms.

Hörnle herself considers two arguments. One is consequentialist, the other rights based. As she does not offer an explicit account as to why victims have a right to have expressive harms addressed, I will join her in offering a consequentialist argument. That is not to say that intrinsic or rights-based arguments are not feasible, but they would certainly require more elaboration than is possible here. Also, even if it is intrinsically valuable to address expressive harms, that alone does not justify the huge costs of having criminal law institution for promoting intrinsic goodness (Husak 2016). If that is so, we need to at least supplement this argument with a consequentialist twist anyways to make the costs worth it.

The main reason I see why the state should care about expressive wrongs is that the effects on the victim will have further detrimental effects on cooperation, trust in the institutions, and crime reporting. Sociologists have suggested that the more the state, the criminal justice system, and rules are perceived as fair and just, the more people tend to adhere to the rules (Tyler 1990). This is especially important when we look at the reality of criminalization. Many victims and offenders come from similarly socially impoverished communities. That is not to say that there is no criminality outside of such communities, nor is it to say that the people living in these communities are especially bad. The observation here should simply emphasize the importance of not ignoring secondary victimization of people living in communities which might already have low confidence in the justice system and do not perceive it as just. Also, as people who suffer expressive harms are less likely to report wrongdoing, the state misses out on the chance to rectify the wrongdoings and improve its standing in these communities.

If the perception of justice matters for adherence to the laws—and if adherence to the law is what the state has a business in promoting—then addressing expressive harms seems to be a good method for the state to promote adherence to the law. Again, that is not to say that other reasons do not matter. Some might think that this reasoning misses the central point, namely the intrinsic badness of expressive harms. But these reasons are not excluded here simply because I focus on the consequentialist benefits. Rather, I focus on these because it is somewhat easier to show that the state will appreciate these reasons and thus alleviate the expressive harms.

6.3 Why Care About Punishment?

If it is plausible that the state has a legitimate interest in helping to alleviate the expressive harms imposed on victims of wrongdoing, we still need to figure out in which way exactly this should happen. In the literature, the paradigmatic way of addressing expressive harm is to inflict legal punishment on the offender (Hampton 1992; Hörnle 2019; Glasgow 2015; Wringe 2016). But other ways are open to the state. The state could, for example, simply verbally or symbolically express concern for the victim and emphasize their importance to the state. Or, as I want to suggest, the offender could be coerced to provide some form of restitution, and both the offender and the victim can be given the opportunity to participate in restorative processes. Even though many philosophers have believed that punishment is the only possible way to address expressive harms, this claim has to be argued for.

I want to discuss two types of arguments for the necessity of punishment. The first, which I will refer to as the *retributive argument*, comes closest to the position generally taken by philosophers within this debate. According to the retributive argument, punishment is the only adequate response to expressive wrongdoing as only it can address the moral wrongfulness of expressive harms, instead of just the material and psychological suffering that is imposed on the victim.

The second argument for the necessity of punishment relies on a more contingent feature of punishment. The epistemic argument claims that a state response without punishment fails to convincingly communicate that the state really condemns the offender and really values the victim. As the saying goes: "Actions speak louder than words," and in this context, we could say that punishment speaks louder than corrective sanctions (or purely symbolic expressions, for that matter)—and the victim's interests should be heard clearly. Without punishment, the victim will not be able to believe that the state really cares, and thus the expressive harm cannot be alleviated.

In the next two subsections, I will discuss these two arguments. I will dismiss the retributive argument as it has the same problem the general line of retributivism typically has: It cannot explain the necessary connection between harming an offender and righting a wrong or expressing concern for the victim of the wrongdoing. The epistemic argument, on the other hand, has a better shot at a convincing case for hard treatment of offenders. If corrective sanctions really were to give victims no redress for the loss of perceived self-worth, then corrective sanctions do not get the job done they were supposed to do in the first place: Empowering victims and putting their interests more into the focus of criminal law. The data, however, suggests otherwise. Harshness of sanctions does play a role, but not as much as do restitution and communication of respect during the criminal process.

The Retributive Argument for Harsh Treatment

Why should we opt for punishment of the offender for addressing expressive harms? Hampton's claim that punishment is necessary to do so was challenged from various perspectives: If it is the victim's moral worth that has to be restored, why not have a parade in her honor, thereby clearly establishing that she should be treated in accordance with her moral value (Hanna 2008)? Why not simply make a verbal statement that acknowledges the victim's value and expresses condemnation of what the offender has done (Günther 2014)? Or why not solely make the offender repair the harm done to the victim to adequately counter the demeaning message of the crime? To respond to such questions, Hampton writes:

> [R]etribution is actually a form of compensation to the victim. Whereas tort damages are supposed to be awarded to place the victim in the situation she would have been in had the tortfeasor not acted, retribution is supposed to be inflicted to nullify the wrongdoer's message of superiority over the victim, thus placing the victim in the position she would have been in had the wrongdoer not acted. Hence the real contrast between corrective justice and retributive justice is not that the former is compensatory whereas the latter is not, but rather that each compensates a different form of damage. Corrective justice compensates victims for harms, whereas retributive justice compensates victims for moral injuries. (1991, 1769–70)

This response by Hampton relates to her objective understanding of the expressive wrong that is imposed on victims by crimes. Therefore, we need to raise the same question as in the previous section: What exactly is the moral injury given that it is distinct from the material, emotional, and broader psychological injury to the victim—and why is this distinct property of the wrongness only addressable by imposing punishment on offenders? Hampton needs to give us a concrete answer and cannot simply state that only retribution can adequately address the wrongness of crime (which is independent of physical and psychological harm).

In my reading of Hampton's work, such an answer is hard to find. Where the answer appears to be the clearest, it sounds more like an epistemic or conventionalist approach than a retributive one:

> It is necessary not merely to object to that denial of worth, but to nullify the evidence that her worth is lower than that of the wrongdoer. *Punishment is a particularly good technique for doing so, insofar as it shows that the victim can succeed, either directly or indirectly (through her agent, e.g., the state) in resubjugating the subjugator.* Once he has been punished, the wrongdoer can't be taken to have subjugated or mastered the victim through his actions, thereby lowering her worth relative to his, because the victim (or her agent acting in her name) has been able to force him to undergo an experience something like the one which he inflicted upon her, thereby proving that she has not been subjugated by him, and thus has not lost value relative to his value. (Hampton 1992, 16 emphasis added)

In this formulation, we can see that the epistemic perspective comes in the focus. Hampton talks about "proving" that the victim is not inferior to the offender. But she also says that this should be achieved by doing something similar to what the offender did. If we take this formulation seriously, we will end up with a retributive approach based on the *lex talionis*. But given Hamptons broader context, it is unlikely that she literally means that the offender should undergo the same treatment as the victim did in order to prove that the offender cannot succeed in subjugating the victim. This would entail that addressing moral wrongs requires the offender to be beaten, sexually assaulted, tortured, or killed. Few in modern liberal states will find this appealing (barring, of course, Kershnar 2001). So, the claim has to be that something at least proportional to that which has been done to the victim has also to be inflicted on the offender.

But still, we did not get an explicit argument for why proportional intentional infliction of harm is the most adequate way of subjugating the offender, if we accept that doing so restores moral value at all. At times, Hampton herself admits that punishment is not the only, and maybe even not the most adequate way, of achieving that, after all. This becomes apparent when she turns to the Christian notion of turning the other cheek as a response to wrongdoing:

> Kind treatment towards us by one we have abused *startles* us, makes us pay attention to the one we have hurt, makes us aware *that* we have hurt him, and makes us aware of the injustice of our deed. Accordingly we feel humbled in the face of that kindness. But this experience of being humbled (along with the painful emotions of shame and humiliation that generally accompany it signals that the treatment we have just received is retributive: the victim has responded to us in a way that has "put us in our place," robbed us of our pretense of elevation with respect to the victim. We feel chastened, just as we would have felt had we been punished. (Hampton 1992, 16–17)

So, if the aim of the response is simply to humble the offender, punishment is not always necessary (though it, admittedly, might sometimes be the best way to achieve that aim). If that is true, the retributive strategy fails. First, there is no necessary connection between punishment and addressing expressive wrongs if what Hampton says is true. And if there is no necessary connection, we need to know more about the characteristics that make state intervention successful in doing so.

At this point, the epistemic approach is the more obvious candidate. We need to find the type of state response that best clarifies to victims that the political community cares about their interests and well-being, and that violations of their legitimate interests are not taken lightly. But it remains open which state actions communicate this message to victims and helps them with the expressive harms.

The Epistemic Argument for Harsh Treatment

If expressive retributivists invoke the epistemic argument for hard treatment, they need to address the *conventionality objection* (Hanna 2008; Günther 2014). The objection claims that our current way of expressing our respect for the victim or condemnation of the offender's wrongdoing by using harsh treatment only seems necessary as an adequate response because we are used to expressing ourselves in our society that way. But the contingent fact that this is how we are used to do things hardly offers a good justification for intentionally harming offenders if less harmful alternatives that work just as well to express respect for the victim or condemnation for the offender exist. And the contingency is even more apparent if we take a historical perspective, or a current cross-cultural one. We used to hold (and some still hold) that it is necessary to torture and kill people to express adequate condemnation for some wrongs, or to express adequate respect for the rights and moral status of victims. And even today, some societies still kill people for certain crimes, whereas other societies sentence such offenders to serve years in prison that still allow them to exert some of their freedom. But—and this is crucial—both societies likely claim that their way of expressing condemnation of the offender, or respect for the victim, is adequate. But either one of them is wrong, and then we would need an additional argument for which side is right, or the expression of condemnation or respect really is contingent on historic and cultural circumstances. And if that is true, why not aim for a convention that expresses condemnation of the offender and valuation of the victim with other means than punitive sanctions?

Hörnle takes the conventionality objection seriously. In her paper, she mainly addresses the objection that purely verbal condemnation could substitute a punitive response, but in her argument, she also turns to corrective sanctions:

> Secondly, in order for merely verbal censure to be taken seriously, one would require a high degree of authority and standing of those who express censure. This might work if offender, victim and the general audience share a high degree of respect for the institution expressing it (imagine a "high priest" in religious environments), but in our contemporary secular and egalitarian states, judges cannot be expected to have this kind of authority *qua* their office. It is a common feature of legal systems to work with visible signs of distinction (such as robes and court room architecture) but such efforts will be increasingly less suited to impress contemporary audiences. Solemn words will usually not be sufficient to convey the seriousness of censure. They need to be accompanied by some kind of token in the form of unpleasant treatment to underline the message. *This does not mean that the strong expression "suffering" is appropriate in all cases, but the unpleasant treatment must go beyond the demand to pay financial compensation for the costs the victim had due to the crime.* (2019, 219 my emphasis)

The crucial part of Hörnle's argument here relies on an empirical assumption, namely that "[s]olemn words will usually not be sufficient to convey the seriousness of censure" (2019, 219). She does not, however intuitive the claim is, provide any evidence for it. Her reference after the just quoted sentence leads to a paper by John Kleinig (1991, 417) which makes the same claim, however, also without providing any substantial evidence apart from the common saying that "sticks and stones will break my bones, but words will never hurt me" as well as his own intuitive agreement with this claim.

For the epistemic argument to succeed, we need to have empirical evidence for whether or not different state actions will succeed in communicating respect for the victim and alleviating the expressive harms. Though Hörnle focuses on the condemnatory dimension of sanctions, compensation, and pure communication—we are, of course, mainly interested in the effects of such actions on the victim. This will of course be more complicated and might make the argument messier depending on what the research suggests, but without it we simply cannot judge the merit of the epistemic argument.

Before looking at the evidence, though, we also need to clarify Hörnle's and other's statement that "unpleasant treatment" is necessary for adequate censure. As has been a main issue in this book (see Chapter 2), it is valuable for the discussion to try and give a somewhat clear distinction between punitive approaches and corrective approaches. Corrective approaches typically also involve "unpleasant treatment," in that they coerce offenders to do something (such as pay restitution or do community service) which they normally would not want to do. But as we can see in Hörnle's quote, compensation is clearly inadequate, even though it also entails some form of unpleasant treatment. What Hörnle means is the intentional infliction of harm, i.e., punishment. We thus need to distinguish unpleasant treatment in the context of restitution orders from unpleasant treatment in the context of the intentional infliction of harm on offenders.

What kind of empirical evidence do we need to look at? What we are looking for is data that speaks to expressive harms and how to alleviate them. We have understood expressive harms in this chapter as harms that involve the victim's perception of moral self-worth and their trust in the justice system. Criminal wrongdoing does not only harm victims in material ways, but also in these dimensions as well. So, we need data on what types of state actions alleviate these kinds of harms to the victim. Specifically, we need to know whether punitive sanctions alleviate such harms comparatively better than corrective sanctions do.

Laxminarayan (2013) interviewed victims of crimes in the Netherlands in order to investigate which types of sanctions were successful to reach certain psychological goals of the victims. The psychological dimensions were conceptualized by Orth (2002) as part of investigating secondary victimization, but they broadly fit to parts of what we have been considering when investigating expressive harms, such as:

> "What consequences did the criminal proceedings have on your ability to cope with the crime?"
> "What consequences did the criminal proceedings have on your self-esteem?"
> "What consequences did the criminal proceedings have on how optimistically you view the future?"
> "What consequences did the criminal proceedings have on your trust in the legal system?"
> "What consequences did the criminal proceedings have on your faith in a just world?"
> (Laxminarayan 2013, 946)

The different sanction options that have been investigated included incarceration, compensation from the offender, compensation from the state, community service and acquittal (no sanction). Incarceration was interpreted as a primarily punitive sanction, whereas compensation from the offender was interpreted as what I call corrective sanctions ("restorative" in Laxminarayan's terms). Besides that, demographic information and the satisfaction with the criminal process were also analyzed. Laxminarayan (2013, 949) found that only the satisfaction with the procedure and the compensation from the offender showed a significant improvement of the psychological well-being of the victim as measured in the study. The effect did not differ with the severity of the wrongdoing or other demographic factors. It is interesting that compensation from the state did not have the same effects on well-being as did compensation from the offender, suggesting that compensation alone is not the sole factor for psychological well-being after wrongdoing. Other research suggests a similar importance of compensation for the victim, especially of compensation from the offender (Davis 1992; Erez and Tontodonato 1992; Ruback, Cares, and Hoskins 2008; Shapland 1984).

There is evidence for the importance of satisfaction with the criminal proceeding for psychological well-being from a wide array of research (Davis 1992; Erez and Tontodonato 1992; Ruback, Cares, and Hoskins 2008). Such satisfaction typically requires taking the victim's perspective seriously—that is, taking them seriously as an epistemic agent—and it requires not pressuring them as is sometimes done in cross-examination, and giving them some role to play in the criminal proceeding. These findings are also corroborated by studies investigating the effects of restorative justice. Some studies suggest that the informal part of restorative justice, that is, the conversation and potentially apology by the offender, are more valued by the victim than money or vengeance (Sherman et al. 2005) and that such conferences are associated with reduction in psychological harm of victims (Strang et al. 2006). In a review article, Latimer et al. found that "restorative justice programs are a more effective method of improving victim and/or offender satisfaction [...]

when compared to more traditional criminal justice programs" (2005, 138). These results have to be taken with a grain of salt, however. Participation in restorative procedures is voluntary, and voluntariness might be a confounding factor for the benefits that are correlated with restorative justice. Furthermore, Kunst et al. (2015) argue in a meta-analysis that even though the results are suggestive, they vary from study to study. Also, the authors warn us that there are important methodological limitations in the current research on victim satisfaction with the criminal procedure. After all, not every victim wants to have these procedural rights, and forcing them to participate in restorative procedures might add more distress than it does them good. Also, the success of procedural rights heavily depends on their successful implementation. That is, giving victims a voice in the criminal proceeding but then rudely interrupting them will likely not help with alleviating expressive harms. More research is thus needed to make confident judgments surrounding expressive harms.

So, there is at least some evidence to think that compensation from the offender and procedural rights help alleviate expressive harms, though we should be careful with our confidence in the current research. But what about punitive sanctions? Unfortunately, I know of little direct investigation of the effect of punitive sanctions on expressive harms as understood in this chapter. We have already seen in Laxminarayan's (2013) studies that no such evidence was found. It is of course very much possible that I overlooked such evidence in my search. But with the evidence I found, punitive sanctions do not appear to be very productive in that regard.

Bringing the focus back to the epistemic argument, I think that it is fair to say that the retributivist has a harder case arguing for the necessity of punitive sanctions than has been assumed by some philosophers. If the studies I just outlined are on the right track, then restitution and procedural aspects seem to play a more important role to alleviate the expressive harms than do punitive sanctions. That is not to say that proper punishment will never achieve this aim. But for practical purposes, we need to decide which rationale should guide sentencing in criminal law. If we had perfect knowledge, and if the expressive harms were all that mattered, we would implement individual sentences that perfectly address the expressive harms of each individual—which would sometimes entail punitive sanctions, mostly corrective sanctions, and always procedural acknowledgement.

But we cannot say in advance what will help all victims—and the expressive harm of victims is not the only morally relevant aspect in the debate. As I have rejected strictly retributive accounts here, we have to calculate the harm inflicted on the offender into the decision whether to punish offenders for the sake of alleviating the expressive harms of some victims. Given that corrective sanctions are typically less harsh than punitive ones and given that they are more successful in addressing expressive harms (together with procedural aspects), I think that the correct conclusion to draw from the discussion here is that the corrective rationale should guide our attempts to address expressive harms—at least as long as the empirical evidence points in that direction.

Lastly, I want to address a worry that is sometimes raised against relying too much on restorative justice. Hörnle for example writes that "[s]uch an approach clashes with important principles such as the principle of equality: these [sanctioning] decisions should be left to judges" (2019, 223). Here, the critique aims at those accounts of restorative justice that allow stakeholders to come up with their own sanction recommendation, which might lead to different sanctions for similar wrongs, depending on what the stakeholders agree on. This would violate an important principle of fairness in law.

There are three responses to this worry.

First, we could accept the criticism but make an companions-in-guilt argument. If different sentences for similar wrongdoings is a problem for corrective approaches, it should also be one for punitive approaches. Hörnle's response that sentencing decisions should be left to judges suggests that judges always treat like cases alike. But that is not obviously the case. To the contrary, there is some evidence to think that judges make different decisions in identical cases (Koppen and Kate 1984; also Bagaric 2000 on the problem of inconsistent sentencing in law), and are influenced by irrelevant factors in their decision making (Chen and Loecher 2019; Cho, Barnes, and Guanara 2017; Danziger, Levav, and Avnaim-Pesso 2011; Eren and Mocan 2018; Kneer and Bourgeois-Gironde 2017; Rachlinski and Wistrich 2017; Spamann and Klöhn 2016; Spamann 2020)—which suggests that judges might not be better at upholding the principle of equality than stakeholders would be.

Second, it is unclear whether restorative approaches are really committed to what Hörnle says they are. Haynes et al. write that "evidence suggests that victims are more interested in being treated with dignity and respect than influencing the sentencing decision" (2015, 469). If that is so, the benefits of restorative procedures can be reaped even without allowing stakeholders to make their own sentencing decisions. Furthermore, stakeholder could make suggestions rather than decisions, which would still allow judges to check whether the suggestions are proportional and fit with other recommendations for similar wrongdoings.

The third response is to deny that the implication Hörnle draws is really problematic. As mentioned above, there is some evidence suggesting that people do not mind the outcome of a process that much as long as the procedure is perceived as fair. If that is also true for comparison between different groups who made different sanction recommendations for similar wrongs, then we should rethink the demand of equal sanctions for similar wrongdoings. It is unclear, however, whether these findings generalize—and as far as it is unclear as of now, we cannot rely on this response here. But we have to keep in mind that the idea of fairness of outcome might be less important than we think it is.

To sum up: As far as the epistemic argument goes it suggests that corrective sanctions and procedural aspects of the wrongdoing are the best means of addressing the expressive harms that wrongdoings impose on victims. As such, the corrective approach is the way to go for respecting the victims' interests in criminal law.

6.4 Conclusion

This chapter took a closer look at the interests or rights of victims and asked whether punishment is needed to address expressive harms done to victims. First, I have argued that expressive harms are best understood as the loss of a sense of (moral) worth and a loss of trust in the justice system. Then, I have argued that the state has a legitimate interest in addressing expressive harms (in addition to material harms), as expressive harms, if not addressed adequately, can result in a loss of confidence in the justice system, less cooperation, and less reporting of criminal activity.

But how can expressive harms be best addressed? I have argued that this should be primarily understood as an empirical question, namely: Which state actions best restore the victim's self-esteem and trust in the justice system? Here, I have argued that even though some victims crave revenge, most victims benefit the most when the offender is coerced to provide restitution for the victim, and if the victim is shown respect during the criminal trial. That involves taking her testimony seriously, acting with respect during the criminal process, and proving as much information about the criminal trial as possible. Expressive harms are thus best addressed with corrective sanctions and restorative justice.

It should also be noted that the criminal law is not the only institution which should help with the victim's expressive harms. It is of course the most important one for the context of this book; but for a comprehensive approach, we should also look into (mental) health care and other dimensions to fully take into consideration the expressive harms imposed on victims.

Part III: **Forward-Looking Approaches**

Chapter 7
Deterrence

> But take away desert and the whole morality of the punishment disappears. Why, in Heaven's name, am I to be sacrificed to the good of society in this way? – unless, of course, I deserve it.
>
> C. S. Lewis, *The Humanitarian Theory of Punishment* (1953, 227)

7.1 Introduction

Deterrence has a somewhat unique place in the debate on the justification of punishment. On the one hand, it seems blatantly obvious to laypeople, legal professionals, and legislature that deterrence should be a main aim of criminal law (Carlsmith, Darley, and Robinson 2002; Carlsmith 2008; Crockett, Özdemir, and Fehr 2014; Gromet and Darley 2009). On the other hand, however, there are few philosophers who embrace deterrence confidently as a main aim of criminal law from a normative perspective (Bagaric 1999)—while the criticism of deterrence is all the fiercer from the retributivist side of the debate.

Deterrence is often discussed in the context of utilitarian theories of punishment (Bentham 1789). This is somewhat unfortunate, I think. In the context of utilitarianism, the discussion of deterrence is often overshadowed by objections against utilitarianism in general, which leads to some rather quick and dismissive arguments against deterrence based on general problems of utilitarianism.[16]

Deterrence need not be based on utilitarianism of course (Chiao 2016, 161). We can value deterrence simply because we want to be safe from wrongdoing, that is, independent of the principle to maximize happiness or well-being. Social contract theories also value deterrence for its (supposed) effect of making people respect the contractually agreed upon rights of their fellow citizens (Lee 2018). Either way, we need not resort to utilitarianism to ground deterrence. In this chapter, I want to look at the problems of deterrence theories on their own terms without worrying about the specific problems of the broader theoretical backgrounds motivating the appeal to deterrence.

I should also note here that in these various traditions, deterrence is—as far as I know—never seen as intrinsically valuable. What really matters to those who

---

[16] Deirdre Golash, for example, sums up her discussion of punishment based on deterrence in the context of utilitarianism as follows: "Punishment, conceived simply as the doing of harm to some in order to prevent harm to others, is as morally suspect as quiet euthanasia of the unsightly homeless" (2005, 48).

care about deterrence is that society is made safer, or in other formulations, that the citizens comply with the laws. Deterrence is just one possible way of reaching the aim of law-abidingness. Other—morally less costly—ways of making people stick to the laws are always preferred to punishment (all other things being equal).

Deterrence works by giving citizens prudential incentives to abide by the law. The prudential incentives are negative, that is they consist in the threat and execution of harm on wrongdoers. Some authors such as Lee (2017) have proposed a broader understanding of deterrence which also includes offering the offender moral reasons (rehabilitation) rather than prudential reasons in the form of punishment. Deterrence and rehabilitation, however, bring up very different moral challenges which deserve their separate discussion. In this chapter, I will focus on the narrow understanding of deterrence. Chapter 10 will briefly touch on questions of rehabilitation.

Two types of deterrence in the narrow sense can be distinguished. Specific deterrence is the infliction of punishment on specific offenders with the aim of giving those offenders reasons not to commit a wrongdoing again in the future. General deterrence is the threat and imposition of punishment on offenders with the aim of showing to other would-be offenders that it is imprudent to commit crimes. Any instance of punishment can of course have both specific and general deterrence justifications and effects.

In this chapter, I want to argue that deterrence is a morally justifiable aim of criminal law, but that the data we have to date does not support punitive sanctions over corrective sanctions when measured by their respective deterrent effects. This will show that deterrence is one more aim on the list in this book that can legitimately be pursued through corrective sanctions. I will proceed as follows: First, I will clarify the conceptual messiness of investigating the empirical success of deterrence both for punitive and corrective sanctions (Section 7.2). Most of the criminological data obviously does not have the conceptual distinctions in mind that I have emphasized in this book, and therefore the data has to be interpreted carefully with this caveat in mind—which makes a definite conclusion difficult. Nonetheless, I will argue that the case for the deterrent success of harsh and punitive sanctions is rather weak and that corrective approaches paint a somewhat more promising picture, even though they, too, are not the silver bullet for crime reduction (Section 7.3). Lastly, I will argue that a justification of corrective sanctions based on the deterrence rationale can address all the normative objections that have been brought up against it sufficiently well (Section 7.4).

7.2 The Messiness of Testing Philosophical Theories

As I am a philosopher by training, I can only be an informed reader when it comes to the question of the deterrent effects of punitive and corrective sanctions. But I do have some expertise regarding conceptual issues that clarify—perhaps complicate—the interpretation of the criminological research for either punitive or corrective approaches to criminal law. So that is what I want to do first.

Criminologists are already careful to conceptually differentiate between various preventive effects of criminal punishment. When criminologists find that sending offenders to prison has the effect that the crime rate is lowered for the time of incarceration, then such crime-reducing effects are due to incapacitation, not deterrence. Only if offenders stop committing offenses after being released from prison (or being sanctioned otherwise) does the data speak for the deterrent effects of punitive sanctions. Such and other nuances already complicate the interpretation of the data (Apel and Nagin 2014; Bun et al. 2020).

But more important for me is the following observation: When criminologists look at the effects of fines or imprisonment, this in itself does not speak as to whether they analyze punitive or corrective sanctions. Criminologists are conceptually more neutral in that regard—they are simply interested in the effects of certain specific kinds of sanctions. Philosophers need to decide whether these sanctions are better conceptualized as punishments, as corrective sanctions, or something else altogether. After all, corrective approaches to criminal law similarly demand that offenders pay a certain amount of money as restitution to the victim, or even undergo some form of community service to offer restitution for the harm inflicted on the victim(s) of the wrongdoing. Potentially, some form of incapacitation (e.g., imprisonment or house-arrest), can also be justified from within the corrective rationale (Boonin 2018).

A first attempt of conceptual clarification would be to say that punitive fines are such that they are paid to the government by the wrongdoer in response to a wrongdoing. A "fine" paid to the victim is better conceived of as a corrective sanction rather than a punitive one, as I have argued in Chapter 2. (Though there might be some exceptions where corrective payments are made to the state as a substitute in cases where the victim is not around anymore to receive restitution). The problem now for analyzing the data is the following: If the criminological data suggests that there are deterrent effects if we raise the fine for a certain wrongdoing from $1,000 to $2,000, then such a finding alone does not necessarily speak in favor of punitive rather than corrective approaches. The data simply suggests that demanding more money from offenders will have certain deterrent effects.

Say we raise the sanction for common assault from $7,500 (no prison time) to $10,000 (or 6 months in prison). Making the sanction harsher in that sense can certainly be captured within the punitive rationale, where we intentionally harm offenders in the hopes of a stronger deterrent effect. But the harsher sanction can also in principle be justified within the corrective rationale. If victimologists were to find that the harm inflicted on victims of common assault is inadequately covered by the lower amount of restitution, or without some form of incapacitation, then such a harsher sanction can be justified in the corrective rationale. This, of course, depends on the more difficult question how much restitution is owed for a certain type of wrongdoing. As I will argue in the next chapter, proportionality is a rather vague method of measurement and allows for a quite broad application—which complicates the analysis quite a bit.

But not all sanctions can be covered within the corrective rationale, of course. If wrongdoers do not pose an objective threat to the victim or broader society after their wrongdoing, then incarceration cannot be easily justified within the corrective rationale. What is more, even if some form of incapacitation is justified, house arrest and surveillance are to be preferred to prison, as the former types of sanctions are less harsh while still restoring a feeling of security (let us assume here). Because of that, criminological studies that investigate the deterrent effects of prisons are certainly skewed towards punitive rather than corrective sanctions and the evidence should thus count more for the efficacy of punitive sanctions.

The same complications apply to community service as a type of sanction. As argued in Chapter 2, community service is compatible with the corrective rationale. If the criminological data suggested that a certain type of community service imposed as a sanction has deterrent effects (compared to a fine, let us say), then we need further information to decide whether this speaks only in favor of punitive approaches or also for corrective approaches. Again, if the harshness of the community service goes well beyond what would constitute adequate restitution, then that kind of data would only speak in favor of punitive approaches. But if the community service would be within the limits of corrective approaches, then that data cannot be used as an argument in favor of the deterrent effects of punitive over corrective approaches.

To sum up: The criminological data is even more difficult to adequately assess given the conceptual distinctions elaborated on in this book. Oftentimes, specific sanctions are both compatible with the punitive as well as the corrective rationale, so that the sanctions' deterrent effects cannot be used to strengthen one over the other approach. Nonetheless, we still need to know whether such sanctions have deterrent effects in the first place, and whether we can say at least broadly something about the difference between the effectiveness of punitive and corrective sanctions.

7.3 Criminological Data

Punitive Sanctions

As already noted above, the analysis of the criminological data is notoriously difficult even without the conceptual complications that I introduced. As Bun and colleagues summarize in their recent article:

> [D]espite the rich history of econometric modelling spanning over 40 years, there is arguably no consensus on whether there is a strong deterrent effect of law enforcement policies on crime activity. Empirical studies provide mixed evidence that are insufficient to draw clear conclusions. (Bun et al. 2020, 2305)

If that is correct, we cannot say with any certainty whether harsh sanctions that would skew towards the punitive rationale are effective in deterring offenders. There is some consensus, however, that there is no one-fits-all answer. Whether or not certain sanctions have deterrent effects depends on the details of the sanctions employed and on the circumstances.

Consider imprisonment as a sanction which skews towards being punitive rather than corrective. Apel and Nagin (2014, 1000) take a closer look at three studies which respectively find a significant, marginally significant, and no significant effect of imprisonment on deterrence, measured as the decrease of criminal activity of a certain type in response to an introduction or increase of prison sentences (Helland and Tabarrok 2007; Lee and McCrary 2009; Weisburd, Einat, and Kowalski 2008). A problem with the study that reported a significant effect of prison on the crime rate is that the incarceration was threatened on those offenders who were already sanctioned to pay a fine—and would then be imprisoned if they fail to do so. Also, in this condition, the certainty of imprisonment was extremely high as all the offenders have already been apprehended for other crimes—the effects of the threat of imprisonment might thus be a result of the certainty of the sanction rather than the harshness of the sanction. Previous research suggests that the certainty of the punishment has a stronger deterrent effect than the harshness of the sanctions (Apel and Nagin 2014, 999; Bun et al. 2020). That is not to say that the unpleasantness of the consequence does not matter, but that it is unclear how severe it has to be to find the deterrent effect. Apel and Nagin thus summarize the studies in question in the following manner:

> [T]hese three studies nicely illustrate that the deterrent effect of the threat of punishment is context-specific and that debates about whether deterrence works or not are ill posed. Instead, the discussion should be in terms of whether the specific sanction deters or not and if it does, whether the benefits of crime reduction are sufficient to justify the costs of impos-

> ing the sanction. To illustrate, while Helland and Tabarrok (2007) conclude that the third-strike effect in California is a deterrent, they also conclude, based on a cost-benefit analysis, that the crime-saving benefits are likely far smaller than the increased costs of incarceration. (2014, 1001)

So, rather than asking more broadly whether punitiveness helps, we should ask more precisely which kinds of sanctions help in given circumstances. This strategy is also corroborated by Abt (2017) who focuses on community violence in inner cities, especially committed by young people. There, too, a narrow focus on specific programs appears to be more promising than a holistic approach to crime reduction. Abt (2017, 271) argues that community violence is "sticky," that is, it centers around few people, in very specific areas.

Simply making the punishments for violent crimes harsher does not seem to have any clear deterrent effects and can sometimes even be detrimental to the crime rate (Abt 2017, 277). The most promising avenues when addressing community violence appear to be focused deterrence and cognitive behavioral therapy (CBT). Focused deterrence

> involves the identification of specific offenders and offending groups, the mobilization of a diverse group of law enforcement, social services, and community stakeholders, the framing of a response using both sanctions and rewards, and direct, repeated communication with the individuals and groups in order to stop their violent behavior. (Abt 2017, 276)

These observations still leave open room for detailed interpretation about the effectiveness of punitive sanctions, but that only helps to pin down the general point: There is indeed need for specific sanctions as these add prudential reasons for offenders to adhere to the laws—but in what circumstances such sanctions really help needs to be determined in the context of the given offender group, not as a general approach.

If these findings are on the right track, we should be less focused on the harshness of sanctions than on more specific and focused approaches to address criminal law. We need more data as to which sanctions work best in a given situation—and which alternatives to sanctions can be implemented. Abt for example also mentions CBT, which promises to reduce recidivism at rates as high as 50% for the people who underwent CBT (2017, 275). Here, too, the details are more nuanced and not all programs work equally well—and the success highly depends on how well the execution is.

None of these considerations directly speak to the question as to whether the sanctions employed should be punitive rather than corrective—and it is also not clear how we can clarify this issue in detail. One small step would be to take a look at whether imprisonment does much work for deterrence. As already mentioned above, broad statements about harsh sanctions do not seem to yield any benefits anyway, but a closer look appears to make this case more forceful with the example of incarceration. Sundt and colleagues (Sundt, Salisbury, and Harmon 2016) analyzed data from California, where the state cut on roughly 17% of the imprisonment rate. The researcher found no effect of reduction of imprisonment on the crime rate. That is, while around $453 million in taxpayer money was saved by this initiative, no detrimental effects on public safety were found. These findings also cannot be applied to prisons as a whole. Prisons in the US are notoriously famous for being overcrowded, and the sanctions too punitive. A roughly 20% cut in imprisonment rate thus cannot be generalized to prisons as a whole and their deterrent effects. But here, again, the evidence should make us hesitant to embrace (very harsh) punitive sanctions from the perspective of the deterrence rationale (for a similar perspective on imprisonment in Germany, see Galli 2020).

Corrective Sanctions and Restorative Justice

Let us assume for the sake of the discussion here that having a well-ordered institution that sanctions misbehavior is generally better than having none. But that of course does not answer which types of sanctions best further the aim of law-abidingness, or with which methods we should do so. Above I reviewed some evidence suggesting that the harshness of sanctions is not of primary importance. Here, I want to argue that there is some evidence to suggest that offering stakeholders of the conflict to participate in restorative processes has additional beneficial effects on recidivism.

Two meta-analyses (Latimer, Dowden, and Muise 2005; Sherman et al. 2015), which analyze the data from all the relevant studies on the matter the authors could find, offer promising data to investigate the question in more detail. Some limitations regarding the question in this book, however, should be noted. First, these meta-analyses look at the effect of restorative conferencing—that is, some form of mediation between the stakeholders of the conflict—and not on the effects of the sanctions that were potentially agreed upon in these types of settings. Secondly, the research is still very much in the early stage—especially when applying high standards to the ways in which the data is collected.

Both meta-analyses find that

> restorative justice programs are a more effective method of improving victim and/or offender satisfaction, increasing offender compliance with restitution, and decreasing the recidivism of offenders when compared to more traditional criminal justice responses (i.e., incarceration, probation, court-ordered restitution, etc.). (Latimer, Dowden, and Muise 2005, 138)

In the newer meta-analysis, the effect of restorative justice procedures on recidivism was rather moderate, but unexpectedly, more effective in cases of serious wrongdoing rather than cases of less grave wrongdoings (Sherman et al. 2015, 11–12).

There are some important further caveats. First, researchers can only speculate about why these processes work. It is speculated that the emotional experience might play an important part, which is compatible with the finding that there was a stronger effect in cases of graver wrongdoing—but there is not yet the type of data available that would make drawing such a conclusion justifiable. Furthermore, there is a potential self-selection effect at work in these studies. Participants in restorative processes need to consent to these procedures, and those offenders who consent to participate might be more likely to show these behavioral changes in the future regardless of the success of the program. Finally, it is hard to estimate whether there is really a deterrent effect at play here. If emotions do the work for behavioral changes, then that might not speak in favor of deterrent effects. Coming to understand their moral wrongdoing would better be described as some form of rehabilitation or moral education rather than deterrence.

* * *

In sum, there is promising evidence for some effect of restorative programs on recidivism—but more research should be done to draw more specific and confident conclusion about these issues. Together with the earlier considerations, we can say that having a system of sanctions and restorative procedures certainly adds to the deterrent effects of that institution. But we should be very careful with the harshness of sanctions and the confidence we put into these institutions with regards to their deterrent effects. A justification for harsh sanctions, or only restorative procedures, for example, would certainly overstate the empirical case for deterrence as of now with the available data at hand. But deterrence should not be thrown out completely when theorizing about criminal law—at least from an empirical perspective.

I will thus proceed with the assumption that there is no good reason to think that sanctions have no deterrent effects at all, but equally no reason to think that the harshness of sanctions is doing much work. From an empirical perspective, deterrence is thus still a feasible aim of criminal law, but not one that should be pursued with harsh sanctions. That is at least what I gather from the evidence we have to date.

7.4 Objections against Deterrence-Based Accounts

The problems for deterrence theories have more or less been the same for many hundreds of years. The discussion has typically focused on punitive sanctions, but the same rationale should also apply to corrective sanctions. In a nutshell, these are the main problems brought forward in the debate: First, sanctions solely based on the deterrence rationale do not treat people with adequate respect. Such sanctions threaten people with pain rather than taking them seriously as moral agents who are capable of truly understanding their wrongdoing. Secondly, sanctions based on the aim of general deterrence treat people as mere means, in other words, instrumentalize them. If we sanction individuals with the aim of deterring other would-be criminals, then we use the sanctioned wrongdoer as a means to the end of general deterrence. We should, however, not instrumentalize people—and thus, sanctions based on such a justification fail. Thirdly, sanctions based on the deterrence rationale will lead to morally unjustifiable distributions of sanctions. Within the deterrence rationale, it is sometimes justifiable to sanction people disproportionally, or even sanction innocent people if thereby a high deterrence effect can be achieved.

In this section, I will argue that none of these objections make a convincing case to reject the deterrence rationale as one of the reasons why we should sanction criminal offenders. We should, however, reject approaches that are purely deterrence-based.

Treating People with Respect

The first objection states that deterrence-based theories give citizens the wrong kinds of reasons for adhering to the law. Deterrence threatens citizens with unpleasant consequences, which thereby gives them prudential reasons to stick to the rules. According to the objection, however, what we really want our fellow citizens to do is to adhere to the laws because they respect them—because they see them as justified and well-designed, or because they simply respect the rights of other people. Deterrence theories treat people as mere dogs, as Hegel once put it[17], because such sanctions threaten them with a stick instead of explaining to them the proper (moral) reasons behind the law.

---

[17] "To base a justification of punishment on threat is to liken it to the act of a man who lifts his stick to a dog. It is to treat a man like a dog instead of with the freedom and respect due to him as a man" (Hegel 1820, 246).

Several versions of this objection have been raised in the literature (Hoskins 2011 for an overview), but I want to focus, here, on the paradigm version that claims that citizens are treated without adequate respect if they are given merely prudential reasons for adhering to the law. A prominent formulation of this version of the objection is presented by Antony Duff:

> The law of [a liberal political] community, as its common law, must address its members in terms of the values it embodies—values to which they should, as members of the community, already be committed. It portrays criminal conduct as wrongful in terms of those values; and the reasons that citizens have to refrain from such conduct, the reasons to which the law refers and on which it depends, are precisely the moral reasons that make such conduct wrong. A purely deterrent law, however, addresses those whom it seeks to deter, not in terms of the communal values that it aims to protect, but simply in the brute language of self-interest. It thus addresses them, not as members of the normative community of citizens, but as threatening outsiders against whom the community must protect itself. (2001, 78–79)

We can break down the argument into three parts. First, we need to assume that there are prudential and moral reasons to adhere to the law. Second, the state treats citizens disrespectfully if it only offers prudential reasons to adhere to the law. Third, punishment based on the deterrence rationale only gives prudential reasons to adhere to the law. From that, we can conclude that punishment based on the deterrence rationale is morally problematic because it disrespects offenders. (Strictly speaking, an additional implicit assumption is that this disrespect is sufficiently problematic to dismiss deterrence as a proper ground of criminalization. That does not follow without argument but is not explicitly discussed as far as I know. Rather, it is assumed that the disrespect is sufficient to disqualify deterrence.)

A first complication regarding the difference between moral and prudential reasons is that the state does not offer the prudential reasons for their own sake—they are thus not completely independent from the moral reasons. True, we defined deterrence as only offering prudential reasons. But why does the state within the deterrence framework offer citizens prudential reasons to adhere to the law? For many in the debate, this ultimately rests on some moral motivation (either to maximize happiness, defend the social contract, or simply protect citizens from wrongdoing).[18] So even if the reasons offered by the state are pruden-

---

[18] Note that these reasons need not be moral. The function of the state can simply be to make people get along better—without any insistence on moral values. Even error theorists will likely want states if these really succeed in delivering the benefits they promise. In such a case there is no problem for deterrence theories.

tial, the motivation for offering them is not completely independent from moral concerns.

But still, the critic might press, the state should communicate the moral reasons directly. Giving citizens prudential reasons does not respect them as moral agents.

First, we need to emphasize that if we could make people comply with the law by simply pointing at the moral values, deterrence theorists would be happy to acknowledge that no harm should be inflicted on offenders. Again, providing prudential reasons in the form of threats and impositions of hard treatment is not valuable in itself—quite the opposite—without a good justification it would itself be a wrongdoing in the book of most deterrence theorists. But the need for prudential reasons according to deterrence theories comes from the realization that simply pointing people to the moral reasons that they have violated will not do (von Hirsch (1985) for this motivation of hard treatment).

Duff himself evades this problem by arguing that pointing people to moral reasons needs to involve harsh treatment, as we have seen in Chapter 5. But if the arguments presented there are correct, such a retributive justification fails. Communicating moral reasons does not intrinsically necessitate harsh treatment, so Duff cannot hope to introduce the necessity of harsh treatment without other concerns than the communication of moral reasons.

So let us focus precisely on why offering prudential reasons should be considered as disrespectful treatment. There is of course at least some pull to Duff's intuition that we should take a closer look at the motives people have for abiding by (moral) rules. If we look at everyday interactions, we likely prefer communicating to people why what they did was wrong to simply threatening them. With children, I suspect, the intuition is strongest that people prefer clarifying the wrongness of the action to threatening with harm.

Even if we grant these intuitions, I think that the idea that the state denies the moral agency of offenders by offering prudential reasons is overstretching what is happening with deterrent incentives. The state regulates lots of behavior in our lives with such prudential incentives. In Germany, tobacco products are heavily taxed, and the recycling of plastic bottles is also incentivized with monetary losses if one fails to recycle the bottles.[19] If we want to be consistent, we either have to say that none of these behaviors should be sanctioned or incentivized in any form; or we should admit that such incentives do not take away the (moral) agency in any of these cases. Some libertarians might go with the former route, but I suspect

---

19 Thanks to Rüdiger Bittner for pointing me to these examples.

that most people in the debate do not disagree that the state is justified in incentivizing people to adhere to certain rules, even with some form of hard treatment.

One response to this observation is to say that the criminal law is categorically different than other areas of state action. The criminal law deals with serious moral wrongs, whereas these other examples involve actions that are not as morally important. It is unclear whether this response is correct, and even if it is, it does not seem to bring the point home that the critic needs. First, there are reasonable accounts of the state that do not see such categorical differences between the criminal law and other areas such as contract law or civil law (Chiao 2016). Incentives to recycle are arguably made out of concern for the environment, animals, and future generations of humans. High taxes on tobacco products can also be motivated by moral concerns in addition to prudential ones. Lastly, much of criminal wrongdoing is not as grave as the response by the critique suggest. Theft is certainly immoral, but it might not even compare to the moral importance of environmental policies.

But even if we grant that the criminal law is concerned with more serious moral matters, it does not follow from this observation that offering prudential reasons disrespects the citizens. Quite the opposite, on might suspect:[20] The aim of the prudential reasons is in fact to make people adhere to the laws—that is, morally laden rules. They can do so either by making people see the moral importance of these rules more clearly, or, in the worst case, by giving the reasons at least enough prudential force to ensure (as much as possible) that the laws will be abided by.

To sum up: It remains unclear why giving citizens prudential reasons to abide by the law disrespects them in a morally problematic manner, or even denies their moral agency. It is true that we would prefer citizens to adhere to the law because of respect for their fellow citizens, social contracts, or because they want to do the morally right thing. That is so because most deterrence theories have a substantive normative theory in the background—and it is typically better to respect these normative reasons directly rather than indirectly with the use of prudential reasons. But simply hoping for respect of the moral reasons does not seem to cut it in the real world. If it is a fact that people will not be sufficiently motivated by moral considerations alone, then offering prudential reasons is a (potentially) good avenue to reduce crime rates. By doing that, we do not deny offenders moral agency and neither disrespect them in ways that would be illegitimate for the state.

We can grant the critic that we should also offer ways of making offenders see the moral reasons to adhere to the law (as argued in Chapters 5 and 6, I think re-

---

20 Thanks to Jonas Geske for emphasizing this point in a discussion with me.

Using People as Mere Means

The objection to deterrence theories which claims that people are used merely as a means to the effect of general deterrence is nicely capture in the following passage from Kant:

> Punishment by a court (poena forensis) [...] can never be inflicted merely as a means to promote some other good for the criminal himself or for civil society. It must always be inflicted upon him only *because he has committed a crime*. For a human being can never be treated merely as a means to the purposes of another or be put among the objects of rights to things: his innate personality protects him from this, even though he can be condemned to lose his civil personality. (Kant 1996, 473 [AA VI, 331])

The critique here has two crucial assumptions: First, that punishment based on the rationale of general deterrence uses offenders as mere means. And secondly, that such a treatment is morally problematic enough to dismiss general deterrence from being a legitimate aim of criminal law.

Even though there has been at least some doubt whether the first assumption is correct, I will accept it for the purpose of the discussion here.[21]

As for the second assumption, it has proven extremely difficult to clarify what aspect of using people as a means is actually morally problematic in a way that categorically forbids such actions (Armstrong 1961, 484; Golash 2005, 45; Lewis 1953, 227 for variations of the objection). What I want to argue in the following is that using people as a means is not where the core of the moral problem lies, rather, it is the way we use people as a means. To motivate this critique, I will first argue that instrumentalization in itself is not morally problematic, then, that instrumentalization is often problematic insofar as it involves some other

---

[21] Hoskins writes that "actual inflictions of punishments are not the means by which a system seeks to achieve this aim. Rather, the threat of punishment is intended to do the work" (2011, 372). With this difference, he wants to evade the conclusion that deterrent punishment intentionally harms offenders. Rather, in his view, it punishes offenders as a side-effect of wanting to keep the threat plausible. I have my doubts whether this strategy works, but I will not discuss it in detail here.

form of disrespectful treatment, such as deceit. Lastly, I want to argue that the merely-as-a-means objection ultimately takes its strength from the fact that offenders are being intentionally harmed (and often being treated disrespectfully), rather than being instrumentalized per se.

First: Is instrumentalization always morally problematic? Probably not. Common examples of instrumentalization that are seen as morally acceptable (and typically mentioned in such debates) are using taxi drivers to get from A to B, using cashiers to pay for groceries, or being used when donating blood. There are no objections to such behavior. One response here is that people in these scenarios are not being used merely as a means. According to the critic, there is only a problem in using people merely as a means.

Bittner (2017, 61–64) discusses the example offered by Kerstein (2013) of young and proud hikers who get lost in the mountains. They spot an experienced hiker and know that they will find their way back to the trail if they follow him. Because of their pride, they do not want to acknowledge to the experienced hiker that they got lost, so they keep their distance and use the hiker to get back on track. In such a case, it seems perfectly reasonable to say that the experienced hiker is being used as a mere means (a tool, so to say) to get back on track. And yet there is nothing wrong with that (though, maybe one might say that such behavior is unvirtuous because the young hikers do not acknowledge their flaws, but that is a different problem).

If this example points into the right direction, using someone *merely* as a means also does not seem to be a good way to pinpoint the problem of instrumentalization. But still there is something to the intuition that we do not want to be instrumentalized. If we find out that a good friend has used the friendship merely to get at certain social contacts of ours, we will be furious, and we will be furious precisely because we have been used as a means. But we need to dig deeper to find the core dimension of wrongdoing here. In principle, there is nothing wrong with using people in relationships as mere means, I think. There are a lot of business relationships that are exactly like that, and there are also romantic and sexual relationships that solely exist for the purpose of getting some form of satisfaction out of it, that is, to use the other person merely to achieve satisfaction. If that is so, using people merely as a means in relationships cannot be problematic in principle, too, but rather only if we specify the circumstances of the relationships.

Whatever the correct story about the wrongness of such actions is, simply referring to the fact that a person is being instrumentalized does not seem to be enough. At the very least, the argument would need to include the fact that a person has been instrumentalized against her will, for example. But even that is not so straightforward. Maybe taxi drivers and cashiers do not want to be treated as mere means, but there is nonetheless nothing wrong in such behavior by customers. Again, we need to differentiate between treating people merely as a mean—as an instrument of transportation, say—from treating someone in an otherwise disrespectful manner. If a costumer yells at a cashier, or insults a taxi driver, because that person thinks of them as mere instruments, then the actions are wrongful independent of the fact that someone is used merely as a means. Also, the fact that it would be nicer not to see people as mere instruments does not suffice to ground a categorical prohibition against treating people as such.

What, then, can be said about the problem of punishment based on the rationale of general deterrence? As the general problem of punishment (see Chapter 2) states, punishment is the intentional infliction of harm on wrongdoers. And that is where the specific problem of instrumentalization comes into play:

> [T]he fact is that punishment stands alone as the one instance in which the state not only does an act that predictably harms some of its citizens, but in which it acts with the explicit aim of causing harm. Punishment is utterly anomalous in this respect. This is precisely what makes punishment distinctively difficult to justify in the first place. (Boonin 2008, 62)

Boonin correctly points out that the state harms citizens under varying circumstances. Sometimes, when freeways are built, people need to be relocated and their houses need to be sold. But these are not actions where the point is to harm some of the citizens. That is just an unfortunate side-effect of the project to build more freeways. The fact that it is not the point of the measure also shows in that governments often compensate the people who need to be relocated for their losses. It is thus more easily justifiable to harm certain people in order to benefit others as long as the harming is not done intentionally. The specific problem of general deterrence is that we harm people intentionally for the benefit of others.

It might seem that we are now back to square one and the problem of instrumentalization simply becomes another instance of the problem of punishment more generally. But I think that we did make some progress with the considerations above. The problem of instrumentalization in the variation I have outlined now does not impose categorical restrictions on using people as means. Rather, it simply sets the justificatory burden for deterrence theorists really high, because, as Boonin emphasized, the intentional infliction of harm is typically not what the state should be doing.

How high is the burden ultimately? That is hard to estimate. It is worth emphasizing though that the intentional hard treatment can be vastly different—which has an impact on how high the burden of justification is. Increasing the length of sentences for certain crimes from two years in prison to four years in prison in order to reach deterrent effects has to be evaluated differently when we speak about prisons in the US, for example, where conditions are comparatively harsh, compared to prisons in Norway. A one-fits-all answer for the justifiability of general deterrence is thus not feasible.

I think Derek Parfit framed the problem of instrumentalization in a way that is very applicable to our current discussion. After a long discussion of several different ways of understanding the using-as-a-means formula, he sums his discussion up with the following principle:

> It is wrong to impose harm on someone as a means of achieving some aim, unless
>
> 1) there is no better way to achieve this aim
>   and
> 2) given the goodness of this aim, the harm we impose is not disproportionate, or too great.
>   (Parfit 2011, 229)

This formulation falls in line with our observation that there is no universal restriction on using people as means. Rather, we should acknowledge that using people as means to other ends, especially when doing so with the intention to harm, poses a very high justificatory burden—and because it poses such a high burden, we need to justify it with proportionally high benefits.

To measure the justificatory burden more precisely, we need to get a better grasp of how much harm we are actually talking about. Intentionally harming the offender with an additional $1 fine to hope for general deterrent effects does not pose a high justificatory burden but will obviously not have any deterrent effects. The discussion in Section 7.3, however, makes it very likely that punishment will not have large deterrent effects for the broad public—or that we at the very least do not have reliable criminological data to back such a claim up. Given this high epistemic uncertainty, I do not think that we are justified in intentionally punishing offenders more harshly in order to try to achieve general deterrent effects.

The story might be different with corrective sanctions, however. What would general deterrence look like in such an account? As I have argued, corrective sanctions can take different forms. They can consist in mere financial payments to the victim, in taking part in restorative conferencing, in community service or other types of work in order to compensate for the harm they imposed on the victim(s)—and in some cases even in the form of incarceration.

Imagine now that in a specific case of criminal wrongdoing, a sanction of a monetary payment for the victim would suffice to satisfy all the different values we have that we want to realize with the sanction (that is, restoring fairness, acknowledgement of the victim, etc.). Still, if it were the case that such a sentence would likely not serve a general deterrent purpose, we might be justified to impose community service related to the wrongdoing instead of mere repayment to the victim. The problem again, however, is that we do not know whether doing this has general deterrence effects. We know that there are some effects on recidivism, but we do not know about the other effects of threatening citizens with community service. But if the limited evidence in the case of punitive sanctions speaks against the general deterrence rationale, the same should be true for corrective sanctions —at least until we have more reliable data.

So, what is the status of the merely-as-a-means-objection? If my arguments are correct, then there is no reason to be categorically opposed to general deterrence because of the supposed immorality of using people merely as a means. Even though this is the standard objection voiced in the literature, there is no plausible account of why using people as mere means should always be morally objectionable. Given the grave moral costs of intentionally harming people for the benefit of others, however, the benefits of deterrence have to be proportionally high to be justifiable. To date, we have no evidence to think that harsh punitive sanctions have an effect on general deterrence—at least not any more so than do corrective sanctions. Insofar as having a sanctioning system in the first place has some effects on the behavior of the public, however, general deterrence is at least one additional plausible reason why we should have a criminal law.

Punishment of the Innocent and Disproportional Punishment

The last standard objection against the deterrence rationale is that it would allow for the punishment of the innocent or disproportionate punishment whenever the deterrent effects would favor such treatment of citizens (Duff 2001, 6–8; Mabbott 1939, 152; McCloskey 1957, 471 for variations of the objection). A throw-away remark against deterrence theories that is sometimes made in such a context is that if deterrence is what we aim for, why not torture people who park where they should not, so that no one will ever dare to do so (Armstrong 1961, 484).

In this section, I want to agree that such implications of the theory should make us cautious to embrace a purely deterrent approach to criminal law. But that is a substantially weaker position than what critics of deterrence typically present. Critics typically take the mere possibility of such disproportionate punishment and punishment of the innocent as sufficient ground to dismiss deterrence as a rationale. But this will not do, as I want to argue.

My own guess is that some of the motivation behind thinking that deterrence theories are obviously flawed and not in need of much more detailed criticism comes from the historical connection between the deterrence rationale and purely utilitarian moral theories. This is a fair association as the trophies of most forceful defenders of deterrence are often given to Bentham and Mill, who happen to have offered utilitarian frameworks for deterrence. This led several people to voice (at least in passing) the criticism that adopting a deterrent justification would also include killing the homeless (Golash 2005, 48), or "extended imprisonment with drugs administered regularly to ensure euphoria" (Braithwaite and Pettit 1990, 53).

As argued in the introduction for this chapter, deterrence theories are not committed to utilitarianism, nor is it clear that utilitarianism would really go so far as to recommend these alleged actions. Here, too, I will focus on the deterrence theory regardless of the broader rationale motivating the need for deterrence. First, I want to clarify the type of criticism typically presented in the debate; that is, that the mere possibility of disproportionate punishment or punishment of the innocent is sufficient to dismiss the deterrence rationale. I will argue that such an argument will not do. Nonetheless, there is a better version of the argument to dismiss monistic deterrence theories. Not the mere possibility, but the high uncertainty whether such types of actions would be implemented in criminal law and the high stakes involved should make us wary of accepting only deterrence as a value in criminal law.

To clarify the objection of the critic of deterrence, we need to distinguish between the theoretical and empirical dimension of deterrence theories. Theoretically, deterrence allows for disproportionate punishment and the punishment of the innocent. But whether or not in societies like ours the data actually supports the implementation of such punishments remains unclear. Within the utilitarian framework, for example, that would only be the case if the benefits of the deterrent effects outweigh the disadvantages that are linked to both the pain of punishment itself and the potential horror that a system of punishing the innocent would have. Utilitarians already made the argument that such a conclusion is unlikely (Bagaric 1999) but it is unclear how this could be calculated in detail—all of the arguments I am aware of rely on speculation rather than thorough analysis of the criminological data.

Some critics of utilitarianism admit as much (Duff 2001, 6–8; Mabbott 1939, 152; McCloskey 1957, 468–69)—so the problem cannot be that the deterrence rationale will certainly and systematically lead to disproportionate punishment and punishment of the innocent. We simply do not know as of now with the available criminological research whether this will be the case for societies like ours. The problem thus has to be that deterrence will under certain circumstances demand such punishments. This is exactly how McCloskey puts the problem:

> What it is important to stress here, however, is the difficulty of settling a dispute of the following kind: Is punishment or telishment the more valuable institution? Such a question is not an a priori question but an empirical one for which apparently there are considerations supporting each alternative. I am quite uncertain as to the solution of the empirical question,

and I suggest that if we are honest with ourselves we all must admit to such uncertainty; yet I, and I suspect most other people, am not uncertain in the same way about the moral wrongness of telishment, and this surely is significant. (McCloskey 1957, 475)

"Telishment" here means an institution that would demand the punishment of the innocent and disproportionate punishment under certain circumstances (whether or not these would ever apply). Some people in the debate hold that those systems are not proper systems of punishment (because they disregard the necessity of the retributive principle)—but this should not bother us here.

The quote is representative of the sentiment to locate the central problem in the fact that the deterrence rationale would sometimes demand such forms of punishment. But why exactly is that a moral problem serious enough to warrant dismissing the rationale? As is nicely exemplified in the quote just given, the argument of the critic typically stops at this point. They observe that surely many will find such a system to be immoral—and that is about as far as the argument goes.

This is of course a well-known argumentative move of deontologists against utilitarians (or maybe consequentialists in general). Deontologists point to actions that utilitarianism will sometimes require and observe that surely it cannot be right of a correct moral theory to sometimes require such actions. And that seems to be the meat of the problem here as well. If you do not already buy into the intuition that such punishments are always immoral, it is surprisingly hard to see what should convince you of believing so.

A common example used at this point of the dialectic is that of a mob who threatens to wreak havoc in large parts of a city if a rapist who is suspected to live in their community is not prosecuted immediately (McCloskey 1957: 468–9). Critics now say that deterrence theorists would not hesitate to look for a scapegoat, portray him as the rapist and punish him to the full extent of the law—all while knowing that the person is innocent.

As already detailed above, it is unclear whether deterrence theorist would really be committed to such a view in the example above. That would depend on the costs and benefits of the deterrent punishment and also on all the other available options to prevent the mob from wreaking havoc in the community. But neither the critic not the defendant of deterrence actually calculates the benefits and burdens in question (and it is unclear whether this would be possible in the first place). But why is the mere fact that such an option is at least considered by deterrence theories sufficient to dismiss such rationales? We find a similar dialectical situation that we encounter in general discussions of dilemma-type situations, not just the punishment of the innocent. Are we justified in pushing the man with the large backpack off the bridge? Or in harvesting the organs of a healthy person to rescue ill patients?

Some deontologists might want to give the answer that we are never justified to do so. I do not want to deny the intuition that such behavior is terrible on the face of it. But why should the state not punish a scapegoat if the stakes are really high enough and no other possibility is available? Or, in the other version of the objection, to punish disproportionately if the benefits are promising enough. If the answer is that giving an institution such a power will likely result in terrible consequences, then the deterrence theorists will agree that it should not be done.

At one point in his discussion, Duff alludes to a dialectical dead end close to what we are facing now (without calling it that). He admits that the deterrence theorist can simply bite the bullet that it is sometimes justifiable to punish the innocent or punish disproportionately harshly, at least in high stakes cases where no alternative options are viable (in practice, it is unclear whether there are ever cases where no such options are available). To that, Duff simply responds that "[the deterrence theorists] are, however, unlikely to satisfy the critic, who will still argue that consequentialists cannot find a place for the necessary connection that should obtain between punishment and guilt" (2001, 10).

Here, it is hard to see how the discussion should advance. The deterrence theorist can deny that there should be a necessary connection between punishment and guilt—at best, there should be a robust one that is also implemented in the legislature (Bagaric and Amarasekara 2000). Granted, we might want that robust connection in, say, 99.99% of the cases—but why not accept the deterrence rationale also in the 0.01% of the cases? Furthermore, if it really is only the 0.01% of the cases (which, again, we simply cannot estimate), is this enough to dismiss the deterrence rationale completely? I simply do not see the pull of this specific claim of the critic of deterrence theories, and as can be seen in the case of Duff and others, there is little argumentative effort to go beyond the observation that there should be a necessary connection between punishment and guilt.

Another variation of this objection is that the deterrence theory cannot account for the (supposed) fact that it is at least *pro tanto* wrong to punish the innocent (Duff 2001, 10). There is a broader discussion to be had whether utilitarianism can explain that, but as I have argued in the beginning, deterrence theories are not limited to a grounding in utilitarianism. In social contract theories, for example, where the purpose of punishment is to uphold the rules agreed upon under the social contract, deterrence is used to make sure that such rules are not broken. One of these rules will likely be that no innocent people are being subject to state coercion and violence. Nonetheless, in extreme cases, it might be for the best of the social contract to violate this rule. The rule is still being violated, that is, there is still something *pro tanto* wrong about punishing the innocent— but sometimes such actions can be all-things-considered justified according to the deterrence account.

Even calling dignity into the ring will likely not help resolve the issue here, I think. Some critics have argued that as deterrence theories are (maybe) committed to the occasional punishment of the innocent, the theory violates human dignity (assuming that punishing the innocent is a dignity violation). Even here the deterrence theorist can retort: "I see that this will sometimes be the case, but I simply cannot see how, if the stakes are high enough, violating human dignity in that sense cannot be the right thing to do. We cannot disregard what is happening to the other people if we do not intervene. And in extreme cases, this should be enough to violate an otherwise valid principle in criminal law." Here, I suspect, the same dead end will occur.

At this point, I am not sure whether I see a clear way forward to resolve this particular objection in a satisfying matter. It is also not so clear to me who has the burden of proof at this point in the dialectic. The intuition not to punish the innocent is certainly on the side of the critic of deterrence, but it is unclear whether the intuition should count for much of a burden of proof in extremely unusual cases where the stakes are high—that is, where our intuitions might not be very reliable. Also, critics of retributivism could potentially try to debunk the intuitions that lead retributivists to the dismissal of deterrence (see Chapter 3 for a more detailed view on debunking arguments)—but that would take us too far from the debate here.

I will have to do here with giving a consequentialist argument against a monistic approach to deterrence. This will of course not satisfy the retributivist critique, but at least it will allow us to continue with the point I am trying to bring home here, assuming that the consequentialist argument is convincing. Some authors at least hint at this argument (Braithwaite and Pettit 1990, 52–53; Duff 2001, 9). The argument goes like this: We simply do not know whether implementing strictly deterrent rationales in criminal law would lead to fundamentally flawed sentencing structures. But fundamentally flawed sentencing structures are extremely problematic, to a point at which even a low probability of such a high-risk scenario is not acceptable. We should thus not institutionalize a purely deterrent foundation for criminal law as long as we are not certain of the probabilities and risks involved. Currently, we cannot estimate the probability very precisely, which is why we should err on the site of caution. Thus, a purely deterrent approach to criminal law is currently not morally justifiable.

This argument is still not flawless, as a lot depends on both the probability of problematic sentencing structures and on how severely unjust these would be according to the standards of a moral and political community. But the risk argument should at least make use very wary of using purely deterrent approaches to criminal law because of disproportional punishment and punishment of the innocent.

7.5 Conclusion

What can we take from this discussion? First, there is some important deterrent benefit to having criminal law institution compared to having none. But there is not enough evidence to justify especially harsh sanctions on basis of the deterrence rationale. Given the empirical data, deterrence is thus one additional plausible reason to have criminal law institutions, but not one that justifies punitive sanctions over corrective sanctions.

What about the morality of having deterrence as one of the aims of criminal law? If my arguments in this chapter are correct, we should only be wary of purely deterrent approaches to criminal law—but not those who see deterrence as one of the reasons why we should sanction offenders. Prudential punishment (that is, deterrence) does not disrespect offenders. There is no good reason to think that general deterrence is categorically problematic, even if it uses people as mere means. The crucial problem with deterrence is that the criminological data does not seem to show that there are substantial deterrent effects to harsh punishment. That does not speak to the immorality of general deterrence, but against its actual implementation. Lastly, I argued that a purely deterrent approach would entail some risk of extremely immoral criminal justice institutions. But if we do not take deterrence to be the sole reason why we sanction offenders, these problems do not apply.

What is needed, then, is a framework in which deterrence is just one of the reasons why we should have criminal law institutions that opt for corrective sanctions. And this is exactly what I want to present next. The next chapter argues for a non-foundational pluralist approach to criminal law, in which all the values I have discussed in this book can find their place: That is, fairness, penance and censure, the interests of the victims, and deterrence.

Part IV: **Towards a Pluralistic Theory of Corrective Justice**

Chapter 8
Weaving the Patchwork Rug

> For mysterious reasons, the pluralism that is so prevalent elsewhere in normative ethics is conspicuously absent when we turn to philosophical commentary about the justification of criminal law and punishment.
>
> Douglas Husak, *The Prize of Criminal Law Skepticism* (2020, 28)

8.1 Introduction

Michael Cahill (2011) mentions in a footnote in one of his works on pluralism that he attended a talk by Mitchell Berman. In that talk, Berman argued that most people in the current debate on punishment defend some form of "desert-constrained pluralistic consequentialism." That is, Berman thought that most philosophers in the debate on punishment are pluralists in that they think that even though consequentialism is the most promising justification for punishment, punishment theories should also integrate retributive considerations such as proportionality and the protection of the innocent. Both to Cahill's and Berman's surprise, this empirical observation found significant resistance within the audience filled with legal philosophers. The audience seemed to disagree that the current debate converged on pluralistic consequentialism (without arguing however, as Cahill remembers, against pluralistic consequentialism during the talk).

Ten years later, I find myself in a very similar situation that Berman seemed to have been in. In my estimation, the debate has mostly shifted away from monistic approaches to a justification of punishment. Even the most hardened retributivists do not ignore the relevance of deterrence and rehabilitation (Moore 2010). And even pure consequentialists care about proportionality and about protecting innocent people from punishment (Bagaric 1999). But exactly as Berman did, I would likely hear quite some disagreement if I were to confront legal philosophers with this empirical observation concerning the current state of the debate.

Moore, for example, would say that even though deterrence is important for refining our practice of punishment, it does nothing at all to provide a justification for punishment. Only retribution can do this job successfully. Bagaric claims that we can derive all retributive concerns from the utilitarian rationale alone, and thus can do without adopting a proper retributive perspective. Then, there are several theories that are somewhat in-between. Dagger's fair-play theory of punishment, which I discussed in Chapter 4, sees itself as unified—as introducing both retributive and utilitarian concerns—but Dagger (2018, 156) explicitly does not want to label the account as 'pluralist.' Duff (2001, 107), whom we discussed in Chapter 5, sees censure as the unifying goal of repentance, reform, and reconciliation—which should all matter in theorizing about the justification of punishment.

The prevailing monism and explicit denial of pluralism also applies to utilitarian approaches to punishment, not just the retributive ones mentioned above. Again, according to Bagaric (1999), utility can account for rights, proportionality, and all other retributive likings without direct commitment to retributivism. The early accounts from von Hirsch (1985) held that only deterrence can justify the harsh treatment of offenders, whereas the newer von Hirsch (1993, 14) places the deterrence considerations more strongly within the censure rationale based on desert alone. Husak (2016), a retributivist at heart, argued that even though retribution is the most plausible moral justification for punishment, only deterrence can plausibly explain why we should have an institutionalized system of punishment that consumes millions of tax dollars each year.

So, my first impression is likely to be perceived as equally mistaken as was Berman's. Of course, we can also find explicitly pluralist accounts of the justification of punishment in the literature (Berman 2011; Cahill 2011; Zaibert 2018). But it was still surprising to me to see that most philosophers are (self-described) monists in important ways, even in the current debate. Intuitively, this seems off to me: Justice, fairness, penance and censure, victims' rights, deterrence, rehabilitation and prevention—they all seem to offer plausible motives to respond to wrongdoing. All these facets seem to reflect important sides of how we think about morality and criminal law.

One reason why researchers have been hesitant to accept some form of pluralism is that it comes with several problems. If we allow different reasons to motivate why we should punish (or impose corrective sanctions for that matter), then this might come at the price of theoretical inconsistency and inconsistent sentencing recommendations. While the retributive motive demands proportionate punishment because of the desert of the offender, the utilitarian motive demands deterrence that is attuned to the empirical facts without any unwavering commitment to proportionality. The task in this chapter is to develop a pluralist approach to criminal law that addresses these different worries. By doing that, I hope to invite more philosophers to leave their monistic homes and join pluralism. I will do so in the following way.

In the first three sections, I will address the question which kind of pluralistic framework is, first, best fitting for the result in this book, but secondly also plausible on its own accord. In Section 8.2, I will reject hybrid theories, as they only allow one justifying reason for sanctions. Against this, I will argue that it makes little sense to clearly distinguish between the aims of punishment, for example, and the question of how much to punish. In practice, these are necessarily connected. We are thus better off accepting that many values justify the imposition of sanctions on offenders.

In Section 8.3, I will reject unified theories. Though unified theories are an improvement to monist theories, they still fail because they try to find one single unifying value that combines all these different justifying reasons of criminal sanctions. Instead, I will argue that we are better off accepting a non-foundational pluralist approach.

In Section 8.4, I will outline such a non-foundational framework and give a more detailed description of how such a system would work in practice.

In Section 8.5, I will defend the non-foundational pluralist framework against several objections.

8.2 Hybrid Theories

The most discussed hybrid theories of punishment go back to Hart (1960) and Rawls (1955). The general idea in both versions is very similar. To get at a convincing argument for the justification of criminal punishment, we need to distinguish different questions within the punishment debate. Most importantly, we need to distinguish between the justification of punishment and the justification of whom and how much to punish. Both Hart and Rawls give similar answers to the respective questions.

The justification for the imposition of punishment is utilitarianism (or rather, deterrence): We are justified in punishing offenders in order to make society safer. But the question whom and how much to punish is best answered by retributivism: Only punish the guilty and punish them proportionally to the severity of their wrongdoing.

I want to discuss two reasons for rejecting these hybrid theories. First, they do not fit well with the results of the previous chapters in this book. Hybrid theories have been presented as attempts to combine the two major theories—retributivism and utilitarianism—where one justified punishment and the other determines the amount of punishment. That will not do for my approach. Secondly, hybrid theories do not make good on their own promises. The big appeal of hybrid theories is to solve the problem of monistic retributivism and utilitarianism: Retributivism without utilitarianism leaves open why we should invest so much money into punishing criminals just because it is intrinsically valuable (Husak 2016). After all, there are plenty of intrinsic values the state takes no interest in promoting. Utilitarianism without retributivism, on the other hand, is often said to be committed to very cruel punishment. Hybrid theories seem very promising in that they try to solve both problems by giving each rationale one role to play. But as I will argue, they do not succeed in that.

Against Hybrid Theories

The first problem is that hybrid theories limit themselves to only one rationale to justify punishment (or corrective sanction for that matter). If my arguments in the previous chapters have been convincing, we have at least four legitimate reasons to impose corrective sanctions on offenders: To restore fairness, communicate censure and offer ways to experience feelings of guilt, to express respect for the victim, and to deter offenders from committing offenses in the future. All these are justified and valuable aims to pursue when imposing corrective sanctions on offenders, as I have argued. Hybrid theories cannot accommodate this finding. Per definition, they aim to combine two rationales, only one of which gives reasons to impose criminal sanctions. For that reason, hybrid theories should be dismissed.

Problems of Hybrid Theories

The argument I just presented will only convince you if you already bought the arguments in the previous chapters. But let us assume that you are undecided on these. Even so, I think that hybrid theories cannot uphold their promises to clearly distinguish the different questions and justifications in criminal law.

There is a tension between a utilitarian justification for the imposition of punishment, and the retributive answer to the distribution of punishment. If the aim of punishment is to deter offenders as effectively as possible, then this might entail punishment that is not proportional to the severity of the wrongdoing. If disproportionate punishment is never justified (even if it is more effective), the role of the utilitarian theory seems somewhat symbolic. This tension is contingent, of course. It might be the case that proportional punishment is the most effective way of deterring offenders, but that is an empirical question which is up to debate.

This consideration is only meant to show that the answers or justifications of the different parts of the punishment debate spill over to each other. Another problem that is more important for what I have mentioned above is that the hybrid theory likely neither satisfies the retributivist nor the utilitarian. The retributivist, after all, emphasizes that the wrongdoing of the offender is a valid reason to impose harm on them. If Husak and others are right, the fact that the suffering of the wrongdoer is intrinsically morally valuable does not justify having the institution of criminal law. The hybrid theory is not able to accommodate this position. It does not acknowledge anything other than utilitarianism as a justification for the imposition of hard treatment of offenders. Because of that, it is in important respects a monistic theory in disguise, at least in the relevant aspects for me. If only utilitarianism justifies punishment, while retribution justifies the proportionality requirement, then the justification of punishment is still monistic. This is of course fine if you merely want to have a side-constrained monistic theory of the justification of punishment (even though it is implausible, as argued in this book), but for the purpose of a genuine non-monistic theory, hybrid theories fail. And such non-monistic theories are exactly what we are looking for at this point of the dialectic in this book. We thus need to look further.

8.3 Unified Theories

Unified theories are a more promising candidate for the task we are aiming to solve in this chapter. Unified theories as I want to understand them here aim to accept the legitimacy of different values for the imposition of sanctions but do so with the promise of combining them under one over-arching value. As such, unified theories are foundational. They base the different values that should be considered on one fundamental value. In this subsection, I will focus on one version of such unified theories presented by Thom Brooks (2012) and Tatjana Hörnle (2019) which I take to be the most promising candidates. There are other unified approaches as well, but I have either dismissed these already (see Chapters 4–5), or they strongly identify as non-pluralist approaches. Also, the legal pluralism offered by Brooks and Hörnle offers the best springboard for the account I wish to defend later.

Legal Pluralism and the Unified Theory

Brooks urges us to begin our search for a pluralist approach to criminal law with the notion of crime itself, for "if we cannot justify a particular criminal act or omission, then we cannot justify its punishment" (2012, 127). So, what constitutes a crime, then? To answer that question, Brooks turns to the function of laws in our society. He writes:

> Laws are necessary for the continuation of any political community. This is because there will be inevitable conflicts between community members over time. These conflicts will require some agreed procedures for future conflict resolution. These procedures form a legal system.

> Note that legal systems are not necessary because people are naturally antagonistic per se, but instead because conflicts are inevitable over time in any political community. (2012, 127)

The function of laws in political communities is to offer ways to resolve conflicts among people, and to protect citizens against certain acts. Which acts exactly should be prohibited is defined with the notion of legal rights:

> The criminal law aims at the protection of individual *legal rights*. Our legal rights are substantial freedoms worthy of protection for each member. Each person possesses rights in virtue of their recognized political membership. (2012, 127)

The justification of (criminal) laws in this tradition is functionalist at heart, similar to the project attributed to Thomas Hobbes. People get into conflicts over certain things, and it is important to them that (some of) their interests are protected. These protected interests build the basis for legal rights. So far so good. But "not all rights have equal value. This is because some rights represent more substantial freedoms than others. For example, the right to life free from murder is linked to a more substantial freedom than the right to private property" (Brooks 2012, 127–28).

Let us tie these considerations back into the discussion of the justification of state punishment. Crimes within the functionalist approach are understood as "rights violations that threaten the substantial freedoms protected by law" (Brooks 2012, 128). By imposing punishment on people who interfere with legal rights (that is, with interests that people within a political community want to be protected), the political community ensures (or maybe rather hopes) that the interests will be protected in the future.

This sounds like a paradigm case of consequentialism in punishment theory, but Brooks (and Hörnle, too) emphasize that deterrence is just one of the penal goals unified theories take into consideration. As Brooks tells us:

> The unified theory of punishment *unifies* multiple penal goals. First, punishment is a response to crime. We cannot punish the innocent because they do not present a threat that may violate our rights as substantial freedoms. [...] Secondly, punishment aims to protect rights from criminal violations. [...] Some crimes may require more severe punishments than others because rights that are more central are violated or threatened with violation. So punishment has a distinctive understanding of proportionality in view of rights protection. Punishment *metaphorically* may be said to *express* the community's disapproval. [...] Punishment may also address penal goals such as deterrence and rehabilitation within a more robust understanding of restorative justice. [...] Punishment can and should restore what crime has damaged. (2012, 130–31)

All the classical penal goals of negative retributivism, expressivism, restoration, deterrence, and rehabilitation are said to be combined within the unified theory presented above. The problem, however, is that the functionalist approach simply lacks the tools to justify integrating all these values while still trying to maintain a non-foundational theory, as I want to argue now.

Critique

The functionalist approach as presented above only gives us the regulation of conflicts and protection of some of the interests (or freedoms) of citizens as the central value in criminal law. People will want to resolve their conflicts in a peaceful manner, and they want their property (broadly understood as including bodily integrity, etc.) to be protected. To do that, we need to establish laws as well as the threat and imposition of punishment.

But that is not where the story ends. Brooks and Hörnle not only want to claim that it is the law's job to resolve conflicts, but both want the political community structured in a way that the law resolves the conflicts *in specific ways*, especially taking into account proportionality concerns, due process, and recognition for victims, as we have seen. But where do these rules come from within a functionalist approach?

In principle, there are several ways a political community could resolve the conflicts of its members. It could, for example, protect the interests by threatening citizens with draconian punishments if they violate the rights of their fellow citizens. This, however, would not be a system that either Brooks or Hörnle would want. As Brooks emphasizes, negative retributivism needs to be accounted for by the state to be legitimate. But why? If the protection of rights is the aim, why not do so with a system that ignores negative retributivism? Legal pluralists would likely not want to make the contingent claim that such a system is unlikely to do a good job at protecting individual rights. That would be an empirical question that might go either way—and it is one that is not addressed by either author.

To take a different example than negative retributivism: Why should a system that aims at the protection of legal rights give recognition to victims? Hörnle states that the victim's individual right should

> be described as a multi-faceted right. First, it is a right to have the case examined—unless the alleged rights violation was of a trivial kind; in that case, the public interest in a sensible allocation of limited resources can be the decisive factor. Secondly, if the evidence supports the conclusion that the accused indeed has committed a criminal wrong, the victim has the right to obtain confirmation that her right to non-intervention (for instance, her right to physical integrity) has been violated. Thirdly, this includes the right to have the degree of wrongdoing assessed. The fourth component is that the offender is addressed with a censuring message. If

> wrongdoing has been established, the person who has committed the wrongful act should be confronted with a condemnatory judgment. (2019, 218)

You might agree with all of these aspects from a moral perspective—and I emphatically do, as can be seen in Chapter 6—but Hörnle leaves it unexplained why a functionalist approach will favor such rules over others. Why should we think that a system that gives victims a right to recognition will do a better job at resolving conflicts than one that does it without the involvement of the victim? Similarly, Brooks seems to simply assume that proportionality, due process, and other aspects should play a role in criminal sentencing. But why they should do so, remains somewhat unclear. I think that the functionalist has two broad options to offer an answer to these questions.

The first way is to go the empirical route and argue that Brooks' and Hörnle's proposed rights and principles lead to the most successful way of resolving conflicts peacefully. Neither Brooks nor Hörnle take up the task of showing this, but I do not think that it is all too implausible. In Chapter 6, I have argued that giving victims a say in the criminal process will have various beneficial consequences. Victims are more satisfied with the criminal justice system when they are recognized in the criminal process, which might result in more respect for the rule of law. But these reasons to add specific rights are not necessarily only about how well or peacefully a conflict can be resolved. The state can do a decent job of identifying offenders and ordering sanctions without the victim's involvement. So, why care about these specific suggestions particularly?

This question leads us to the second way of integrating such values into criminal law—a strategy, however, that might go beyond a narrow functionalist account. The second way to help the functionalist approach is to say more about what kinds of individual rights people should or would want to have in a political community. The functionalist approach was introduced in a way that seemed very parsimonious. People will inevitably come into conflict, and they have good reasons to want to resolve such conflicts peacefully. But that is not all, as Hörnle's description of victim's rights clarifies.

As I see it, the functionalist approach cannot circumvent adding more specific interests than simply resolving conflicts peacefully. They have to add that, as a matter of fact, people not only want their property rights (again broadly understood) respected, but they want to be treated in specific ways. They want recognition, due process, proportionality, etc. That is more than a functionalist who is solely looking at how to peacefully resolve conflicts can capture. Nonetheless, adding these details seems to be a promising way of getting at where Brooks and Hörnle want their theory to go.

And here is where the non-foundational pluralist comes into play. It is likely a mischaracterization that people want a political community with the sole aim of resolving conflicts peacefully (neither seems such a narrow aim prudential). Rather, people also want their political community to resolve conflicts in a certain way, respecting certain principles. It might be that implementing such safeguards and more specific individual rights also adds to resolve conflicts more peacefully, but that is not the reason why people value these principles. Even if a draconian punishment system did a somewhat better job at resolving conflicts, people might still prefer due process and proportional punishment to such a system. They simply care about these things, not because they help to better resolve conflicts, but (for example) because such values might be conducive to their flourishing or happiness.

If that is a more plausible route to solve the problem of integrating these specific values, then we need an account that has the conceptual space for such claims. The functionalist account as introduced here does not get the job done. It only focuses on resolving conflicts. Simply assuming that there is a notion of individual rights or freedom that encompasses all these details of how to address wrongdoing will not do—and there is no argument for such an all-encompassing notion of rights in Brooks' or Hörnle's articles. If, however, the unified theory simply looks at the types of freedoms and rights people want to have, such as a right to due process, then we are closing in on a non-foundational pluralist approach. There is nothing that undergirds all these different values but for the fact that they matter to people and are beneficial to societal cooperation or individual flourishing. Thus, we can turn to non-foundational pluralism to solve the problems of a unified theory.

8.4 Non-Foundational Pluralism

Even though unified theories do a better job at offering a plausible pluralistic account than hybrid theories, they still fail to motivate the different values that both laypeople and legal scholars typically want to integrate into criminal law. We do not get at the types of values that we are after in this book with a parsimonious notion of legal rights alone. If that is correct, the most plausible candidate for a suitable theory is non-foundational pluralism. According to this account, fairness, penance and censure, victims' rights, deterrence, and rehabilitation all matter for how we should approach criminal law. What is more, the different values cannot be subsumed under a single rationale, they have to be taken seriously for their own sake (while they can still be motivated by the benefits they have for society, cooperation, individual flourishing, etc.).

Restorative justice as an approach to criminal law has sometimes been described as such a non-foundational account, interestingly enough, especially by critics who see this as a reason to dismiss restorative justice. The values typically associated with restorative justice do not map perfectly with those I try to defend in my project—but the general structure of a non-foundational pluralism still stands.

So let us take a closer look at why critics find this pluralism to be a problem:

(1) Multiple and unclear goals: The advocates of restorative justice put forward a variety of stated RJ [i.e., restorative justice] goals: That, for example, the victim be "restored"; the offender be made to recognize his wrong; the "conflict" between victim and offender be healed; the breach in the community's sense of trust be repaired; the community be reassured against further offending; and fear of crime be diminished [...]. The goals may be ambitiously but vaguely formulated; for example, that the aim is to "repair harm", but without considering whether this should address purely the consequential harms of the conduct, or should involve a normative response of some kind [...]. Several goals may be proposed simultaneously, without priorities among them specified. Some purported goals appear to have analogical rather than literal meaning. Restorative processes are supposed, for example, to resolve the "conflict" between offender and victim [...], but crimes are different from disputes in that the offender seldom claims to be entitled to what he takes—so what "dispute" is being resolved? RJ processes are said to "restore" the bonds of community frayed through the offense, but it is not explained what kind of bonds have been damaged or how this restoration is to take place. Such overbreadth of purpose dilutes the guidance that RJ conceptions can provide. An injunction to seek numerous imprecisely delineated good ends tells us little about what particular purposes should be pursued, and how those ends should be achieved. (Hirsch, Ashworth, and Shearing 2003, 22–23)

There are many dimensions of the objection against pluralism in here. For now, we are only interested in the problem that a non-foundational pluralism is doomed to impracticality as it is unclear how the different aims relate to each other and the correct type of sanction. To address this objection, I will explain in this section how a pluralistic approach as I hinted at in this book would integrate the different aims within a more or less straightforward approach to criminal law.

To do that, let us quickly recap the results of the previous chapters.

Fairness. Some crimes are best conceptualized as taking unfair advantages of other law-abiding citizens or unfairly disadvantaging citizens. As such, crimes violate a fundamental fairness norm according to which all parties in a cooperative endeavor should respect certain limitations of their freedom for the sake of productive cooperation. Corrective sanctions can counteract the unfair advantage that offenders gain when committing crimes, or counteract the unfair disadvantage that victims suffer when being wronged. Institutionalizing this fairness norms with corrective sanctions pays respect to this fundamental norm that people hold and furthermore helps strengthening cooperation in modern Western market communities.

Penance and Censure. When offenders are confronted with their wrongdoing, we expect them to show some form of remorse. Remorse is valuable in that it signals understanding of the wrongdoing on part of the offender, is a good indicator of a change of heart (if remorse is authentic), and expression of remorse gives somewhat reliable reason to expect the offender to actually change their future behavior (though remorse is not strictly necessary for these results). All these considerations taken together give us reasons to design criminal law in a way that incentivizes remorse (without forcing offenders to experience it). One good way to incentivize the experience of remorse is to institutionalize restorative justice settings. These have no guarantee of success, but as long as the data suggests that they make remorse (and by extension, all the benefits just mentioned) more likely, we have good reasons to adopt it. Furthermore, we can express censure towards the offender's behavior by imposing corrective sanctions on them. Whether these will be sufficient to communicate censure is still up to debate for future research.

Victim's Rights. Crimes have far-reaching impacts on victims that often go beyond the material harm they suffer. Often, the victim's perception of justice within that society, the perception of her own self-worth, and of her moral standing are impacted. A society that addresses such impacts is better off than one that does not. Restoring the sense of justice and self-worth of victims might be valuable in itself, but it is also valuable from a societal perspective, as such responses will likely strengthen the trust in the criminal law institutions, which, in turn, could result in more productive cooperation. Corrective sanctions and restorative procedures can achieve the aims just mentions.

Deterrence. A fundamental reason why we want to institutionalize responses to (criminal) wrongdoing is to make society safer. It has to be emphasized, though, that deterrence theorists do not care about punishment as an intrinsic value. If there are more effective and less (morally) costly ways of achieving peaceful cooperation, then every deterrence theorist should prefer such alternative actions to punishment. There are such alternative actions. Even though the criminological data is hard to estimate for now, there is no strong reason to suspect that a system of corrective sanctions will do a worse job in deterring offenders than a system of punishment. To ensure more effective means of changing offenders' behavior, it is also advisable to make use of restorative justice.

That is the result of the book in a nutshell, and I hope to have shown that it is less incoherent than critics expected of corrective pluralistic approaches. All the different values that I have looked at (which is not a comprehensive list, of course), recommend very similar responses to wrongdoing. The aim of criminal law should always be to repair the harm done to the victim. That means both the material harm and their feeling of self-worth and trust in the justice system as suggested in Chapter 6. The severity of the sanction can be measured with reference to the impact the wrongdoing had on the victim (more on that below). Where possible, criminal wrongdoing should be addressed via restorative justice. If that is not possible, the offender should nonetheless be coerced to offer adequate restitution. If the wrongdoing had a severe impact on the victim, or if the restorative process was unsuccessful in repairing the victim's sense of self-worth etc., then sanctions should entail community service or other more burdensome types of sanctions than mere repayment of money for the harm that was inflicted on the victim. In cases where the offender is deemed dangerous, some form of incapacitation is justifiable which stands in proportion to the wrongdoing and the danger posed by the offender. The incapacitation should be the least burdensome for the purpose of restoring safety. Prisons will often be too harsh, as house-arrest and monitoring can successfully achieve a restoration of security without intruding as heavily on the rights of the offender.

8.5 Objections to Pluralistic Theories in Criminal Law

If we accept the argument for endorsing pluralism in criminal law laid out above, what other objections should we worry about? First, different values lead to different sentencing recommendations. If we care about deterrence, we might be committed to other lengths and types of sentences than when we care about fairness, or penance. Depending on the circumstances, deterrence might suggest more or less harsh punishment, whereas fairness mostly requires sanctions that are proportional to the loss the victim suffered from the wrongdoing. I argued that all values broadly point towards the direction of corrective sanctions and restorative justice, but the concrete sanction recommendation can still vary vastly. Secondly, it is unclear whether a pluralistic approach with an emphasis on restorative justice can respect the demands of proportionality. And as argued earlier (see Chapters 4 and 5) accounts that violate the proportionality of punishment are at the very least in the need of explanation. So, my account has to make a statement on proportionality as well.

Embracing (Some) Inconsistency

I have three general responses to the problem of inconsistency. The first involves making a companions-in-guilt argument emphasizing that the problem of inconsistency equally applies to monistic theories. The second response is to argue that the inconsistency is less likely to yield practical problems than the critic suggests. This is so, because the values which we should incorporate into criminal law suggest largely similar sanctions, as I have argued throughout this book. The third response is to argue that some wiggle room for different types and lengths of sanctions is nothing to be worried about. Rather, we can see this as a helpful feature in theorizing about criminal law.

Regarding the first response, we should remind ourselves that the pull of the objection comes from the idea that pluralistic theories do not recommend clear sanctions as different values might vary in what concrete sanctions they output. But this problem also applies in a similar form to all theories. This is so, because there is almost never a clear path from the value to the specific sanction. The lex talionis might offer such a very clear way of getting from the value to the specific sanction, but no one in the Western debate defends such an approach. So even pure retributivists have a hard time of deciding what specific sanction is adequate for the value of proportional suffering. Is prison the adequate sanction for battery? Or maybe old-fashioned corporal punishment? Or maybe a substantial fine? The value of proportional harm itself does not seem to answer this question in any specific way. So monistic theories might have a similar problem of inconsistency when different accounts of proportionality—as in the case of the retributivist—suggest different kinds of sanctions. This observation does not help us solve the problem of which sanction to decide upon, but at least it puts pluralist theories in good company in that regard.

As to the second response: Many hybrid, unified, or pluralist theories have faced the objection of inconsistency before (Kaufman 2008; Lacey 1988, 48–49). In this book however, I have argued for a specific approach to criminal law, namely one that focuses on restorative justice for addressing wrongdoing and on corrective sanctions that aim to repair the harm that was done to the victim and potentially the affected community. I have made it my central aim to show that all the proposed values (fairness, penance and censure, victims' rights, and deterrence) favor such approaches to criminal law. Because of that, the inconsistency is evaded. If it is true that from the perspective of all these values, sanctions should aim to restore the harm done to the victim, then the classical worry of inconsistency is evaded.

There is, however, some inconsistency with regards to the question how the corrective sanctions should look like in detail. While the penance rationale only makes a suggestion concerning how to address wrongdoings (namely via restorative justice procedures), fairness aims solely at repairing the harm done to the victim, while deterrence and the victims' rights perspective sometimes favor sanctions that are somewhat burdensome for offenders. To make the point of potential inconsistency more precise: Except for the victims' rights and deterrence approach, corrective approaches respect the principle of least infringement (see Chapter 2). That is, all values except deterrence and victims' rights favor sanctions that repair the harm done to the victim with the least burden imposed on offenders. Victims' rights and deterrence approaches, however, (sometimes) favor sanctions that are more burdensome than mere repayment at least, even if they still stay within the rationale of repairing the harm done to the victim. By making the sanctions more burdensome than mere repayment, we might be able to reach a higher deterrent effect or express more clearly to the victim that the state or community respects their rights and takes their moral injury seriously.

Here is one example to illustrate this difference. Imagine that an offender stole the laptop of the victim in a coffee store. After the offender is apprehended, we are tasked with finding the right type of sanction for them. According to the fairness rationale, the offender should give the laptop back (or, if lost, make a payment of restitution of equivalent value) and compensate the victim for emotional distress and potential losses that were linked to the crime. According to the value of penance, the victim should be given the chance to address the offender for the wrongdoing. In the best case, the offender will experience remorse and not only pay restitution with gritted teeth, but also accept that the sanction is justified and apologize.

The problem comes into play when we look at how we can best realize the value of deterrence and the rights or interests of the victim. Simply giving back the laptop and paying some amount of compensation as mentioned above might not be enough to give us reasons to think that the offender will not commit such a crime again, thereby not satisfying the value of deterrence; and it might not give the victim a good reason to think that the offender genuinely feels bad about the crime and that the state took the crime seriously (this will likely depend on the success of the restorative procedure, however), thereby not taking the value of protecting the interests of the victim seriously. Taking these two values seriously, then, might give us a good reason to make the sanction more burdensome to the offender than the values mentioned in the previous paragraph have suggested. Deterrence and victim's rights might warrant more than mere repairment in order to be realized.

Here, we (as a community, or the political representatives of the community) have to decide. Do we go above what fairness and penance would require and make the sanction more burdensome to ensure a better deterrent and communicative effect? My point here is not to answer this question, but rather to ask whether having to make this decision is a problem for pluralist approaches. I do not think that it is. First, we should note against the proposed objection that the theory is not necessarily inconsistent simply because such a question can be raised. There will be cases where corrective sanctions that solely aim to repair the damage done to the victim (and do so within a restorative setting) also suffice to express adequate respect for the victim without any need for further deterrence. The problem is not theoretical inconsistency, but the need for practical decision and policy making.

Having the choice to opt for different kinds of sanctions, however, should be seen as an advantage of the theory, not as a problem. It gives us leeway to take the criminological factors into account when addressing real-world problems, rather than giving an abstract one-fits-all solution to the problem of punishment.

Imagine that the situation in a certain community is such that mere payments of restitution and restorative procedures are not sufficient to express respect for the victim—that is, victims will generally feel let down by the justice systems without somewhat harsher sentences, and therefore lose trust in the system. In such cases, having a good justification for going beyond mere payments of restitution and opt for more demanding corrective sanctions such as community service comes in handy.

Of course, a strong proponent of the principle of least infringement could still argue that the communicative dimension of burdensome sanctions does not justify making repairing the harm done to the victim harsher than is necessary. I happen to disagree with such a view and argued that the communicative dimension is quite important (see Chapter 6). But the arguments are not so clear-cut. Maybe the critic is right, and we should care less about communicating respect to victims, or maybe it should be left to the democratic community to decide how much worth should be given to such considerations. Or maybe we should strive for divorcing our sense of self-worth from how we are treated by wrongdoers. This might be psychologically difficult, but it is a proposal worth considering.

The bottom line is that these different considerations concerning how seriously to take communicative aspects of wrongdoing (or deterrence, for that matter) only diversifies our discussion in criminal law—which we should appreciate. For policy purposes, a definitive answer is needed, of course—and as already mentioned, I happen to think that the arguments for allowing harsher corrective sanctions for the sake of deterrence and communication are morally and prudentially convincing. In detail: For low-severity wrongdoings, mere financial restitution and a restorative process (if wanted by the victim) should suffice to reach the values in question. For mid-level wrongdoings, community service will often be a more adequate sanction. This is so because such wrongdoings typically express more disrespect for the victim, and we have a justified interest to deter such wrongdoings. I personally think that it is still a good idea to have some leeway in the actual decision making in cases where the victim is satisfied with the restorative process, and where it is clear that the offender will likely not reoffend. In such cases, the response should be as in low-level crimes, with proportional restitution. In cases of high-level wrongdoing, the state is well-advised to consider some form of incapacitation (again, the least infringing type of incapacitation available) besides restorative settings and corrective sanctions that are perceived as burdensome.

That is the response to the objection of inconsistency. Yes, pluralism does allow for a flexible way of responding to wrongdoing, but still, we can establish clear guidelines for sentencing. These should typically be proportional to the severity of the wrongdoings. But why proportionality?

Proportionality

Before addressing the worry regarding proportionality in pluralistic and restorative settings in detail, more has to be said about the role of proportionality in criminal law. Even though it might seem obvious what proportionality entails on the face of it, the details in the debate are quite messy.

Let us start with some conceptual clarifications. First, the difference between *cardinal* and *ordinal* proportionality (Hirsch and Ashworth 2005, 138–40):

Cardinal proportionality defines the exact amount of punishment that is proportional to the wrongdoing. One example of a cardinal account of proportionality is the *lex talionis*. The *lex talionis* tries to give a rather straightforward measure of the types and lengths of punishments that are deserved for certain kinds of wrongdoing—an eye for an eye, a tooth for a tooth.

Ordinal proportionality, on the other hand, does not give absolute measures of proportionate punishment, but rather only defines the upper and lower limits of punishment for the worst (least bad) crimes, and then goes on to say that wrongdoings and their punishments have to be measured among these scales. There is thus some relativity built into ordinal proportionality. Some countries can define the worst crime as murder, and the highest punishment as 25 years in prison with the chance of parole. Others can define the highest amount of punishment for the same crime as torture to death. Both would introduce ordinal proportionality scales.

Ordinal proportionality also requires *parity, rank-ordering,* and *spacing* (Hirsch and Ashworth 2005, 139–40). Parity requires that like cases are given like punishments. If two offenders commit the same crime, with the same harm inflicted on victims, and the same intent, then they should be punished roughly equally. Rank-ordering requires that punishments be ranked according to the severity of the crime. Give the highest punishment to the severest crime, the lowest punishment to the least bad crime—and order accordingly in between. Spacing requires that there be no "jumps" in the mapping of punishments and severity of crimes. If we look from an imagined mid-point, two crimes that are equally distant in severity from this midpoint, should also have equally distant punishments from the mid-point.

For the discussion in this chapter, we can skip cardinal proportionality. Barely anyone in the debate defends the lex talionis anymore (but see Kershnar 2001, chap. 8), and no viable alternative measures for cardinal proportionality have been introduced. We will thus focus on ordinal proportionality, as do the other researcher in the debate.

First let us emphasize the problem of relativity for ordinal proportionality. As mentioned above, ordinal proportionality has no built-in measure to assess how much punishment is needed for the worst kind of wrongdoing. It would be completely compatible with ordinal proportionality to punish murder with a $10,000 fine, and then scale down for the less severe wrongdoings. But such a scaling will be unappealing for many people. So, we need a more detailed account of ordinal proportionality that does not stay agnostic on such measures.

To see how ordinal proportionality can be defined more clearly, we can turn to the question why we should care about proportionality in the first place. Three accounts are especially prominent in the literature: First, a strictly utilitarian justification for the proportionality of punishment, secondly, a justification based on the interests of laypeople, and thirdly, a justification based on censure.

Von Hirsch and Ashworth (2005, chap. 9) argue that only censure can give an adequate specification of how ordinal proportionality should be understood. In the following, I will take a closer look at their justification for ordinal proportionality and argue that they are mistaken to solely base proportionality on concerns regarding censure. As is the theme in this chapter, I think that a pluralistic understanding of proportionality gives us a more plausible account.

Utilitarian theories of punishment have always been confronted with the objection that they are committed to disproportionate punishment (see Chapter 7 in this book). The main answer to this critique can already be found in Beccaria and Bentham, and can be summarized as follows:

> When people offend [...], it is preferable that they commit lesser offences rather than serious crimes. Hence, the state should grade its prescribed sanctions according to the seriousness of offences, so that potential offenders would be induced (to the extent that they decide to offend at all) to prefer petty thefts over burglaries, burglaries over violent crimes and so forth. Failure to observe the principle of proportionality in sentencing would result in a misdirected structure of disincentives: those choosing to offend might as soon commit grave crimes as lesser ones. (Hirsch and Ashworth 2005, 132)

The main problem of such accounts is that the commitment to proportionality is "weak and prone to exceptions" (2005, 132). If petty crimes are rampant, whereas serious crimes are rare, it might be all-things-considered best to topple the proportionality requirement and adjust the length of the sanctions to the criminological data. As argued in Chapter 7, we simply cannot calculate how likely such scenarios are, but as the critic emphasizes: The sheer possibility of something like disproportional punishment being morally permissible within a certain rationale is sufficient to dismiss said rationale entirely—though as we have seen, this claim has to be weakened to be plausible.

The second strategy to argue for proportionality is to claim that proportionality best reflects the interests of the citizens and thus will result in stronger law-abidingness among citizens:

> The German criminal law scholar Claus Roxin contends, for example, that a penalty structure in which penalties are kept commensurate with the gravity of crimes will be perceived as more just, and being so perceived, will better strengthen citizen's self-restraint and respect for law. (Hirsch and Ashworth 2005, 133)

For this argument to succeed, we need to take into account the empirical evidence. As von Hirsch and Ashworth argue, there is some reason to think that Roxin is correct in his assumption that laws which are perceived as just will have the effects he assumes (Bottoms 2003), but the exact evidence is hard to calculate (Frisch 1998).

But the central problem according to von Hirsch and Ashworth lies in the account's failure "to recognize that proportionality is not just a prudential but an ethical principle" (2005, 133). They emphasize that we should not only think that proportionality is the smart thing to do, but that we feel like it is the right thing to do (2005, 133).

Thus, von Hirsch and Ashworth argue that proportionality should be a function of the censure that offenders deserve for their wrongdoing:

> Once one has created an institution with the condemnatory implications that punishment has, it is a requirement of justice, not merely of efficient crime prevention, to punish offenders according to the degree of reprehensibleness of their conduct. (2005, 134)

Von Hirsch and Ashworth are likely correct in their observation that to most people, proportionality requirements are not a mere matter of prudence. Nonetheless, I think they are too quick to dismiss the other considerations because of that.

First, even if von Hirsch and Ashworth are right about their normative claim, they did not solve the problem they were tasked with solving. We still do not know how to narrow down the upper limits of ordinal proportionality, even if we think that censure is the appropriate ground for the proportionality of sanctions. Von Hirsch and Ashworth more or less admit that this is the case (2005, 142–44). So even though they have an argument for proportionality at hand, they do not really have a solution to the problem of anchoring the upper and lower bounds of proportionality.

Here is where I think we should come back to the two accounts that von Hirsch and Ashworth were too quick to dismiss entirely from consideration. Imagine, for example, that the criminological data suggests that there is no difference in deterrent effects between a one year and a ten-year prison sentence for battery. If that is so, we are justified in scaling certain punishments at one year of prison instead of ten years simply because there is no more benefit to gain from adding more years in prison.

Von Hirsch and Ashworth would still be correct in thinking that we should not give free rein to the consequentialist, as this might result in sanctions that are fundamentally at odds with our intuitive notion of proportionality—and an institution that is fundamentally at odds with the intuitions of its citizens might have a hard time gaining their trust. But other than von Hirsch and Ashworth, I do not think that even a deeply held intuition regarding proportionality should be above grounds of criticism. If disproportionate punishment would have immensely great benefits, then at some point we should really rethink our deeply held norm of proportionality.

Finally, von Hirsch and Ashworth suggest measuring the gravity of the wrongdoing and the intensity of the sanction via the impact the wrong has on the victim. This, I think, is more promising—and brings me back to restorative justice and its way of handling proportionality. But before going to restorative justice, let me quickly summarize the somewhat messy takeaway from this subsection.

The idea that there is a clear criterion for the anchoring points for ordinal proportionality is a chimera. The censuring approach gives us good reasons to care about ordinal proportionality in principle, and thus limit the effect of utilitarian violations of proportionality. But utilitarian (and other) considerations can nonetheless illuminate how we should rank different wrongdoings and thus the accompanied sanctions. This will be a messy process, and it is likely not up to a single philosopher to lay out the details of exact proportionality. Rather, it seems plausible to me to see this as a societal, democratic task—where philosophers should still discuss the suggestions made in public debates. But similar to the discussion about sanctions, we should acknowledge that there is a plurality of values that should be taken into considerations when debating proportionality. All this does not give us exact proportionality measures into our hands, but these clarifications help us investigate to what extent proportionality poses a problem to restorative justice and corrective sanctions.

Restorative Justice and Proportionality

Von Hirsch and Ashworth admit that some form of proportionality can be built into restorative justice. For that, they imagine a "making amends model," which aims at making the offender repair the harm done to the victim—which roughly fits the model proposed in this book. Then, they go on to argue that the censure argument for the proportionality of punishment should also apply to the making amends model as they understand it:

> This argument extends to the making-amends model, where what is to be negotiated is not just a verbal apology, but a burden undertaken by the offender that is designed to convey that apologetic stance. If the basis for the imposition lies in its recognition of wrongdoing, its degree of onerousness necessarily conveys how reprehensible the conduct is treated as being. This implied valuation should, then, bear a reasonable relation to the actual degree of reprehensibleness of the conduct—that is, to its seriousness. The upshot is a requirement of proportionality. (It should be noted, moreover, that this requirement has not been "externally" derived from traditional criminal-justice principles; it derives from the logic of making-amends itself.) (2005, 120)

This is also roughly the argument I have made at several points in this book where critics have claimed that restorative justice models or corrective sanctions do not offer adequate sanctions. They do because what is decided upon in the restorative justice setting is not just verbal censure but is also a burden for the offender—a sanction—albeit one that solely aims at repairing the harm done to the victim and is thus limited by that rationale.

Nonetheless, von Hirsch and Ashworth worry that proportionality might be violated within restorative justice settings:

> In this kind of negotiated disposition [i.e., restorative justice settings], however, it would not seem feasible to import the kind of rigorous ordinal-proportionality requirements that a desert model envisions for criminal punishments [...]. This is because considerable leeway would be needed for the parties to choose a disposition that they feel conveys regret in a satisfactory manner. (2005, 120)

Keep in mind that I have argued in the previous section that the idea that the desert (or censure) model envisions "rigorous ordinal-proportionality requirements" is vastly overstated. But let us nonetheless take the objection seriously. The idea here is that restorative justice might lead to disproportionate sanctions because it gives some decision power to stakeholders of the conflict. By doing that, some measure of subjectivity is introduced, because the victims themselves together with other stakeholders of the conflict can decide what kind of sanctions would be best for their needs. As such, every party will likely take into account their own interests. If one victim thinks that adequate respect to them can only be communicated with a sanction that is above what would normally be considered proportionate, then restorative justice seems to be committed to that type of sanction, thereby violating proportionality.

But this argument does not suffice to overthrow restorative justice as a procedure to address criminal wrongdoing. Instead of leaving the sanction completely up to the stakeholders, we can allow the stakeholders in a conflict to have some authority over the type of sanction that is decided upon. As argued above, ordinal proportionality always only gives a broad direction for which sanctions will be proportionate for a certain wrongdoing. Mere repayment and community service are still roughly proportional to the severity of the wrongdoing—measured, for example, by the impact the wrongdoing had on the victim—, and stakeholders (but also judges and social workers) can be given leeway to decide upon which specific form of repayment or community service is most adequate for the stakeholders.

At the same time—as pluralism suggest—leaving the decision up to the stakeholders is not the only value we care about. We also care about rough proportionality and parity. Is the leeway then problematic? If one offender simply has to repay the loss, and another offender has to do community work for several weekends—would that be too much leeway in the decision process?

Again, I am not sure. There is some research that suggests that people care more about procedural justice than outcomes (Tyler 1987; 1990). If that turns out to be correct, giving more leeway to the stakeholders in the conflict to make the sanctions better fit their individual needs is preferable. If, however, people will be unhappy with giving one offender a restitution sentence and another a community service sentence for the same offense—then there is good reason to argue that such leeway should be limited. This is not a rebuttal against restorative justice, however. Restorative justice would even work without giving stakeholders the power to make sentencing recommendations. That is, in such cases we would employ victim-offender mediation with the aim of giving the victim a voice and the offender the chance to apologize to the wrongdoing.

Either way, restorative justice as a procedure of addressing criminal law is not off the table. Here, I will not decide how much leeway should be given to individuals in making their own sentencing recommendations. My only aim was to show that proportionality is not a knock-out concern that speaks against restorative justice. At best, proportionality can be understood broadly and easily be respected in restorative justice. At worst, stakeholders should not be given much leeway in making sentencing recommendations. Whatever the result, restorative justice and corrective sentences remain justified.

8.6 Conclusion

In this chapter I have outlined a non-foundational pluralist approach to criminal law. If the results of the previous chapters in this book are correct, we need a framework that combines fairness, penance and censure, victims' rights and deterrence to play into the justification of corrective sanctions. Hybrid and unified theories fail as plausible accounts for that aim (but also for independent concerns). We should thus approach criminal law through a non-foundational pluralist perspective.

Such an account is not inconsistent. I have argued that all the rationales considered in this book favor corrective sentences, and some favor restorative procedures of addressing wrongdoing. But even if all rationales favor corrective sanctions, the pluralist theory might still suggest different ranges of corrective sanctions. To some extent, this is true. If it were not for the communicative and consequentialist dimension, mere payments of restitution would suffice. But communicative and consequentialist concerns might warrant more burdensome corrective sentences such as community service. Because of that, sentencing decisions should take into account how much these additional considerations apply in a given situation and judge accordingly.

Would that violate proportionality? Not in a problematic manner, I think. It would in principle allow for some difference in sentencing recommendations for similar crimes (mere restitution where deterrence is not necessary, community service where it is necessary for the same wrongdoing). I suspect that this range of sentencing guidelines will not pose too many difficulties. If, however, the public will regard these variations as illegitimate proportionality violations, then the criminal law institution can impose similar types of corrective sanctions for similar wrongdoings. This, however, would have the drawback that the sanction types will not be made with the specific needs of the victims in mind. Here, we simply have to weigh the importance of proportionality versus most helpful and precise sentencing recommendations. All of this, however, is compatible with the type of theory outlined in this chapter.

Chapter 9
Objections to Corrective Approaches to Criminal Law

> We must take seriously the abolitionist challenge that state punishment cannot be justified and should be abolished.
>
> Antony Duff, *Punishment, Communication, and Community* (2001, xv)

9.1 Introduction

I have presented the positive arguments in favor of corrective approaches, and I did so with a keen eye on empirical research relevant to the normative debate on the justification of criminal law. Along the way, I discussed some problems of the different approaches trying to justify legal sanctions. What remains to be done, now, is to take a closer look at general objections to corrective approaches. When the objections can be successfully addressed, the defense of corrective approaches will be complete as far as this book is concerned. There will be no systematic structure in this chapter, and I will simply go through several objections that have been raised against corrective approaches.

9.2 Problems with Corrective Approaches

Let us begin with some primarily pragmatic concerns, albeit, if convincing, with grave moral implications.

Poor Offenders

For the first one, we have to start with the empirical observation that many crimes are committed by people with impoverished social backgrounds—in short: Poor offenders (Clear 2007; Western 2006). There are two important problems associated with imposing corrective sanctions on such offenders. First, as the offenders are poor, "it can take months or years to extract [the compensation] from offenders; in the meantime their victims may suffer" (Lippke 2020, 330–32). Secondly, by demanding poor offenders to pay up for their crimes, we make their situation even worse, which would have detrimental consequences for the offenders and potentially the families or communities who are dependent on the offender (Lippke 2020, 324; Mumola 2000). Lippke's aim in raising these problems is to argue against an offender-focused compensation scheme and in favor of a state-funded compensation scheme for victims. I think that he is right to worry about the impacts of corrective sanctions on both offenders and victims, but wrong to dismiss restitution paid by the offender as the best solution to these problems.

Let us first turn to the problems for the victim. It is true that many crimes severely impact victims financially—and in some cases, as argued in Chapter 6, the material and financial problems are the cause of secondary problems for the victims (poverty, loss of trust in the justice system and diminished perception of moral self-worth). For that reason, there already are some government-funded compensation programs for victims in certain countries (Braun 2019). Furthermore, victims can also demand compensation in civil procedures. These, however, can also take some time to go through, which would impact the victim negatively as just said.

The problem for corrective approaches according to Lippke is that offenders often cannot immediately pay up to the harm they have done, and that thereby more harm is visited upon victims. I think that this part of the objection is plainly on point. If corrective approaches aim to alleviate the harm done to victims, but the contingent empirical circumstances make it such that often times this cannot happen immediately, then that poses a downside to corrective theories (note, however, that punitive sanctions would not really do a better job here either).

The problem with Lippke's response, however, is that he takes the objection to show that the corrective rationale needs to be dismissed. But that is not what the argument succeeds to show. It is indeed beneficial to implement a state- or NGO-funded compensation scheme that can immediately alleviate the harm that offenders cause to their victims without much bureaucratic hassle. But these payments of restitution can still be conceptualized and communicated as the offender's restitution. This can be done in a formal and legal manner, by clarifying that the offender incurred a debt to the government or the NGO which can be paid in a slower manner, as is often done with daily rates. At the same time, the victim can immediately receive money that is send as restitution from the offender, in his or her debt. This could allow us to keep the important communicative effects of payments of restitution from the offender rather than a third-party (Chapters 5 and 6), while still addressing the objection Lippke raised.

From a moral perspective such an acknowledgement is important because it is the offender who is the adequate person to pay the victim restitution, not the taxpayers. Not having the offender pay up thus would amount to not taking the offender's responsibility seriously. Lippke evades this problem by punishing the offender in addition to the government funded compensation scheme, but as argued in this book, there is no convincing argument for sanctioning offenders independent of the aim to restore the harm done to the victim.

Acknowledging the offender as being responsible for restitution has also psychological benefits for the victim. In Chapter 6, we have taken a closer look at what types of sanctions help most in restoring the victim's feeling of justice and perceived moral self-worth. There, I have argued that the empirical evidence suggests that it makes an important difference for the victim if the compensatory payment is framed as being paid by the offender or by a third-party (Laxminarayan 2013). I do not know of any direct studies researching whether simply framing the restitution as the offender's—even though being initially paid by the state or NGO's—has the same effect as direct restitution by the offender. That would be important to know for the success of such sanctions. But the limited evidence that we have suggests that having the payment of restitution be made in the offender's name is preferable to simply paying through a third-party.

This response to the first version of the objection directly leads us to the second one. If we insist that it is the offender who has to pay up, the government perpetuates their poverty and thus impacts the families and other dependent people negatively. To address the full scope of this objection, we need to take a look at what else we could do. Retributivists such as Lippke still suggest that poor offenders should be punished for the wrongs they committed. Punishment, however, typically either consists in fines which the offender has to pay, or incarceration in the case of more serious wrongdoings. In actual practice, not being able to pay the fines for the wrongdoing can, in turn, lead to incarceration of the offender. This, however, has a dire impact on the offenders themselves, their families and even communities, which is especially visible in the US with its culture of mass incarceration in the last decades (Mumola 2000).

So, the retributive solution does not really solve the problem put forward to speak against the corrective rationale. At the very least, both accounts are in the same boat, and a punitive alternative is thus not more appealing than the corrective approach. This, in turn, would give us reasons to stick with the corrective approach, even if it were unable to solve this problem (and assuming that we do not want to abolish sanctioning poor offenders altogether).

This response might be good enough for a defense of corrective approaches in comparison to punitive approaches, but the response still leaves us with a bitter taste. What else could be done? One solution which I want to outline here is community service (punitive theorists could maybe also take this route to offer a solution to the problem). If the offender owes, let us say, $10,000 as restitution to the victim, and the state or an NGO pays up first, then the government can either extract the money in rates that are manageable for the offenders and their families, or by sentencing them to community services which will at some point cover the costs. As argued in Chapter 2, corrective approaches can adopt community service as a type of sanction without resorting to the punitive rationale. The community service does not aim to harm the offender, but rather to simply extract the amount of compensation that victims are justified in demanding. Such a sanction would of course still involve coercive treatment, but such coercive treatment is justifiable from within the corrective rationale—and it can be designed in a way to have the least collateral damage for the offender.

That response is still not optimal. But we are not dealing with optimal circumstances here, of course. The fact of poverty and criminality in such demographics falls outside the scope of just criminal law. As a society, we are certainly well-advised to tackle these issues, but the criminal law alone does not seem to be the way to achieve this. For the purpose at hand, we can confidently conclude that poor offenders are no reason to dismiss the corrective rationale.

Rich Offenders

But what about rich offenders? With rich offenders, a different objection can be raised with regards to corrective approaches (for an overview, Boonin 2008, 259–61). If offenders do not have to fear punishment as a response to wrongdoing, then they can simply "pay" to commit certain crimes. Imagine that there is an especially gruesome millionaire, who, for whatever reason, loves to beat people up. According to the corrective approach, so the criticism goes, the millionaire simply has to pay the victim after beating them up. Imagine, for the sake of the argument, that the losses incurred to victims of battery are roughly around $50,000. If that amount can easily be paid, we might have to fear gruesome millionaires running around our streets, beating up people, and then simply paying them the required amount of money. A system of criminal law that lets this happens is simply abhorrent—and corrective approaches should be dismissed as they do not have the tools to address such behavior adequately.

To address this objection in detail, it will be important to carefully clarify the exact nature of the problem. I want to distinguish three readings of the problem. A justice-based reading, a communicative reading, and a deterrence-based reading.

According to the justice-based reading of the objection, justice would not be restored when the offender is allowed to simply pay up for beating up other people. But within a rather narrow understanding of justice, this does not seem to be quite right. If I owe you $10,000, for whatever I did (either loaned it, or damaged something from you), then repaying that money will re-establish a just distribution regardless of whether or not I am rich. If I damage your property right that you have to your bodily integrity (understood in a libertarian fashion), then justice will be restored when I pay you the required amount of money to restore that property as much as possible. If the critic assumes a retributive reading of justice, in which intentionally harming offenders is necessary to restore justice—then I can only point to Part II of this book and the observation that retributivists fail to convincingly justify such an understanding of justice. If we accept a corrective approach to justice, simply providing the adequate compensation is all that needs to be done. But even when giving this answer, I myself feel that this cannot be the full story—it feels like something is missing. But as justice is doing just fine, we need to turn to the other interpretations of the objection.

More pressing, I think, are the communicative- and deterrence-based readings of the problem. The communicative reading of the objection states that offenders who simply pay up (with no severe burden being imposed by the sanction) do not express adequate respect for the victim of the wrongdoing. We have encountered versions of this objection in Chapters 5 and 6. Typically, making sanctions burdensome and accepting such sanctions on part of the offender is a good way of communicating either remorse about the wrongdoing or acknowledgment for the victim, though this is strictly speaking neither necessary nor sufficient (sometimes we can express remorse without being burdened, and sometimes being burdened does not express remorse). Paying $50,000 does not seem very burdensome to millionaires, so we often times cannot be sure whether the offender really communicates respect for the victim, or even experiences remorse—or so the objection goes.

Similarly for the deterrence-based version of the objection, we might worry that such sanctions will not do a great job of incentivizing brutal millionaires to respect the bodily integrity of other people. If the worst that can happen to gruesome millionaires who want to beat up other people is to pay an amount of money that they barely care about, then what else is there to deter them from regularly committing such actions? Thus, for adequate communication and deterrence, punishment is needed over and above corrective sanctions.

David Boonin has offered a response to the deterrence-based objection against corrective approaches. His strategy to address the objection is to argue that the harm inflicted by rich offenders is more serious than the harm inflicted by poor offenders:

> Since the wealthy offender has barely been harmed by his action, he has barely been deterred from repeating it. This means that he has caused much more harm to his secondary victims—more subjective anxiety and a greater decrease in their objective level of security—than has the typical offender. Thus, he owes much greater compensation to his secondary victim than does the typical offender. (Boonin 2008, 260)

The reasoning here is somewhat awkward, I think, as his argument does not rest on direct harm to victims. Rather, if the corrective sanctions would not deter rich offenders as reliably as other offenders, then in virtue of that fact their wrongdoings have a more harmful impact on secondary victims who now fear for their security. Therefore, we have to impose a stricter corrective sanction, one that will not lead to people fearing their security. This can either be done with harsher corrective sanctions, or by other measures such as ankle monitors, etc. If wearing an ankle monitor for a month, say, restores the wrongfully violated objective security of the community where the wrongdoing happened, then corrective approaches can justify harsher measures for rich offenders, thereby addressing the rich-offender-objection.

This argument is unconvincing in my view, because the additional harm to secondary victims does not result from the action of the offender, but from the action of the state, that is, the corrective sanction. But then sanctioning the offender even more because the state chose the wrong sanction seems weird. It would be more reasonable to argue that from the very beginning, the offender should be sanctioned more harshly than the corrective rationale itself would allow—but that is not a conclusion that Boonin would like to accept. The somewhat complicated structure of the argument is the result of Boonin's attempt to stay strictly within the corrective rationale as he understands it. But a more direct response is available to the corrective theorist. By doing that, we can evade the somewhat inelegant argument of saying that rich offenders should be sanctioned more harshly because our initially considered sanction failed to reliably deter them, thereby causing secondary harm to the community. It is unclear why the offender should step up for that shortcoming of the state.

A better way to address the rich-offender-objection, I think, is to precisely state which facts we should consider when we are faced with such wrongdoings. Preventing wrongdoings matters in criminal law, as argued in Chapter 7, and people who run around the town beating up people for the fun of it are a danger to our society. We have good reasons to prevent such persons from roaming free. Rich offenders are not a special case in that regard. If we know that there is a random person who beats people up for the fun of it, we need to take stricter measures than simply making them pay restitution for the harm they have imposed on others (though we should also do that). Once we know that the motive of the offender was such that future wrongdoings are likely, we can work with that knowledge.

What can we do about people with such unusual motivations to commit criminal wrongdoing? Punishment only partly helps. There will also be people who are willing to accept a year-long prison sentence when it buys them the opportunity to beat up a person they hate. The corrective rationale has no special problem here, except maybe because the burden is somewhat lower as sanctions are not as harsh as in the punitive framework.

But I want to argue that we can partly address this problem without resorting to the punitive rationale. As argued before, the corrective rationale offers various ways of addressing wrongdoing. Simply paying restitution is one form of sanction compatible with it. But if for whatever reason we deem mere restitution to be inadequate, say because more deterrence is needed, then there are other types of sanctions we can chose from. We can sanction the offender not only to repay the money, but to make them participate in a restorative justice process. True, a rich offender who beats people up for fun might not be the most likely to come to recognize their wrongdoing—but if the victims wish for such a procedure, it would simply be more burdensome and more of a hassle to the offender. Furthermore, the payment of restitution can be supplement with community work to put up more of a burden while still providing adequate restitution for the victim. The idea that within the corrective framework offenders simply pay for their crimes in monetary terms is imprecise. A corrective approach can be fine with such a sanction when the offender recognized their wrongdoing, for example. But in other cases, the corrective rationale prefers different types of compensation to just paying money.

Still, the critic might press, corrective sanctions simply have a lower deterrent effect than punitive sanctions. To stay within this admittedly unusual example: in a punitive framework, we can disincentive more brutal millionaires than in the corrective framework, as the sanctions are harsher in the punitive framework.

That is correct, but it is unclear whether this consideration is enough to make a case against the corrective rationale. It would only show that we need punishment for the limited case of wrongdoers as described in the objection. We have no idea, of course, how many such weird cases exist. As we have seen in Chapter 7, we have no evidence from criminology to think that punitive sanctions do a better job at deterring the general public than corrective sanctions. Quite the opposite, corrective sanctions, restorative justice, and therapy appear to do a better job at securing law-abidingness. And there is no data I know of on the types of offenders the rich offender objection envisions.

Furthermore, the state has options outside of the criminal law to do something about such offenders. If it is determined by the criminal proceeding that an offender had as a motivation for their wrongdoing the sheer lust for violence, then therapy and surveillance can be justified not as a form of punishment, but as forward-looking preventive treatment. In accordance with the principle of least infringement, we should still provide the security for the general public by infringing as little as possible on the rich offender's rights or interests. But it is typically not disputed that the state can have the authority for such preventive actions without resorting to punishment in the sense we are interested in.

So, the rich offender objection is no death blow to corrective theories. First of all, even if successful, the objection does not grant the state a general right to punishment. If at all, it would justify punishing a very peculiar subgroup of offenders. But even with these types of offenders, corrective approaches do not come unprepared. A corrective system can sanction offenders to community service and restorative processes rather than simply repaying money, and it also has good reasons to put such offenders under surveillance or coerce them to try therapy. That is only assuming, of course, such offenders are indeed motivated in the way the rich-offender-objection describes them.

What about the communication-based objection? As argued in Chapter 6, we have good reasons to account for the expressive or communicative effects of wrongdoings on victims, especially their perceived sense of moral self-worth and justice restoration. Offenders who think that they can beat people up simply because they have the money to pay restitution appear to express disrespect towards victims, a disregard of their interests and moral status. We have good reasons to address these disrespectful dimensions of the wrongdoing, all the more in cases of senseless battery. Again, the rich offender is not an unparalleled case here. Other offenders can be similarly disrespectful, if they are, for example, motivated by a racist belief that the victim is morally worthless.

But if what I said in Chapter 6 is correct, punishment does not help in this picture. There is little evidence to think that simply punishing offenders does a good job at rectifying the expressive harms done to the victim. There is some evidence, however, that restitution-orders, restorative justice, and giving the victim a say in the criminal proceeding do indeed help with such expressive wrongs. If the critic does not give us any reasons to believe that things would be different with rich offenders, we should expect corrective sanctions to help here as well.

Thus, rich offenders who beat people up for the fun of it are not a reason to dismiss corrective theories.

There Is No Adequate Restitution for Some Losses

A frequently voiced criticism against corrective theories is that some wrongdoings and the harms they inflict on victims cannot be adequately addressed with restitution (Dagger 1991, 32; Hoekema 1991, 338–39; Tunick 1992, 160; Walker 1993, 68). Corrective approaches are thus necessarily incomplete. And at least in such cases, they need to be supplemented with a punitive approach. This would not entail dismissing the corrective rationale completely. For many crimes, restitution can meaningfully be offered by the offender, and for these we should indeed do so. But the corrective rationale I want to defend here aims to be comprehensive—the objection thus needs to be addressed.

Two paradigmatic types of wrongdoing that are often mentioned as the crux for corrective theories are rape and murder.[18] With murder, there is a very direct sense in which restitution is not possible: The victim is not alive anymore and thus cannot receive any form of restitution. With very serious wrongdoing such as rape, the objection has a different dimension. Rape victims can be given payments of restitution for the harm they suffered, but monetary payments are inadequate to repair the harm that has been inflicted on them—the very idea of paying for the harm suffered might even be an insulting one.

Corrective approaches thus need a response to these different versions of the objection. First, how to deal with wrongdoings where there is no recipient to receive restitution? Second, can restitution really adequately repair the harm done to the victim in cases of serious wrongdoing?

For the first version of the objection, we need to be careful again to distinguish different readings of the argument. One reading would be that the very fact that there is no recipient anymore undermines corrective theories. A different reading suggests that corrective theorists do not allow us to deal with the dangers of murderers successfully.

To me, the first variation has already been successfully addressed by Boonin (2008, 241). He argues that with the help of three principles—each of which is independently accepted in current law—the objection can be addressed. The first principle (transferability claim) states that a debt owed to one person can be transferred to another person. If a person dies, the debt can be transferred to the estate of the person, or a relative of the person. That much is uncontroversial. The second principle (substitutability claim) states that if a person cannot pay up exactly what they owe, they nonetheless should pay as much as possible. That should also be uncontroversial. If I owe you $10,000, but can currently only pay half of it, then I should pay half if it now, and the rest whenever I reasonably can. The third principle (pricing claim) states that it is in principle possible to put a price on a hu-

---

[18] There is some evidence that corrective approaches are promising for addressing hate crimes, though the data is very limited and much depends on the quality of the restorative process (Walters 2014; Walters, Paterson, and Brown 2020). There are of course many more cases where restitution and restorative justice could be difficult to apply, such gender-based violence more broadly, acts of terrorism, or mass-murder. As outlined in the Introduction, I will not be able to cover all instances of wrongdoing, though such a detailed approach of corrective justice should be investigated more in the future.

man's life. That principle, too, is already operating in law and used by insurance companies and is thus uncontroversial in that regard.

Boonin's defense now goes as follows: According to the corrective rationale, a murderer would incur the debt of restoring their victim to a level of well-being equal to the one before the wrongdoing. That is not possible for murder. But according to the substitutability claim, the offender would still owe an amount as close as possible to the value of the life. According to the pricing claim, the value of a life can be determined. Thus, the murderer ought to compensate the amount of money as much as possible. But the victim is dead, they cannot be compensated. Still, according to the transferability claim, the amount owed can be transferred to the victim's estate, descendants, or, as a last resort, also to the state. If all that is correct, the corrective rationale can account for murder.

Admittedly, the case of murder commits corrective theories to somewhat awkward responses. Is paying money really a substitute for the loss of life? Is giving the money back to the family really adequate? Suppose this is not so, in what way exactly would punishment help with addressing this gap in the corrective theory? If corrective sentences cannot offer adequately restitution for such a wrongdoing, punishment cannot do so either for the very same reason. The victim does not get anything out of the offender being sentenced to life in prison. So, punishment does not really add to the corrective theory in this regard at all. And as we do not have a plausible independent justification of punishment as justice-restoring mechanism (see Part II of this book), this objection does not offer a plausible reason to prefer punitive to corrective theories. The honest answer simply seems to be that in some cases, the moral values that we would like to realize cannot be fully achieved. The dead cannot be brought back, and they cannot be adequately compensated. But if punishment also does not help with this problem, there is no reason to dismiss the corrective theory because of that. We simply have to accept the limits of what we can achieve with restitution.

What about the deterrence consideration? Do we need to resort to the punitive rationale for that reason? Murderers have a huge impact on the society at large in terms of the feeling of security, at least for the community in which the wrongdoing occurred. In order to restore the feeling of insecurity, the corrective approach can justify forms of monitoring, rehabilitation, or incarceration. The details depend on the circumstances of the action. We are probably well-advised to incarcerate or heavily monitor a murderer who acted intentionally. Manslaughter that resulted from a "heat-of-the-moment" action will be more difficult to consider. It is unclear whether these actions can really be deterred because they are per definition actions that result from extremely strong momentary urges. Also, it is unclear whether such a person will be a danger for society for the rest of their life, although some rehabilitative treatment and monitoring is likely still advisable—and justifiable from within the corrective rationale.

There is also the open question whether the family should be conceptualized as direct victims. Note that corrective theories in principle are not committed to any specific view on criminalization and the scope of victims of wrongdoings that can justifiably demand restitution. Obviously, there is the direct victim, but there could also be more indirect victims of wrongdoing that might have a justified claim to restitution. If the whole neighborhood of where a murder occurred has a right to some form of restitution because of the loss of feeling of security, then that needs to be included in the sanction that the offender is sentenced to. I am not committed to any specific view here. But again, there is nothing in the corrective approach that speaks against using non-punitive measures to prevent wrongdoing in the future. Given that we have no criminological evidence that murder will be rampant without punishment over and above restitution (see Chapter 7), the objection does not hold.

Let us now turn to the second variation of the objection: Some wrongs cannot be adequately repaired. To some, it might seem insulting to think that moral wrongs such as rape can be corrected by the offender paying restitution to the victim. It might seem to belittle the wrong that has been inflicted on the victim and add insult to injury. These are often cases where emotions run high—but we should nevertheless ask whether there is really a problem for corrective theories.

As a first response to the objection, we can again make a companions-in-guilt argument. After all, the criticism against corrective theorists is raised by proponents of punishment. Does punishment help with such wrongs?[19] Lippke (2020, 321), when pushing this objection, emphasizes the emotional harm and loss of dignity such wrongdoings typically have as a result. In Chapter 6, however, I argued with reference to victimological research that punishment alone does not seem to do a good job to help with such repercussions of wrongdoing for the victim. Corrective sanctions and giving the victim a say in the criminal process have a greater impact on the victim's perceived moral self-worth, feeling of justice restoration,

---

[19] Boonin has a response in which he emphasizes that there will always be some cases where punishment is not applicable. When a sick person suffering from late-stage cancer decides to murder several nurses, the offender will not be around long enough for proper punishment and cannot really be made to suffer for their wrong in any interesting sense. Because of that, the mere fact that sometimes there are wrongdoings where restitution is not applicable is not enough to dismiss the corrective rationale, except if we are willing to dismiss the punitive rationale because of that same reason, too. This response, however, misses a more interesting perspective of the objection, namely that corrective sanctions are in some sense normatively inadequate to deal with serious wrongdoing.

and trust in the system. The emotional harm such wrongdoings typically inflict on victims is better accounted for within the corrective rather than punitive approach.

Even if that is correct, the critic is still right that there will be many cases in which the emotional harm cannot be completely repaired. Especially in cases of wrongdoing with traumatic consequences for the victim, the hope that sanctions will make it as if nothing happened appears to be naïve and misguided. But two things have to be kept in mind here.

First, even if corrective sanctions and procedural aspects will not always fully address the emotional harm, corrective theories are still the way to go if there are no better alternatives at hand. The fact that the theory sometimes does not have the tools to completely restore victims is not a reason to dismiss it if there is no better alternative. Secondly, we should not have a narrow focus on sanctioning alone. Sanctioning offenders is certainly one important component of addressing the harms of serious wrongdoings, but it is not the only one. There are also other ways of showing support for the victim and thereby addressing the emotional harm of the wrong, such as offering therapeutic measures or immediate financial help to relieve worries about hospital costs and other things. Sanctioning offenders is just one part of a more comprehensive attempt to address such harms to the benefits of the victim and the broader society.

So yes, strictly speaking there are repercussions of wrongdoings that the corrective theory will not be able to fully address. But that is not a reason to dismiss corrective approaches. Quite the opposite: Corrective approaches still promise the most productive way of addressing these serious aspects of wrongdoing—at least when taken in addition with other measures that have nothing to do with sanctioning or criminal law in the narrow sense. The irreparability of certain wrongdoings is thus no reason to reject the corrective rationale.

Differences between Criminal Law and Civil Law

Most Western criminal law institutions roughly distinguish between criminal and civil wrongdoings. Criminal wrongdoings are typically responded to with punishments, while civil lawsuits are concerned with questions of compensation for victims. If the corrective approach I advocate here wishes to abolish punitive sanctions, it in effect gets rid of criminal law in that sense. Institutions following the corrective approach would only have the civil law left (and other types not relevant here, such as contract law, etc.). A system that only acknowledges civil wrongdoing, however, is extremely problematic (Husak 2020, 46–47). Criminal law is typically concerned with moral wrongs, whereas civil law is concerned with harms which can simply be compensated. Also, criminal law typically requires a higher burden of proof for the conviction of wrongdoers than civil law. Abolishing criminal law results in abolishing these important aspects of the criminal law, which we simply cannot accept. Therefore, we should not abolish the criminal law.

There are some broadly corrective theorists who agree with the slogan that we should abolish the criminal law. Joseph Ellin, for example, writes: "The idea is that criminal law as a body of rules, along with most prisons and police, would be abolished. Most of what is now considered a crime would be treated as a tort" (2000, 299; similarly Barnett 1977, 490). I am not so sure, however, that the authors also agree to abolish the typical standard of proof in criminal law ("beyond reasonable doubt")—at least they do not seem to say so explicitly in the papers that critics cite.

The critique might rest on some form of misunderstanding what corrective theories want to abolish. When corrective theorists say that they want to abolish the criminal law and instead focus on civil law, they mean first and foremost the types of sanctions, not the procedural aspects. That is to say, corrective theories can still address certain wrongdoings with a higher burden of proof, while addressing others with a lower one. Furthermore, they can still distinguish between morally charged restitution orders for wrongdoing (as in criminal law), and more morally neutral compensation orders as in civil law (a tree in your garden destroyed the fence of your neighbor). Nothing in the idea of abolishing punitive sanctions commits to a stance on any of these other aspects of criminal law, they are simply a different matter.

Furthermore, some authors deny that there should be a strict distinction between criminal law and civil law in the first place. In the public law tradition (Chiao 2016), there is no principled difference between criminal law, civil law, contract law, etc. Ultimately, all these institutions aim at the enforcement of rules, albeit for different types of wrongs. Also, all these branches share the same rationale. They enforce rules in order to make cooperation more stable and smoother within a given political community. Criminal law typically does so with harsher sanctions than does civil law, but that does not change the fact that the general function of both types of sanction is the same.

Should different types of rules be enforced with different standards of proof in such a framework? That depends. If there are good reasons to do so, the public law tradition can incorporate it. For especially harsh sanctions, we want to make really sure that we only sanction those who actually did violate a certain rule—otherwise the point of rule-enforcement for wrongdoing is somewhat undermined (Chiao 2016, 155–61). Whether or not less serious wrongdoings such as contract breaches should have a lower burden of proof needs to be answered with regards to the question how much that would help to stabilize cooperation. If we need to allow for some false positives in order to make people in general more likely to stick to contracts, then so be it. If people lose trust in the justice system if the standard of proof is too low and too many innocent people are made to pay compensation, then that would be a reason to make the standard of proof high. The point here is not to give a definite answer, but rather to show that the question of sanction is silent on the question of burden of proof.

Does this book advocate to abolish the criminal law? Not in the sense that Husak worries about. It is true that corrective theories as understood in this book advocate to abolish punitive sanctions. But that alone does not say anything with regards to other aspects of criminal law, especially those mentioned by the critic. We should ask how high the standard of proof for given crimes should be independently of whether or not we are concerned with criminal law. As Husak (2020, 46) hints at, high standards of proof typically involve high procedural costs. A lot of evidence has to be gathered by the defendant or state attorney to make a case beyond reasonable doubt, whereas less work has to be done when the standards of proof are lower. We might thus want to only accept high burdens of proof in cases where a lot is at stake. The claims of corrective theories are thus compatible with accepting different kinds of standards of proof.

Lastly, abolishing punitive sanctions does not necessarily entail abolishing the difference between serious criminal wrongdoings and minor civil wrongs. I have argued in several chapters of the book that corrective sanctions, especially when accompanied by restorative processes, communicate to the offender, the victim, and the community that a (serious) moral violation has taken place (Chapters 5 and 6). Even within the corrective framework, we treat battery different from, say, a tree in your garden that has fallen on your neighbor's fence (assuming the latter is a paradigmatic case of a tort, not one that gravely endangered the neighbor). In principle, for the latter case, there would be nothing out of place if an insurance company would cover the costs of a new fence and the work to build it. In the case of battery, however, not taking the offender into the equation would result in a failure to acknowledge the actions as a wrong done by the offender, that is, as an action that they should personally take responsibility for, and the need for the victim to receive the acknowledgement from the offender. These differences in how we typically respond to different kinds of mishaps (not to call the falling tree a wrong) can thus still be accounted for in the corrective framework if all I have argued for in this book is correct.

To sum up: Abolishing punitive sanctions is neutral on the question what the standard of proof for different kinds of wrongdoings should be. Also, even if we abolish punitive sanctions, we can still maintain a difference between serious wrongdoings and lesser harms. The slogan that corrective theorists want to abolish the criminal law should thus not worry us.

Crimes as Public Wrongs

Corrective sanctions are primarily concerned with the victim of the wrongdoing and the question how the offender can provide adequate restitution for the harm inflicted on the victim. To some, this is an odd focus. When we ask the question why we should criminalize certain actions in the first place, some authors have suggested that the state should only criminalize public wrongs (Duff and Marshall 2010). The reason for criminalization would not be that a person has suffered an unrightful loss, but that a public wrong has been committed.

Unfortunately, the debate surrounding public wrongs is complicated as there is some disagreement on what public wrongs are in the first place (Wall 2018), and whether public wrongs should be the basis of criminalization (Edwards and Simester 2017). We will not be able to decide this dispute in this subsection, but it is worthwhile to address some of the central themes of the debate in the context of corrective theories. Two dimensions of the public wrong theory stand out: First, criminal wrongs are conceptualized as not only the business of the victim, but as being an important matter for the society at large. As Duff and Marshall put it, a public wrong is a "matter of public interest in the sense that it properly concerns all members of the polity by virtue simply of their shared membership of the political community" (2010, 71). A corrective approach would then be inadequate as it mischaracterizes the nature of criminal wrongdoings. The second, related, dimension of the objection is that the public has a stake in the criminal proceeding. That is, even if the victim chooses not to pursue the wrongdoing in court, the public might still have a legitimate interest in the wrong as it is a public wrong, not just a private wrong against the victim. The corrective approach again misses this dimension and should thus be dismissed.

In the same spirit, Husak asks the corrective theorist to clarify:

> What role would the public continue to play in a radically reconfigured system of criminal justice? Would all legal disputes be public? Or would none be? If a line between the public and the private would continue to be drawn, what would be its foundation? And would it not simply reintroduce the criminal category under a different guise? These questions pose further challenges for criminal law skeptics. (2020, 51)

Again, the corrective framework I imagine here does not necessary abolish criminal law with all its differences to other branches of law. Rather, it only aims to abolish punitive sanctions. All of the other questions raised by the public wrong defendant are independent from the question whether punitive or corrective sanctions are most appropriate.

This response also clarifies a related worry outlined above. Accepting that victims have a justified claim to restitution does not say anything about whether or not the public also has a justified claim to make against the offender. The state can still be the central institution who oversees the handling of criminal wrongdoing (see Chapter 8 for a more detailed outline) even if the sanction should be corrective rather than punitive. I have argued in Chapters 5, 6, and 7 that there are good reasons to give the stakeholders of the conflict some leeway in handling the conflict on their own, that is, meeting in restorative procedures and making own suggestions for the most helpful and adequate types of restitution for their individual case. But there is nothing in the corrective framework that speaks against the government's prerogative to have a veto right and overturn these suggestions. But for that, the government needs sound reasons. If it can give such reasons, the corrective approach can coherently allow for such a veto right by the state.

That is also the case for situations where the victim does not want to address the wrongdoing or does not want any restitution after a successful restorative procedure. From the perspective of the victim, the state has no business in telling them to demand the restitution. But the political community might have an independent interest in the criminal wrong, in part maybe because there were indirect victims involved. Imagine, for example, that the victim forgives the offender, but that the people in the neighborhood have legitimate worries that the wrongdoer might commit robbery again in the future. In that case, if the worries are well-justified, the political community might be justified in deciding on additional sanctions that cover these additional harms that go beyond the direct harm inflicted on the victim, or to take actions outside of the criminal law to protect the community from further harm (for more on secondary victims and harm to the society, see Boonin 2008, chap. 5.3).

So, a corrective theory does not in itself take a stance on the public wrong perspective. Wrongs are always against individuals, but they might also rightfully concern the public at large. Because of that, the state can still have legitimate interests in criminal procedures and sentencing decisions, even if the victim's harm is in the focus of attention. Also, if the community is harmed, it can legitimately pursue restitution for their losses as well, even if victims themselves do not want to receive restitution. Also, if without a payment of restitution, the offender might be legitimately thought to be a danger to society, the state might take measures to reduce that risk.

A different version of the objections claims that only punitive sanctions can adequately address public wrongs (Wall 2018). If that were the case, the corrective approach really would be inadequate. If there are public wrongs, and if public wrongs can only be adequately addressed with punitive sanctions, then punitive sanctions are needed, and the corrective rationale is not comprehensive.

The problem here is that the objection needs an independent argument as to why public wrongs require punitive sanctions. Given that none of the current theories of punishment offer a good justification of punitive sanctions, as I have argued in this book, the fact that some wrongs concern the public as a whole will also not add to this. If that is correct, and if the argument against corrective sanctions based on public wrongs does not succeed without such an independent motivation, there is no reason to dismiss the corrective rationale.

Victimless Crimes

A substantive problem for the corrective approach is that there are victimless crimes that need to be accounted for. Corrective approaches do not seem to be well-equipped to handle such crimes. If there is no victim, there is no one who was harmed and should receive restitution. But we still need to do something about crimes without victims. Thus, the objection claims, we need to at least supplement the corrective approach with punitive sanctions in some cases of wrongdoing.

The crucial question here is whether there are victimless crimes that pose a problem for corrective theories. A lot depends on our understanding of victimless crimes—three of which we can distinguish for the discussion at hand. First, there are crimes such as tax fraud where the victims are not easily identifiable or easy to individualize. Secondly, there are *mala prohibita* wrongs which often do not directly have a victim, such as running a red light at night where no one could be harmed. Thirdly, there might be some crimes which are wrong in virtue of their violating a moral code rather than harming other individuals directly or violating their rights. Examples of such cases are drug use and certain sexual acts.

As to the first problem, the victims in such cases are somewhat abstract. It is the community of taxpayers who is wronged when one person does not do their part (assuming the taxes are justified). This is a paradigmatic case of free riding as discussed in Chapter 4. There, I have argued that the corrective rationale does have something sensible to say about such crimes. Unfair crimes in that sense should be addressed with corrective sanctions in order to rectify the unfair advantage of the offender and/or the unfair disadvantage of the victims. Tax frauds enjoy the same societal benefits such as roads, hospitals, health care, public education, etc., that other citizens do—but they do not hold up their end of the bargain. Imposing corrective sanctions thus corrects for that wrong imposed on abstract victims. In that sense, it should not be a problem that we cannot easily individualize the victims of the wrong.

There is, however, indeed a sense in which abstract victims limit the applicability of the corrective rationale. Restorative justice as a way of approaching wrongdoings is less clearly applicable in such cases than in cases where the victim is identifiable. That is not to say that such procedures are not useful at all. Even when dealing with abstract victims, public apologies or restorative processes with representatives of the victims might be a prudential way of addressing the wrongdoing. This, of course, depends on the type of wrongdoing. But even if restorative processes are less applicable in such cases, corrective sanctions can still be applied to wrongdoings involving abstract victims and thus such cases do not pose a challenge to the corrective rationale.

Mala prohibita wrongs are more complicated for several reasons. First, there is no clear consensus on how to understand mala prohibita wrongs (with some people arguing that the category is confused in the first place). But for the purpose of the discussion here, we can work with the broad understanding Douglas Husak has proposed: "For present purposes, I construe an offense as an instance of malum prohibitum when the conduct proscribed is not wrongful prior to or independent of law" (2008, 104–5). Mala prohibita are often contrasted with mala in se wrongs, which are wrongful not just because the legislature posits so, but independent of the law. Battery, assault, rape, murder, etc., are thus mala in se wrongs, whereas money laundering, regulatory offenses, license offenses, etc., are often seen as mala prohibita wrongs.

This is where things get even more complicated. Duff and Husak agree that a substantial number of mala prohibita wrongs are at least partly also mala in se wrongs. That is, driving under the influence is a malum prohibitum in that there need to be positive laws about driving vehicles in the first place for such actions to be unlawful. At the same time, wrongfully endangering the well-being of others is a wrong independent of the law. Thus, such offenses are often labelled as hybrid wrongs (Husak 2008, 113).

Insofar as such mala prohibita are also partially mala in se, the corrective theory should have the conceptual tools to cover such offenses. Because in cases where driving under the influence, not stopping at a red light, etc., wrongfully endanger other people, these people are owed restitution for the unrightful endangerment of their well-being. So far, so good.

There will however still be cases where this is not so obviously the case. Husak takes the example of money laundering, which does not unlawfully set back any legitimate interests of other parties. Or take the example of running a red light at the dead of night. There is no ground for restitution in such cases, as no one is wrongfully put at risk (let us assume here). How, then, could restitution in principle be justified?

Two answers are possible. The first is to take Husak's route and admit that there are no plausible grounds for criminalization in such cases. If we take that route, however, there is no special problem for corrective theories. If there really are no grounds for criminalizing such actions, then we should neither impose punitive nor corrective sanctions. There simply is nothing to sanction in such cases. If a certain action does not endanger another citizen, nothing should be done about it.

The second route is to argue for the criminalization of inchoate offenses (Husak 2008, 160). Inchoate offenses are such where the *type* offense harms individuals, but not every *token* offense inflicts harm on any particular individual (the harmfulness of attempts are also covered under this header, but they pose their own issues and are disregarded here). If the harm of a *type* offense is serious enough that we want to strictly criminalize such wrongdoing, then we are better off also sanctioning those instances of the wrong that happen to harm no one. Strictly speaking, there is no direct ground to sanction such offenders as they did not harm anyone, but we sanction them nonetheless so as to uphold the general rule.

Again, my aim here is not to argue whether or not (and on what grounds necessarily) such wrongs should be criminalized. If they should not be criminalized, this is not a specific problem of corrective theories. If they should, and if the prevention of harm is the reason for that, then the corrective rationale can be applied. Admittedly, the corrective theory does not work as smoothly as it does in other cases, as the restitution would probably have to be paid to some substitutional entity as no victim has been directly harmed. Nonetheless, the rationale can be applied.

Interestingly enough, Husak draws a similar conclusion to what I offered here regarding mala prohibita wrongs—but for different reasons. As he is skeptical that there is a convincing justification for criminalizing mala prohibita wrongs in principle, he suggests that "[a] more ambitious project than I undertake here would go on to describe the conditions under which legitimate state interests should be pursued through free markets, systems of taxation, civil law, state-sponsored advertising campaigns, and the like" (Husak 2008, 119) instead of imposing punitive sanctions on mala prohibita offenses. As Husak suggests, civil law procedures are also an option—which in my terminology falls under corrective approaches. Or we should not sanction such offenders at all and rather try to discourage such behavior in other ways, such as marketing campaigns. Anyways, the corrective approach should be able to cover mala prohibita wrongs.

Lastly, there are truly victimless crimes. Not victimless crimes as in the case above where sometimes single instances of types of wrongs do not involve direct victims. Rather, we lastly need to talk about truly victimless crimes as in the case of drug use, certain sexual relationships, sex work, etc. Here we are interested in types of wrongdoing that do not harm other people than the agents themselves (if at all). When drug use leads to violence, or to abandoning the duties towards one's children, then these actions cause harm, are not victimless, and are thus covered by the corrective theory. But what about truly victimless crimes?

There are two ways to respond to the victimless crime objection. The first is to say that these should simply not be criminalized. This is also my go-to response, though it would require more argument than I can provide in this subsection. The general idea is that as long as such actions do not harm others, we should not criminalize them, and thus not sanction them. That does not necessarily mean we should not discourage such actions as a society, or help people deal with them responsibly. If adults with no responsibilities to others want to do cocaine on the weekend with friends and have a good time, then they should not be criminalized for doing so if no harm to others results from such actions. They can be discouraged in many different other ways—with marketing campaigns or heavy taxation—but they will not be subject to the criminal law.

The second response would entail accepting that self-harm should be criminalized and then ask whether corrective accounts could capture the wrongness of self-harm. Corrective accounts would indeed have some trouble here. It seems weird to sanction an offender (and victim at the same time) to restore the harm they have done to themselves (though this is not absolutely absurd, we can imagine the state forcing the victim to try rehabilitation as a form of self-restitution).

But the idea of sanctioning self-harmers fails because it does not seem to be coherent, at least on a deterrent view. If the sanction is supposed to nudge the person not to do self-harm again, then the sanction needs to be harsher than the self-harm inflicted with the drug use, for example, to be an effective deterrent to people. But then the state simply makes life worse for self-harmers than it would have been if the state would just let self-harmers harm themselves. The idea that sanctions help in this picture seems confused. And if the state simply chooses to offer rehabilitative treatment to people who impose harm on themselves, then there is no problem for the corrective theory, as we leave the realm of imposing criminal sanctions. There certainly needs to be a good justification for coercing people to undergo rehabilitative treatment, but this need not happen under the banner of criminal law at all.

Victimless crimes thus also do not pose problems to corrective theories, at least not anymore than to punitive theories.

The Public Wants Punishment

It has been objected that corrective approaches are impracticable as they will not find support in the wider public. The public is supposedly largely punitive, and the criminal law has to account for that (Brooks 2016). In Husak's words:

> These sociological facts are crucial and cannot be ignored by skeptical reformers. I am doubtful that alternative means to sanction wrongdoers and mollify victims would be adequate to satisfy those who call for justice. If the criminal law were fundamentally altered, all bets would be off as to how the public in general and victims in particular would respond. In view of the ubiquity of the foregoing demands, one can only wonder how citizens would react to a systematic call to dismantle the criminal justice system. Few criminal law skeptics purport to have any sociological evidence about how their ideas are likely to be received in a democratic state. (2020, 52)

As Husak (2020, 52–53) rightly notes in his paper, there has been ample research emphasizing the victim's and the public's vindictive attitudes. And it is indeed true that we should not disregard the potential societal costs were we to simply implement policy changes which citizens are fundamentally at odds with. The issue with this objection, however, is that victims and the larger public might not be against these changes, after all.

First, we should take a second look at the empirical evidence for Husak's claim. In order to do that adequately, we have to keep in mind that the public will not necessarily share the conceptual distinction between punitive and corrective sanctions we use in this book—neither do those who research public attitudes about punishment. Nonetheless, we have already gone through some research in this book in which we made the case that laypeople are far more concerned with corrective justice than critics have anticipated, and sometimes even more so than with retributive justice.

In Chapter 3 we took a look at two different justice-restoring mechanisms: Punitive and corrective sanctions. There, we analyzed the data on the public's attitudes on punishment. Newer research findings overhaul the evidence that Husak relies on, which claims that people are primarily retributive or punitive. Part of the research Husak (2020, 52–53) relies on made the mistake in the design of the studies that people only had the option to punish transgressors or do nothing at all. Of course, with such a setup researchers find a preference to punish transgressors. But the research design simply did not include the option of other actions for participants. If you give people additional options, such as compensating the victim rather than punishing the transgressor, researchers find a preference for that kind of compensation over punishment (Dhaliwal, Patil, and Cushman 2021; Doorn, Zeelenberg, and Breugelmans 2018; Doorn et al. 2018; Heffner and FeldmanHall 2019).

That is of course not to say that there is a lack of evidence for the punitive attitudes of people. As Husak rightly notes, anthropologists have observed preferences for punishment in virtually all societies (Curry 2016; Curry et al. 2021; Curry, Mullins, and Whitehouse 2019), and there is some evidence that preferences for rudimentary forms of punishment appear early in the development of children

(Kanakogi et al. 2017; McAuliffe, Jordan, and Warneken 2015; Li et al. 2016; McAuliffe et al. 2017; Yang et al. 2018). But as we have seen in Chapter 3, this is only part of the picture. Other ways of dealing with wrongdoing are available to us, with restitution and restorative justice processes being similarly prevalent in all cultures and our psychology (Petersen et al. 2012).

When we take a look at surveys of the public, we can indeed find preferences for punitive approaches. These preferences are somewhat lowered, however, when people take more time to think about these issues and are better informed about the criminal law before deciding on whether they prefer incarceration to alternative sanctions, such as community service and rehabilitation (Cullen, Fisher, and Applegate 2000). True, many still want punitive sanctions, but a significant proportion of participants emphasize how important other justice-restoring mechanism are to them. Not only do these findings make a dent into the retributivist's empirical case, but the research also hints at some epistemic doubts about punitiveness, as punitiveness appears to correlate with lower cognitive effort and few information about criminal wrongdoing (Aharoni et al. 2019; 2020; Gollwitzer et al. 2016, see Chapter 3 for more details). Also, not only do people care about alternative justice-restoring mechanisms than punishment, but they also seem to care more about the communicative message of punishments than about the punitiveness itself (Sarin et al. 2021; Funk, McGeer, and Gollwitzer 2014, see Chapters 3 and 5 for more details). Punitiveness is thus not holy to the public as communicating censure appears to take precedence over such punitive concerns.

The same is true for the victim's perspective that Husak uses for his objection. Philosophers have used the victim's perspective in order to argue for the necessity of punishment, as we have seen in Chapter 6. When we take a systematic look at the research, however, we find that the punitiveness of the sanctions is not what matters most to the victim—at the very least it is not the sole aspect in the criminal proceeding that they care about (Erez and Tontodonato 1992; Laxminarayan 2013; Shapland 1984). What appears to matter most is some form of acknowledgment—both from the offender in the form of apologies, but also from the state in the form of being granted procedural rights. Sanctions certainly matter, but corrective sanctions have the additional benefit of addressing the costs of wrongdoings imposed on victims, which are also often a source of stress for victims in the aftermath of wrongdoing. Lastly, restorative procedures, at least when consented to by the victim, offer another great avenue to communicating the respect to the victims which they often times care more about than the punitive sanction imposed on the offender itself.

Again, all of this should not suggest that there are no pure punitive interests, of course. But the objection stated that corrective approaches will find barely any resonance in the public at all and that we might even have to fear serious repercussions from the suggested changes to the criminal law—but a more systematic overview of the research does not seem to support that worry. The "sociological evidence" that Husak asked for certainly found its way into the argument of corrective theorists.

Also, corrective approaches should certainly be wary of marketing issues. Simply saying "Let's stop punishing offenders" is not a good communication strategy for the broader public. The corrective approach takes the offender's responsibility seriously and has no interest whatsoever in letting them off the hook easily. The point, especially here, is to show that the corrective rationale better realizes all the values that punitive sanctions aim to realize as well. There is of course no issue at all in calling corrective sanctions "punishments" for practical matters, as long as the underlying rationale is clear. "Abolishing the criminal law" is a very broad slogan in the context of a complex and nuanced philosophical debate. It is useful for philosophical analysis not to mix together punitive and corrective approaches, as I have argued. But for the purpose of public communication, we might be better off saying things like "Let's coerce offenders to finally make good on the harm they inflict on victims"—that is, things that do not sound like radical abolitionism.

As a last point: We should keep in mind that we have come a long way in a relatively short amount of time when it comes to the punitiveness of our criminal law. Most people in the public sphere no longer want public executions and torture in most Western countries. Going from public torture in the past (and sometimes in the present) to prisons as they are in Norway, for example, is an impressive development. Status quo bias might suggest that it is hard to change course, but history seems to tell otherwise—and shows that it is worth it.

9.3 Conclusion

In this chapter, I have discussed several general objections against corrective approaches to criminal law. None of these show that corrective approaches are either fundamentally flawed or need to be supplemented in parts with punitive approaches. If all that is correct, and if the positive arguments in favor of corrective approaches are convincing, we have made a good case for adopting a corrective rationale in criminal law.

Chapter 10
Epilogue

> "More research should be done."
> More or less every empirical paper nowadays.

10.1 A Messy Conclusion

Other philosophers and I, too, tend to be happier when we can say that we have solved a philosophical problem in such a book-length project, or have rejected one central theory, or defended our pet theory sufficiently well. I am not sure that any of these aims have been reached in this project. But this has not been for the lack of trying. Even though I think that a judicial system following the corrective rationale has a more convincing moral justification to offer, I have not shown that legal punishment is necessarily immoral. Other defendants of restorative justice or corrective justice more generally sometimes tend to think that they have shown that (Boonin 2008; Golash 2005), but I disagree. Sometimes, in single instances, punishment can surely be morally justified. Maybe there will even be circumstances where a society is actually better off putting the punitive rationale at the basis of their criminal law. Maybe if the trust in the state is low or if the need for deterrence is high, a punitive system would be justified. But for our current Western societies, we are very likely better off using corrective sanctions to realize the different values the citizens and the criminal law are after.

I call this conclusion "messy" since the moral justification depends on many empirical findings. Whether or not victims can restore their feeling of self-worth and their trust in the judicial system with punishment or corrective sanctions is such an empirical question. Or whether we need harsh punitive sanctions for deterrence. Or whether we need punishment to reliably communicate to the members of our society the importance of the shared values. I have surveyed what I take to be the best empirical research pertinent to these questions we have to date. But as some of these questions have only recently been more rigorously tested, many of the conclusions remain tentative. And because my arguments heavily rely on empirical research, it could easily be the case that most of the positive arguments in this book turn out to be on the wrong track after ten more years of research.

This worry is especially pressing when we consider the state of the empirical research in the last decades. Many studies from the past failed to replicate, that is, researchers fail to get the same findings when doing a study again and again (Collaboration 2015). Others worry that even if studies replicate, most findings from the laboratory cannot easily be taken as evidence for what we should do in the real-world (Klein et al. 2014; Yarkoni 2020), especially in such a vastly complex system such as the criminal law.

Also, at least in my estimation, philosophers and psychologists are only starting to really work together as opposed to working in parallel on this topic. To really investigate the success of philosophical theories that depend on empirical data, it is paramount that we design the research in a way that really speaks to the philosophical context. As has been observed in experimental philosophy more generally, this is not an easy feat (Pölzler and Wright 2019), and we will have to work together to make this happen in the debate on the justification of punishment. This is also why I advertised this project as being exploratory in spirit. As I tried to motivate in Chapter 1, I feel like the interdisciplinary approach to the philosophy of punishment is still in its early stages. If I succeeded to show that the interdisciplinary approach is correct in the first place, I see this as an absolute win. Much of the contemporary philosophical discussion in this debate does not really acknowledge this perspective.

So, from a marketing point of view, the conclusion I draw in the book might not be really attractive. All conclusions in the respective chapters of this book about why we should prefer corrective rationales to punitive ones are drawn with what I take to be the required amount of modesty, and I do not claim to have shown that punishment is always immoral, neither that there can never be contexts in which a society is better off with a punitive system. But from a general scientific and meta-theoretical point of view, such a modest conclusion seems to me to be perfectly reasonable—maybe even the only right conclusion to draw. Punishment is such a complex phenomenon that it would be rather surprising to find a simple solution. A conclusion such as "always impose sanction x, and do not mind the specific context" would certainly warrant a healthy amount of skepticism, simply because the phenomenon itself is so complex.

10.2 It Is Not All about Sanctions

Another important limitation of this book that I want to emphasize is that I work within a very classical debate in criminal law: The moral justification of legal punishment. Because of that choice, I focus on the justification of legal sanctions and argue that we are better off putting the corrective rationale at the center of the criminal law, rather than a punitive rationale. But that alone does not say much about which behavior to sanction in the first place. That is, I do not give a full theory of criminalization. And I also do not say how much of a role sanctioning should play in our society in the first place. Especially when it comes to the aim of reaching rule-abidingness in society, we might be better off not putting all our resources into the criminal law. We might intuitively think of sanctions when we think about law-abidingness, but this might be more due to our psychology than due to good arguments.

I have hinted at this perspective in the Chapter 7, but I cannot give it the space in this book it would otherwise deserve. For example, I could not talk about rehabilitation in any detail. There are interesting contemporary debates on rehabilitation and neuro-intervention which I could not give any consideration in this book. It is its own huge topic, and it should be considered together with the debate that I chose to focus on, without any emphasis on which debate is more important. As far as I can see, the debate there looks extremely promising for promoting law-abidingness without any focus on sanctions at all. If we can develop medical treatment that will reduce recidivism, we might be better off not sanctioning offenders after all (except for the communicative effects for the victim perhaps).

Also, as only hinted at in Chapter 7, the long-term strategies to lower crime rates might have more to do with mental health, social justice, and other aspects rather than the criminal law with its focus on sanctions. If we really want to lower crime rates, we might want to invest more in mental health of especially young people, drug treatment, combating unemployment, homelessness, and poverty in general. Also, the more we learn about the origins of criminality, the more can we attempt to achieve early-detection models to help prevent wrongdoing in the first place. That is not to say that we should pre-emptively punish individuals and violate their privacy rights. But as Wright et al. (2015) argue, there are many stations in life where we can already suspect a higher risk of becoming an offender. If we keep researching, communicating, and informing the public about these issues, we can promote a safer society without solely relying on sanctions.

These are just some of the areas of research which are relevant for the topic I am interested in, but that have nothing directly to do with the justification of sanctions in criminal law. For a comprehensive approach, we should pay as much attention to these research areas as we do to the classical debate on the justification of punishment. Or maybe we should focus on these research areas even more strongly—which brings me to my next point.

10.3 It Is Not All about Philosophy

Some philosophers might not consider this book to be a genuinely philosophical enterprise. Almost all of my arguments heavily depend on empirical premises, and the book is rather skeptical when it comes to the success of purely conceptual or armchair arguments with regards to the debate on punishment. For retributivism, fairness, community values, the interests of victims, and deterrence, my strategy was to show that philosophical arguments without reference to empirical research do not succeed. There is no good argument for the objective or intrinsic worth of retribution, the restoration of fairness, protecting community values, respecting victims, or rejecting deterrence. For all these values, we need to take a closer look at how different sanctions actually impact our perception of whether or not the values in question are realized. Also, I have argued that we need instrumental motivations for why the criminal law should incorporate these values in the first place. As such, my arguments imply that philosophers alone cannot get the problem of punishment resolved, especially when they want to make a positive case concerning what to do in criminal law (rather than making negative arguments as to which theories we should reject).

If that is true, this has implications for the importance of philosophy when it comes to questions and problems that philosophers took to be entailed in their job description for hundreds of years—at least speaking for the debate on punishment specifically. But I do not think that more modesty on what philosophy can do is out of place here. This fits into the broader meta-philosophical debate that we have had for a while regarding what philosophy can actually achieve. Here, of course, we are only concerned with the justification of punishment, not philosophy in general. But the lesson is important, nonetheless. We philosophers have discussed these problems for quite some time now, and no clear results have been found yet. What we did manage to do, however, is to clarify different justifications, their premises, and problems. Particularly, I see my job as a philosopher to clarify these limits of what our profession can achieve in the debate. Our job is to keep our colleagues' arguments in check by analyzing them with scrutiny—and to find the parts of the arguments that are no longer in our own area of expertise.

It remains to be seen whether this change in methodology will do any better for the aim of finding a consensus in the debate. I have some doubts, as there is not only disagreement on the content of the debate, but also on the methodology. But I am slightly optimistic that if we accept the empirically informed methodology defended in this book, we can also find consensus more easily. This is so, as much depends on empirical facts that can be more easily researched and found consensus on than statements of value. That is not to say that we will not disagree on the empirical research, but only that there is a clearer way of proving people wrong with regards to empirical matters than with regards to moral matters. And if that is correct, this project might have a slight advantage in finding consensus over the purely philosophical projects. We will see about that.

10.4 Last Conclusion

I began the book by outlining two central aims. First, I wanted to show that those arguments in the debate on the justification of punishment that hold the biggest promise directly rely on empirical assumptions about our attitudes to punishment, the epistemic reliability of these attitudes, the interests of victims, and the effects of sanctions. The second aim was to take a closer and more systematic look at the empirical research that we have to date in regard to these arguments and show that they support corrective approaches to criminal law more than they support punitive approaches—at least in the context of Western criminal law institutions that are typically in the focus of the debate that I am interested in. I hope to have been successful in making a convincing case for both claims.

References

Abt, Thomas P. 2017. "Towards a Framework for Preventing Community Violence among Youth." *Psychology, Health & Medicine* 22 (S1): 266–85. https://doi.org/10.1080/13548506.2016.1257815.

Aharoni, Eyal. 2021. "Bias at the Surface or the Core? A Comment on the Psychology of the Trial Judge." In *Law and Mind. A Survey of Law and the Cognitive Sciences*, edited by Bartosz Brożek, Jaap Hage, and Nicole Vincent, 207–14. Cambridge: Cambridge University Press. https://doi.org/10.1017/9781108623056.010.

Aharoni, Eyal, and Alan J. Fridlund. 2012. "Punishment without Reason: Isolating Retribution in Lay Punishment of Criminal Offenders." *Psychology, Public Policy, and Law* 18 (4): 599–625. https://doi.org/10.1037/a0025821.

Aharoni, Eyal, and Alan J. Fridlund. 2013. "Moralistic Punishment as a Crude Social Insurance Plan." In *The Future of Punishment*, edited by Thomas Nadelhoffer, 213–29. Oxford: Oxford University Press. https://doi.org/10.1093/acprof:oso/9780199779208.003.0010.

Aharoni, Eyal, and Morris B. Hoffman. 2021. "Evolutionary Psychology, Jurisprudence, and Sentencing." In *The SAGE Handbook of Evolutionary Psychology*, edited by Todd K. Shackelford, 221–42. SAGE Publications Ltd. https://doi.org/10.4135/9781529739428.n11.

Aharoni, Eyal, Heather M. Kleider-Offutt, Sarah F. Brosnan, and Sharlene Fernandes. 2020. "Slippery Scales: Cost Prompts, but Not Benefit Prompts, Modulate Sentencing Recommendations in Laypeople." *PLOS ONE* 15 (7): e0236764. https://doi.org/10.1371/journal.pone.0236764.

Aharoni, Eyal, Heather M Kleider-Offutt, Sarah F. Brosnan, and Julia Watzek. 2019. "Justice at Any Cost? The Impact of Cost–Benefit Salience on Criminal Punishment Judgments." *Behavioral Sciences & the Law* 37 (1): 38–60. https://doi.org/10.1002/bsl.2388.

Aharoni, Eyal, David Simpson, Eddy Nahmias, and Mario Gollwitzer. 2022. "A Painful Message: Testing the Effects of Suffering and Understanding on Punishment Judgments." *Zeitschrift Für Psychologie* 230 (2): 138–51. https://doi.org/10.1027/2151-2604/a000460.

Anderson, Jami L. 1997. "Reciprocity as a Justification for Retributivism." *Criminal Justice Ethics* 16 (1): 13–25. https://doi.org/10.1080/0731129x.1997.9992024.

Anderson, Jami L. 1999. "Annulment Retributivism: A Hegelian Theory of Punishment." *Legal Theory* 5: 363–388. https://doi.org/10.1017/S1352325299054014.

Anomaly, Jonathan. 2017. "Trust, trade, and Moral Progress: How Market Exchange Promotes Trustworthiness." *Social Philosophy and Policy* 34 (2): 89–107. https://doi.org/10.1017/s026505251700022x.

Apel, Robert, and Daniel S. Nagin. 2014. "Deterrence." In *Encyclopedia of Criminology and Criminal Justice*, edited by Gerben Bruinsma and David Weisburd, 998–1005. New York: Springer.

Armstrong, K. G. 1961. "III. – The Retributivist Hits Back." *Mind* LXX (280): 471–90. https://doi.org/10.1093/mind/lxx.280.471.

Ash, Michael. 1972. "On Witnesses: A Radical Critique of Criminal Court Procedures." *Notre Dame Law Review* 48: 386–425.

Awad, Edmond, Sohan Dsouza, Azim Shariff, Iyad Rahwan, and Jean-François Bonnefon. 2020. "Universals and Variations in Moral Decisions Made in 42 Countries by 70,000 Participants." *Proceedings of the National Academy of Sciences* 117 (5): 2332–37. https://doi.org/10.1073/pnas.1911517117.

Axelrod, Robert, and William D. Hamilton. 1981. "The Evolution of Cooperation." *Science* 211 (4489): 1390–96. https://doi.org/10.1126/science.7466396.

Bagaric, Mirko. 1999. "In Defence of a Utilitarian Theory of Punishment: Punishing the Innocent and the Compatibility of Utilitarianism and Rights." *Australasian Journal of Legal Philosophy* 24: 95–144.

Bagaric, Mirko. 2000. "Consistency and Fairness in Sentencing – The Splendor of Fixed Penalties." *California Criminal Law Review* 2 (1). https://doi.org/10.2139/ssrn.235759.

Bagaric, Mirko, and Kumar Amarasekara. 2000. "The Errors of Retributivism." *Melbourne University Law Review 124* 24 (1).

Bagaric, Mirko, and Kumar Amarasekara. 2001. "Feeling Sorry? – Tell Someone Who Cares: The Irrelevance of Remorse in Sentencing." *The Howard Journal of Criminal Justice* 40 (4): 364–76. https://doi.org/10.1111/1468-2311.00215.

Balvig, Flemming, Helgi Gunnlaugsson, Kristina Jerre, Henrik Tham, and Aarne Kinnunen. 2015. "The Public Sense of Justice in Scandinavia: A Study of Attitudes towards Punishments." *European Journal of Criminology* 12 (3): 342–61. https://doi.org/10.1177/1477370815571948.

Barnett, Randy E. 1977. "Restitution: A New Paradigm of Criminal Justice." *Ethics* 87 (4): 279–301. https://doi.org/10.1086/292043.

Bastian, Brock, Jolanda Jetten, and Fabio Fasoli. 2011. "Cleansing the Soul by Hurting the Flesh: The Guilt-Reducing Effect of Pain." *Psychological Science* 22 (3): 334–35. https://doi.org/10.1177/0956797610397058.

Baumeister, Roy F., Arlene M. Stillwell, and Todd F. Heatherton. 1994. "Guilt: An Interpersonal Approach." *Psychological Bulletin* 115 (2): 243–67. https://doi.org/10.1037/0033-2909.115.2.243.

Benn, Stanley I. 1958. "An Approach to the Problems of Punishment." *Philosophy* 33 (127): 325–41. https://doi.org/10.1017/S0031819100055017.

Bennett, Christopher. 2008. *The Apology Ritual. A Philosophical Theory of Punishment.* New York: Cambridge University Press. https://doi.org/10.1017/cbo9780511487477.

Bennett, Christopher. 2019. "How Should We Argue for a Censure Theory of Punishment?" In *Penal Censure. Engagements within and Beyond Desert Theory*, edited by Antje du Bois-Pedain and Anthony E. Bottoms, 67–84. Oxford: Hart Publishing. https://doi.org/10.5040/9781509919819.ch-004.

Bentham, Jeremy. 1789[1988]. An Introduction to the Principles of Morals and Legislation. New York: Prometheus Books.

Berker, Selim. 2009. "The Normative Insignificance of Neuroscience." *Philosophy & Public Affairs* 37 (4): 293–329. https://doi.org/10.1111/j.1088-4963.2009.01164.x.

Berman, Mitchell N. 2011. "Two Kinds of Retributivism." In *The Philosophical Foundations of Criminal Law*, edited by R. A. Duff and Stuart Green, 433–57. Oxford: Oxford University Press. https://doi.org/10.2139/ssrn.1592546.

Bilz, Kenworthey. 2016. "Testing the Expressive Theory of Punishment." *Journal of Empirical Legal Studies* 13 (2): 358–92. https://doi.org/10.1111/jels.12118.

Bittner, Rüdiger. 2017. *Bürger Sein.* Berlin: De Gruyter. https://doi.org/10.1515/9783110569858.

Blair, Robert James Richard, Lawrence Jones, Fiona Clark, and Margaret Smith. 1997. "The Psychopathic Individual: A Lack of Responsiveness to Distress Cues?" *Psychophysiology* 34 (2): 192–98. https://doi.org/10.1111/j.1469-8986.1997.tb02131.x.

Boonin, David. 2008. *The Problem of Punishment.* Cambridge: Cambridge University Press. https://doi.org/10.1017/cbo9780511819254.

Boonin, David. 2018. "Punishment, Restitution, and Incarceration." In *Rethinking Punishment in the Era of Mass Incarceration*, 122–43. New York: Routledge. https://doi.org/10.4324/9781315170602-8.

Bottoms, Anthony E. 2003. "Some Sociological Reflections on Restorative Justice." In *Restorative Justice and Criminal Justice: Competing or Reconcilable Paradigms?*, edited by Andrew von Hirsch,

Julian V. Roberts, and Anthony E. Bottoms, 79–113. Oxford/Portland: Hart Publishing. https://doi.org/10.5040/9781472559333.ch-005.

Bougie, Roger, Rik Pieters, and Marcel Zeelenberg. 2003. "Angry Customers Don't Come Back, They Get Back: The Experience and Behavioral Implications of Anger and Dissatisfaction in Services." *Journal of the Academy of Marketing Science* 31 (4): 377–93. https://doi.org/10.1177/0092070303254412.

Boyd, Robert, Herbert Gintis, Samuel Bowles, and Peter J. Richerson. 2003. "The Evolution of Altruistic Punishment." *Proceedings of the National Academy of Sciences* 100 (6): 3531035. https://doi.org/10.1073/pnas.0630443100.

Braithwaite, John. 2000. "Survey Article: Repentance Rituals and Restorative Justice." *The Journal of Political Philosophy* 8 (1): 115–31. https://doi.org/10.1111/1467-9760.00095.

Braithwaite, John. 2002. "In Search of Restorative Jurisprudence." In *Restorative Justice and the Law*, edited by Lode Walgrave, 150–67. Devon: Willan Publishing. https://doi.org/10.2139/ssrn.330989.

Braithwaite, John, and Philip Pettit. 1990. *Not Just Deserts: A Republican Theory of Criminal Justice*. Oxford University Press. Oxford: Oxford University Press. https://doi.org/10.1093/acprof:oso/9780198240563.001.0001.

Braun, Kerstin. 2019. *Victim Participation Rights. Variation across Criminal Justice Systems*. London: Palgrave Macmillan. https://doi.org/10.1007/978-3-030-04546-3.

Brennan, Jason. 2017. "Corporal Punishment as an Alternative to Incarceration." In *Rethinking Punishment in the Era of Mass Incarceration*, edited by Chris W. Surprenant, 294–308. New York: Routledge. https://doi.org/10.4324/9781315170602-18.

Brooks, Thom. 2003. "Kant's Theory of Punishment." *Utilitas* 15 (2): 206–24. https://doi.org/10.1017/s0953820800003952.

Brooks, Thom. 2004. "Is Hegel a Retributivist?" *Bulletin of the Hegel Society of Great Britain* 25 (1–2): 113–26. https://doi.org/10.1017/s0263523200002044.

Brooks, Thom. 2012. *Punishment*. London and New York: Routledge. https://doi.org/10.4324/9780203929421.

Brooks, Thom. 2016. "Punitive Restoration: Giving the Public a Say on Sentencing." In *Democratic Theory and Mass Incarceration*, edited by Albert Dzur, Ian Loader, and Richard Sparks, 140–61. Oxford: Oxford University Press. https://doi.org/10.1093/acprof:oso/9780190243098.003.0007.

Bublitz, Jan Christoph. 2020. "Die Genealogie Der Vergeltung, Oder Warum Retributiven Intuitionen Nicht Zu Trauen Ist. Ein Beitrag Zu Einer Neuropsychologisch Informierten Strafrechtswissenschaft." In *Recht – Philosophie – Literatur. Festschrift Für Reinhard Merkel Zum 70. Geburtstag*, edited by Jan Christoph Bublitz, Jochen Bung, Anette Grünewald, Dorothea Magnus, Holm Putzke, and Jörg Scheinfeld, 459–92. Berlin: Duncker & Humblot. https://doi.org/10.3790/978-3-428-55566-6.

Bun, Maurice J. G., Richard Kelaher, Vasilis Sarafidis, and Don Weatherburn. 2020. "Crime, Deterrence and Punishment Revisited." *Empirical Economics* 59 (5): 2303–33. https://doi.org/10.1007/s00181-019-01758-6.

Burgh, Richard W. 1982. "Do the Guilty Deserve Punishment?" *The Journal of Philosophy* 79 (4): 193–210. https://doi.org/10.2307/2026220.

Cahill, Michael T. 2011. "Punishment Pluralism." In *Retributivism. Essays on Theory and Policy*, edited by Mark D. White, 25–48. Oxford: Oxford University Press. https://doi.org/10.1093/acprof:oso/9780199752232.003.0003.

Carlsmith, Kevin M. 2006. "The Roles of Retribution and Utility in Determining Punishment." *Journal of Experimental Social Psychology* 42 (4): 437–51. https://doi.org/10.1016/j.jesp.2005.06.007.

Carlsmith, Kevin M. 2008. "On Justifying Punishment: The Discrepancy Between Words and Actions." *Social Justice Research* 21 (2): 119–37. https://doi.org/10.1007/s11211-008-0068-x.

Carlsmith, Kevin M., John M. Darley, and Paul H. Robinson. 2002. "Why Do We Punish? Deterrence and Just Deserts as Motives for Punishment." *Journal of Personality and Social Psychology* 83 (2): 284–99. https://doi.org/10.1037/0022-3514.83.2.284.

Carlsmith, Kevin M., Timothy D. Wilson, and Daniel T. Gilbert. 2008. "The Paradoxical Consequences of Revenge." *Journal of Personality and Social Psychology* 95 (6): 1316–24. https://doi.org/10.1037/a0012165.

Caruso, Gregg D. 2016. "Free Will Skepticism and Criminal Behavior: A Public Health-Quarantine Model." *Southwest Philosophy Review* 32 (1): 25–48. https://doi.org/10.5840/swphilreview20163214.

Caruso, Gregg D. 2017. *Public Health and Safety: The Social Determinants of Health and Criminal Behavior.* ResearchersLinks Books.

Caruso, Gregg D. 2019. "Free Will Skepticism and Its Implications: An Argument for Optimism." In *Free Will Skepticism in Law and Society: Challenging Retributive Justice*, edited by Elizabeth Shaw, Derk Pereboom, and Gregg D. Caruso, 43–72. New York: Cambridge University Press. https://doi.org/10.2139/ssrn.2758311.

Caruso, Gregg D. 2020. "Buddhism, Free Will, and Punishment: Taking Buddhist Ethics Seriously." *Zygon* 55 (2): 474–96. https://doi.org/10.1111/zygo.12599.

Caruso, Gregg D. 2021. *Rejecting Retributivism.* Cambridge: Cambridge University Press. https://doi.org/10.1017/9781108689304.

Chavez, Alex K., and Cristina Bicchieri. 2013. "Third-Party Sanctioning and Compensation Behavior: Findings from the Ultimatum Game." *Journal of Economic Psychology* 39: 268–77. https://doi.org/10.1016/j.joep.2013.09.004.

Chen, Daniel L., and Markus Loecher. 2019. "Mood and the Malleability of Moral Reasoning: The Impact of Irrelevant Factors on Judicial Decisions." *SSRN Electronic Journal.* https://doi.org/10.2139/ssrn.2740485.

Chiao, Vincent. 2016. "What Is the Criminal Law For?" *Law and Philosophy* 35 (2): 137–63. https://doi.org/10.1007/s10982-015-9247-8.

Cho, Kyoungmin, Christopher M. Barnes, and Cristiano L. Guanara. 2017. "Sleepy Punishers Are Harsh Punishers." *Psychological Science* 28 (2): 242–47. https://doi.org/10.1177/0956797616678437.

Cholbi, Michael. 2010. "Compulsory Victim Restitution Is Punishment: A Reply to Boonin." *Public Reason* 2 (1): 85–93.

Christie, Nils. 1977. "Conflicts as Property." *The British Journal of Criminology* 17 (1): 1–15. https://doi.org/10.1093/oxfordjournals.bjc.a046783.

Christie, Nils. 1986. "The Ideal Victim." In *From Crime Policy to Victim Policy*, edited by Ezzat A. Fattah, 17–30. London: Palgrave Macmillan. https://doi.org/10.1007/978-1-349-08305-3_2.

Cimino, Aldo. 2012. "The Evolution of Hazing: Motivational Mechanisms and the Abuse of Newcomers." *Journal of Cognition and Culture* 12 (1–2): 161–162. https://doi.org/10.1163/156853711X591242.

Clear, Todd R. 2007. Imprisoning Communities: How Mass Incarceration Makes Disadvantaged Neighborhoods Worse. Oxford: Oxford University Press.

Collaboration, Open Science. 2015. "Estimating the Reproducibility of Psychological Science." *Science* 349 (6251): aac4716. https://doi.org/10.1126/science.aac4716.

Cottingham, John. 1979. "Varieties of Retribution." *The Philosophical Quarterly* 29 (116): 238–46. https://doi.org/10.2307/2218820.

Coverdale, Helen Brown. 2013. *Punishing with Care. Treating Offenders as Equal Persons in Criminal Punishment*. PhD diss., The London School of Economics and Political Science (LSE).

Coverdale, Helen Brown. 2018. "Punishment and Welfare: Defending Offender's Inclusion as Subjects of State Care." *Ethics and Social Welfare* 12 (2): 117–32. https://doi.org/10.1080/17496535.2017.1364398.

Coverdale, Helen Brown. 2021. "Caring and the Prison in Philosophy, Policy and Practice: Under Lock and Key." *Journal of Applied Philosophy* 38 (3), 415–30. https://doi.org/10.1111/japp.12415.

Crockett, Molly J., Yagiz Özdemir, and Ernst Fehr. 2014. "The Value of Vengeance and the Demand for Deterrence." *Journal of Experimental Psychology: General* 143 (6): 2279–2286. https://doi.org/10.1037/xge0000018.

Cullen, Francis T., Bonnie S. Fisher, and Brandon K. Applegate. 2000. "Public Opinion about Punishment and Corrections." *Crime and Justice* 27: 1–79. https://doi.org/10.1086/652198.

Curry, Oliver Scott. 2016. "Morality as Cooperation: A Problem-Centred Approach." In *The Evolution of Morality*, edited by T. K. Shackelford and R. D. Hansen, 27–51. Basel: Springer International Publishing. https://doi.org/10.1007/978-3-319-19671-8_2.

Curry, Oliver Scott, Mark Alfano, Mark J. Brandt, and Christine Pelican. 2021. "Moral Molecules: Morality as a Combinatorial System." *Review of Philosophy and Psychology*, 1–20. https://doi.org/10.1007/s13164-021-00540-x.

Curry, Oliver Scott, Daniel Austin Mullins, and Harvey Whitehouse. 2019. "Is It Good to Cooperate? Testing the Theory of Morality-as-Cooperation in 60 Societies." *Current Anthropology* 60 (1): 47–69. https://doi.org/10.1086/701478.

Cushman, Fiery. 2015. "Punishment in Humans: From Intuitions to Institutions." *Philosophy Compass* 10 (2): 117–33. https://doi.org/10.1111/phc3.12192.

Cushman, Fiery, Arunima Sarin, and Mark K. Ho. 2022. "Punishment as Communication." In *Oxford Handbook of Moral Psychology*, edited by John Doris and Manual Vargas, 197–209. Oxford: Oxford University Press. https://doi.org/10.31234/osf.io/wf3tz.

Dagger, Richard. 1991. "Restitution: Pure or Punitive?" *Criminal Justice Ethics* 10 (2): 29–39. https://doi.org/10.1080/0731129X.1991.9991901.

Dagger, Richard. 2011. "Social Contracts, Fair Play, and the Justification of Punishment." *Ohio State Journal of Criminal Law* 8 (2): 341–68.

Dagger, Richard. 2018. *Playing Fair: Political Obligation and the Problems of Punishment*. Oxford: Oxford University Press. https://doi.org/10.1093/oso/9780199388837.001.0001.

Danziger, Shai, Jonathan Levav, and Liora Avnaim-Pesso. 2011. "Extraneous Factors in Judicial Decisions." *Proceedings of the National Academy of Sciences* 108 (17): 6889–92. https://doi.org/10.1073/pnas.1018033108.

Darley, John M., and Thane S. Pittman. 2003. "The Psychology of Compensatory and Retributive Justice." *Personality and Social Psychology Review* 7 (4): 324–36. https://doi.org/10.1207/s15327957pspr0704_05.

Davis, Michael. 2008. "Punishment Theory's Golden Half Century: A Survey of Developments from (about) 1957 to 2007." *The Journal of Ethics* 13 (1): 73–100. https://doi.org/10.1007/s10892-008-9040-0.

Davis, Robert C., Barbara Smith, and Susan Hillenbrand. 1992. "Restitution: The Victim's Viewpoint." *Justice System Journal* 15 (3): 746–58. https://doi.org/10.1080/23277556.1993.10871158.

Deutchman, Paul, Mark Bračič, Nichola Raihani, and Katherine McAuliffe. 2021. "Punishment Is Strongly Motivated by Revenge and Weakly Motivated by Inequity Aversion." *Evolution and Human Behavior* 42 (1): 12–20. https://doi.org/10.1016/j.evolhumbehav.2020.06.001.

Dhaliwal, Nathan, Indrajeet Patil, and Fiery Andrews Cushman. 2021. "Reputational and Cooperative Benefits of Third-Party Compensation." *Organizational Behavior and Human Decision Processes* 164: 27–51. https://doi.org/10.31234/osf.io/c3bsj

Dignan, James. 2005. *Understanding Victims and Restorative Justice*. Maidenhead: Open University Press.

Dijk, J. J. M. van. 2000. "Implications of the International Crime Victims Survey for a Victim Perspective." In *Integrating a Victim Perspective within Criminal Justice*, edited by Adam Crawford and Jo Goodey. Aldershot: Ashgate Dartmouth.

Doorn, Janne, and Lieve Brouwers. 2018. "Third-Party Responses to Injustice: A Review on the Preference for Compensation." *Crime Psychology Review* 3 (1): 59–77. https://doi.org/10.1080/23744006.2018.1470765.

Doorn, Janne van, Marcel Zeelenberg, and Seger M. Breugelmans. 2018. "An Exploration of Third Parties' Preference for Compensation over Punishment: Six Experimental Demonstrations." *Theory and Decision* 85 (3): 333–51. https://doi.org/10.1007/s11238-018-9665-9.

Doorn, Janne van, Marcel Zeelenberg, Seger M. Breugelmans, Sebastian Berger, and Tyler G. Okimoto. 2018. "Prosocial Consequences of Third-Party Anger." *Theory and Decision* 84 (4): 585–99. https://doi.org/10.1007/s11238-017-9652-6.

Duff, Antony. 2001. *Punishment, Communication, and Community*. Oxford: Oxford University Press.

Duff, Antony. 2002. "Restorative Punishment and Punitive Restoration." In *Restorative Justice and the Law*, edited by Lode Walgrave, 82–100. Devon: Willan Publishing.

Duff, Antony. 2003. "Penance, Punishment and the Limits of Community." *Punishment & Society* 5 (3): 295–312. https://doi.org/10.1177/1462474503005003004.

Duff, Antony. 1986. *Trials and Punishments*. Cambridge: Cambridge University Press.

Duff, Antony. and S. E. Marshall. 2010. "Public and Private Wrongs." In *Essays in Criminal Law in Honour of Sir Gerald Gordon*, edited by James Chalmers, Fiona Leverick, and Lindsay Farmer, 70–85. Edinburgh, Edinburgh University Press. https://doi.org/10.3366/edinburgh/9780748640706.003.0016.

Duff, Antony. 2007. *Answering for Crime: Responsibility and Liability in the Criminal Law*. Hart Publishing. Oxford/Portland: Hart Publishing.

Duus-Otterström, Göran. 2017. "Fairness-Based Retributivism Reconsidered." *Criminal Law and Philosophy* 11 (3): 481–98. https://doi.org/10.1007/s11572-015-9382-1.

Eder, Andreas B., Vanessa Mitschke, and Mario Gollwitzer. 2020. "What Stops Revenge Taking? Effects of Observed Emotional Reactions on Revenge Seeking." *Aggressive Behavior* 46 (4): 305–16. https://doi.org/10.1002/ab.21890.

Edwards, James, and Andrew Simester. 2017. "What's Public About Crime?" *Oxford Journal of Legal Studies* 37 (1): 105–33. https://doi.org/10.1093/ojls/gqw010.

Ellin, Joseph. 2000. "Restitutionism Defended." *The Journal of Value Inquiry* 34 (2–3): 299–317. https://doi.org/10.1023/a:1004770105668.

Ellsworth, Phoebe C., and Lee Ross. 1983. "Public Opinion and Capital Punishment: A Close Examination of the Views of Abolitionists and Retentionists." *Crime & Delinquency* 29 (1): 116–69. https://doi.org/10.1177/001112878302900105.

Eren, Ozkan, and Naci Mocan. 2018. "Emotional Judges and Unlucky Juveniles." *American Economic Journal: Applied Economics* 10 (3): 171–205. https://doi.org/10.1257/app.20160390.

Erez, Edna, and Pamela Tontodonato. 1992. "Victim Participation in Sentencing and Satisfaction with Justice." *Justice Quarterly* 9 (3): 393–417. https://doi.org/10.1080/07418829200091451.

Farnham, Daniel. 2008. "A Hegelian Theory of Retribution." *Journal of Social Philosophy* 39 (4): 606–24. https://doi.org/10.1111/j.1467-9833.2008.00445.x.

Fehr, Ernst, and Urs Fischbacher. 2004. "Third-Party Punishment and Social Norms." *Evolution and Human Behavior* 25 (2): 63–87. https://doi.org/10.1016/s1090-5138(04)00005-4.

Fehr, Ernst, and Simon Gächter. 2002. "Altruistic Punishment in Humans." *Nature* 415 (6868): 137–40. https://doi.org/10.1038/415137a.

Feinberg, Joel. 1965. "The Expressive Function of Punishment." *The Monist* 49 (3): 397–423. https://doi.org/10.5840/monist196549326.

FeldmanHall, Oriel, Peter Sokol-Hessner, Jay J. van Bavel, and Elizabeth A. Phelps. 2014. "Fairness Violations Elicit Greater Punishment on Behalf of Another than for Oneself." *Nature Communications* 5 (1): 5306. https://doi.org/10.1038/ncomms6306.

Finnis, John. 1972. "The Restoration of Retribution." *Analysis* 32 (4): 131–35. https://doi.org/10.2307/3327910.

Flew, Antony. 1954. "The Justification of Punishment." *Philosophy* 29 (111): 291–307. https://doi.org/10.1017/S0031819100067152.

Friehe, Tim, Svenja Hippel, and Anne Schielke. 2021. "Appeasing Yourself or Others? – The Use of Self-Punishment and Compensation and How It Influences Punishment." *Journal of Economic Psychology* 84: 102379. https://doi.org/10.1016/j.joep.2021.102379.

Frisch, Wolfgang. 1998. "Schwächen Und Berechtigte Aspekte Der Theorie Der Positiven Generalprävention." In *Positive Generalprävention: Kritische Perspektive in Deutsch-Englischen Dialog*, edited by B. Schünemann, A. von Hirsch, and N. Jareborg, 125–146. Heidelberg: C. F. Müller.

Funk, Friederike, Victoria McGeer, and Mario Gollwitzer. 2014. "Get the Message: Punishment Is Satisfying If the Transgressor Responds to Its Communicative Intent." *Personality and Social Psychology Bulletin* 40 (8): 986–97. https://doi.org/10.1177/0146167214533130.

Galli, Thomas. 2020. *Weggesperrt. Warum Gefängnisse Niemanden Nützen*. Hamburg: Edition Körber.

Garvey, Stephen P. 1999. "Punishment as Atonement." *UCLA Law Review* 46 (6): 1801–58.

Garvey, Stephen P. 2003. "Restorative Justice, Punishment, and Atonement." *Utah Law Review* 1: 303–17.

Gaus, Gerald F. 1991. "Does Compensation Restore Equality?" In *Compensatory Justice: Nomos XXXIII*, edited by John W. Chapman, 45–81. New York: New York University Press. https://doi.org/10.18574/9780814790144-005.

Genn, Hazel. 1988. "Multiple Victimization." In *Victims of Crime: A New Deal?*, edited by Mike Maguire and John Pointing, 90–100. Milton Keynes and Philadelphia: Open University Press.

Gert, Heather J., Linda Radzik, and Michael Hand. 2004. "Hampton on the Expressive Power of Punishment." *Journal of Social Philosophy* 35 (1): 79–90. https://doi.org/10.1111/j.1467-9833.2004.00217.x.

Giacomantonio, Mauro, and Antonio Pierro. 2014. "Individual Differences Underlying Punishment Motivation." *Social Psychology* 45 (6): 449–57. https://doi.org/10.1027/1864-9335/a000211.

Glasgow, Joshua. 2015. "The Expressivist Theory of Punishment Defended." *Law and Philosophy* 34 (6): 601–31. https://doi.org/10.1007/s10982-015-9235-z.

Golash, Deirdre. 2005. *The Case Against Punishment, Retribution, Crime Prevention, and the Law.* New York and London: New York University Press. https://doi.org/10.18574/9780814733295-002.

Gollwitzer, Mario, Judith Braun, Friederike Funk, and Philipp Süssenbach. 2016. "People as Intuitive Retaliators: Spontaneous and Deliberate Reactions to Observed Retaliation." *Social Psychological and Personality Science* 7 (6): 521–29. https://doi.org/10.1177/1948550616644300.

Gollwitzer, Mario, and Markus Denzler. 2009. "What Makes Revenge Sweet: Seeing the Offender Suffer or Delivering a Message?" *Journal of Experimental Social Psychology* 45 (4): 840–44. https://doi.org/10.1016/j.jesp.2009.03.001.

Gollwitzer, Mario, Milena Meder, and Manfred Schmitt. 2011. "What Gives Victims Satisfaction When They Seek Revenge?" *European Journal of Social Psychology* 41 (3): 364–74. https://doi.org/10.1002/ejsp.782.

Goodmark, Leigh. 2018. "Restorative Justice as Feminist Practice." *The International Journal of Restorative Justice* 1 (3): 372–84. https://doi.org/10.5553/ijrj/258908912018001003003.

Goodwin, Geoffrey P., and Dena M. Gromet. 2014. "Punishment." *Wiley Interdisciplinary Reviews: Cognitive Science* 5 (5): 561–72. https://doi.org/10.5553/ijrj/25890891201800100300.

Greene, Joshua D. 2014. "Beyond Point-and-Shoot Morality: Why Cognitive (Neuro)Science Matters for Ethics." *Ethics* 124 (4): 695–726. https://doi.org/10.1086/675875.

Griffin, Brandon J., Jaclyn M. Moloney, Jeffrey D. Green, Everett L. Worthington Jr., Brianne Cork, June P. Tangney, Daryl R. Van Tongeren, Don E. Davis, and Joshua N. Hook. 2016. "Perpetrators' Reactions to Perceived Interpersonal Wrongdoing: The Associations of Guilt and Shame with Forgiving, Punishing, and Excusing Oneself." *Self and Identity* 15 (6): 1–12. https://doi.org/10.1080/15298868.2016.1187669.

Gromet, Dena M., and John M. Darley. 2006. "Restoration and Retribution: How Including Retributive Components Affects the Acceptability of Restorative Justice Procedures." *Social Justice Research* 19 (4): 395–432. https://doi.org/10.1007/s11211-006-0023-7.

Gromet, Dena M., and John M. Darley. 2009. "Punishment and Beyond: Achieving Justice Through the Satisfaction of Multiple Goals." *Law & Society Review* 43 (1): 1–38. https://doi.org/10.1111/j.1540-5893.2009.00365.x.

Günther, Klaus. 2014. "Criminal Law, Crime and Punishment as Communication." In *Liberal Criminal Theory: Essays for Andreas von Hirsch*, edited by A. P. Simester, Antje du Bois-Pedain, and Ulfrid Neumann, 123–39. Oxford: Hart Publishing. https://doi.org/10.5040/9781474200868.ch-007.

Hampton, Jean. 1991. "Correcting Harms Versus Righting Wrongs: The Goal of Retribution." *UCLA Law Review* 39 (6): 1659–1702.

Hampton, Jean. 1992. "An Expressive Theory of Retribution." In *Retributivism and Its Critics*, edited by Wesley Cragg. Stuttgart: Franz Steiner Verlag.

Hanna, Nathan. 2008. "Say What? A Critique of Expressive Retributivism." *Law and Philosophy* 27: 123–50. https://doi.org/10.1007/s10982-007-9014-6.

Hanna, Nathan. 2009. "Liberalism and the General Justifiability of Punishment." *Philosophical Studies* 145: 325–349. https://doi.org/10.1007/s11098-008-9234-0.

Hanna, Nathan. 2017. "The Nature of Punishment: Reply to Wringe." *Ethical Theory and Moral Practice* 20 (5): 969–76. https://doi.org/10.1007/s10677-017-9835-9.

Hanna, Nathan. 2020. "The Nature of Punishment Revisited: Reply to Wringe." *Ethical Theory and Moral Practice* 23 (1): 89–100. https://doi.org/10.1007/s10677-019-10047-1.

Hart, H. L. A. 1955. "Are There Any Natural Rights?" *The Philosophical Review* 64 (2): 175–91. https://doi.org/10.2307/2182586.

Hart, H. L. A. 1960. "The Presidential Address: I—Prolegomenon to the Principles of Punishment." *Proceedings of the Aristotelian Society* 60 (1): 1–26. https://doi.org/10.1093/aristotelian/60.1.1.

Hart, H. L. A. 2008. *Punishment and Responsibility: Essays in the Philosophy of Law.* 2nd ed. Oxford: Oxford University Press. https://doi.org/10.1093/acprof:oso/9780199534777.001.0001.

Haynes, Stacy Hoskins, Alison C. Cares, and R. Barry Ruback. 2015. "Reducing the Harm of Criminal Victimization: The Role of Restitution." *Violence and Victims* 30 (3): 450–69. https://doi.org/10.1891/0886-6708.vv-d-13-00049.

Heffernan, William C., and John Kleinig. 2000. From Social Justice to Criminal Justice. Poverty and the Administration of Criminal Law. Oxford: Oxford University Press.

Heffner, Joseph, and Oriel FeldmanHall. 2019. "Why We Don't Always Punish: Preferences for Non-Punitive Responses to Moral Violations." *Scientific Reports* 9 (1): 13219. https://doi.org/10.1038/s41598-019-49680-2.

Hegel, G. W. F. 1820. *Hegel's Philosophy of Right.* Translated by T. M. Knox. New York: Oxford University Press.

Helland, Eric, and Alexander Tabarrok. 2007. "Does Three Strikes Deter? A Nonparametric Estimation." *Journal of Human Resources* 42 (2): 309–30. https://doi.org/10.3368/jhr.xlii.2.309.

Henrich, Joseph. 2009. "The Evolution of Costly Displays, Cooperation and Religion Credibility Enhancing Displays and Their Implications for Cultural Evolution." *Evolution and Human Behavior* 30 (4): 244–60. https://doi.org/10.1016/j.evolhumbehav.2009.03.005.

Henrich, Joseph. 2016. *The Secret of Our Success: How Culture Is Driving Human Evolution, Domesticating Our Species, and Making Us Smart.* Princeton: Princeton University Press. https://doi.org/10.1515/9781400873296.

Henrich, Joseph. 2020. The WEIRDest People in the World. How the West Became Psychologically Peculiar and Particularly Prosperous. New York: Farrar, Straus and Giroux.

Henrich, Joseph, Richard McElreath, Abigail Barr, Jean Ensminger, Clark Barrett, Alexander Bolyanatz, Juan Camilo Cardenas, et al. 2006. "Costly Punishment Across Human Societies." *Science* 312 (5781): 1767–70. https://doi.org/10.1126/science.1127333.

Hirsch, Andrew von. 1985. Past or Future Crimes. Deservedness and Dangerousness in the Sentencing of Criminals. Manchester, Manchester University Press.

Hirsch, Andrew von. 1993. *Censure and Sanctions.* Oxford: Clarendon Press. https://doi.org/10.1093/acprof:oso/9780198262411.001.0001.

Hirsch, Andrew von, and Andrew Ashworth. 2005. *Proportionate Sentencing. Exploring the Principles.* Oxford: Oxford University Press. https://doi.org/10.1093/acprof:oso/9780199272600.001.0001.

Hirsch, Andrew von, Andrew Ashworth, and Clifford Shearing. 2003. "Specifying Aims and Limits for Restorative Justice: A 'Making Amends' Model?" In *Restorative Justice and Criminal Justice: Competing or Reconcilable Paradigms?*, edited by Andrew von Hirsch, Julian V. Roberts, Anthony Bottoms, Kent Roach, and Mara Schiff, 21–41. Oxford and Portland, Oregon: Hart Publishing. https://doi.org/10.5040/9781472559333.ch-002.

Hoekema, David A. 1991. "Trust and Obey: Toward a New Theory of Punishment." *Israel Law Review* 25 (3–4): 332–50. https://doi.org/10.1017/s0021223700010451.

Hoffman, Morris B. 2021. "The Psychology of the Trial Judge." In *Law and Mind. A Survey of Law and the Cognitive Sciences*, edited by Bartosz Brożek, Jaap Hage, and Nicole Vincent, 165–92. Cambridge: Cambridge University Press. https://doi.org/10.1017/9781108623056.008.

Holroyd, Jules. 2010. "Punishment and Justice." *Social Theory and Practice* 36 (1): 78–111. https://doi.org/10.5840/soctheorpract20103614.

Hörnle, Tatjana. 2019. "The Role of Victims' Rights in Punishment Theory." In *Penal Censure. Engagements Within and Beyond Desert Theory*, edited by Antje du Bois-Pedain and Anthony E. Bottoms, 207–226. Oxford: Hart Publishing. https://doi.org/10.5040/9781509919819.ch-011.

Hoskins, Zachary. 2011. "Deterrent Punishment and Respect for Persons." *Ohio State Journal of Criminal Law* 8 (2): 369–84.

Hosser, Daniela, Michael Windzio, and Werner Greve. 2008. "Guilt and Shame as Predictors of Recidivism." *Criminal Justice and Behavior* 35 (1): 138–52. https://doi.org/10.1177/0093854807309224.

Husak, Douglas. 2008. *Overcriminalization: The Limits of the Criminal Law*. New York: Oxford University Press. https://doi.org/10.1093/acprof:oso/9780195328714.001.0001.

Husak, Douglas. 2016. "What Do Criminals Deserve?" In *Legal, Moral, and Metaphysical Truths: The Philosophy of Michael S. Moore*, edited by Kimberly K. Ferzan and Stephen J. Morse, 49–62. Oxford: Oxford University Press. https://doi.org/10.1093/acprof:oso/9780198703242.003.0004.

Husak, Douglas. 2020. "The Price of Criminal Law Skepticism." *New Criminal Law Review* 23 (1): 27–59. https://doi.org/10.1525/nclr.2020.23.1.27.

Inbar, Yoel, David A. Pizarro, Thomas Gilovich, and Dan Ariely. 2013. "Moral Masochism: On the Connection between Guilt and Self-Punishment." *Emotion* 13 (1): 14–18. https://doi.org/10.1037/a0029749.

Institute, Credit Suisse Research. 2021. *Global Wealth Report 2021*. Zürich, Switzerland: Credite Suisse AG.

Jacobs, Jonathan. 2016. "Resentment, Punitiveness, and Forgiveness. An Exploration of the Moral Psychology of Punishment." In *The Routledge Handbook of Criminal Justice Ethics*, edited by Jonathan Jacobs and Jonathan Jackson, 58–75. London and New York: Routledge. https://doi.org/10.4324/9781315885933.

Kanakogi, Yasuhiro, Yasuyuki Inoue, Goh Matsuda, David Butler, Kazuo Hiraki, and Masako Myowa-Yamakoshi. 2017. "Preverbal Infants Affirm Third-Party Interventions That Protect Victims from Aggressors." *Nature Human Behaviour* 1 (2): 0037. https://doi.org/10.1038/s41562-016-0037.

Kant, Immanuel. 1996. "The Metaphysics of Morals." In *Practical Philosophy*, edited and translated by Mary J. Gregor, 353–604. Cambridge: Cambridge University Press. https://doi.org/10.1017/cbo9780511813306.013.

Kasachkoff, Tziporah. 1973. "The Criteria of Punishment: Some Neglected Considerations." *Canadian Journal of Philosophy* 2 (3): 363–77. https://doi.org/10.1080/00455091.1973.10716049.

Kaufman, Whitley. 2008. "The Rise and Fall of the Mixed Theory of Punishment." *International Journal of Applied Philosophy* 22 (1): 37–57. https://doi.org/10.5840/ijap20082214.

Kauppinen, Antti. 2014. "Ethics and Empirical Psychology – Critical Remarks to Empirically Informed Ethics." In *Empirically Informed Ethics: Morality between Facts and Norms*, edited by Markus Christen, Carel von Schaik, Johannes Fischer, Markus Huppenbauer, and Carmen Tanner, 279–305. New York: Springer. https://doi.org/10.1007/978-3-319-01369-5_16.

Keller, Livia B., Margit E. Oswald, Ingrid Stucki, and Mario Gollwitzer. 2010. "A Closer Look at an Eye for an Eye: Laypersons' Punishment Decisions Are Primarily Driven by Retributive Motives." *Social Justice Research* 23 (2–3): 99–116. https://doi.org/10.1007/s11211-010-0113-4.

Kershnar, Stephen. 2001. *Desert, Retribution, and Torture*. Lanham: University Press of America.

Kerstein, Samuel J. 2013. *How to Treat Persons*. Oxford: Oxford University Press. https://doi.org/10.1093/acprof:oso/9780199692033.001.0001.

Ketelaar, Timothy, and Wing Tung Au. 2003. "The Effects of Feelings of Guilt on the Behaviour of Uncooperative Individuals in Repeated Social Bargaining Games: An Affect-as-Information

Interpretation of the Role of Emotion in Social Interaction." *Cognition & Emotion* 17 (3): 429–53. https://doi.org/10.1080/02699930143000662.

Klein, Richard A., Kate A. Ratliff, Michelangelo Vianello, Reginald B. Adams, Štěpán Bahník, Michael J. Bernstein, Konrad Bocian, et al. 2014. "Investigating Variation in Replicability." *Social Psychology* 45 (3): 142–52. https://doi.org/10.1027/1864-9335/a000178.

Kleinig, John. 1991. "Punishment and Moral Seriousness." *Israel Law Review* 25 (3–4): 401–21. https://doi.org/10.1017/s0021223700010517.

Kneer, Markus, and Sacha Bourgeois-Gironde. 2017. "Mens Rea Ascription, Expertise and Outcome Effects: Professional Judges Surveyed." *Cognition* 169: 139–46. https://doi.org/10.1016/j.cognition.2017.08.008.

Koppel, Stephen, and Mark R. Fondacaro. 2017. "The Retribution Heuristic." In *The Routledge Handbook of Criminal Justice Ethics*, edited by Jonathan Jacobs and Jonathan Jackson, 191–202. London/New York: Routledge.

Koppen, Peter J. van, and Jan Ten Kate. 1984. "Individual Differences in Judicial Behavior: Personal Characteristics and Private Law Decision-Making." *Law & Society Review* 18 (2): 225–48. https://doi.org/10.2307/3053403.

Kunst, Maarten, Lieke Popelier, and Ellen Varekamp. 2015. "Victim Satisfaction with the Criminal Justice System and Emotional Recovery." *Trauma, Violence, & Abuse* 16 (3): 336–58. https://doi.org/10.1177/1524838014555034.

Lacey, Nicola. 1988. *State Punishment*. New York: Routledge. https://doi.org/10.4324/9780203046067.

Latimer, Jeff, Craig Dowden, and Danielle Muise. 2005. "The Effectiveness of Restorative Justice Practices: A Meta-Analysis." *The Prison Journal* 85 (2): 127–44. https://doi.org/10.1177/0032885505276969.

Laxminarayan, Malini. 2013. "The Effect of Retributive and Restorative Sentencing on Psychological Effects of Criminal Proceedings." *Journal of Interpersonal Violence* 28 (5): 938–55. https://doi.org/10.1177/0886260512459385.

Lee, Ambrose YK. 2016. "Defending a Communicative Theory of Punishment: The Relationship between Hard Treatment and Amends." *Oxford Journal of Legal Studies* 37 (1): 217–237. https://doi.org/10.1093/ojls/gqw003.

Lee, David S., and Justin McCrary. 2009. *The Deterrent Effect of Prison: Dynamic Theory and Evidence*. Princeton, NJ: University of Princeton, Industrial Relations Section.

Lee, Hsin-Wen. 2017. "Taking Deterrence Seriously: The Wide-Scope Deterrence Theory of Punishment." *Criminal Justice Ethics* 36 (1): 2–24. https://doi.org/10.1080/0731129x.2017.1298879.

Lee, Hsin-Wen. 2018. "A New Societal Self-Defense Theory of Punishment—The Rights-Protection Theory." *Philosophia* 46 (2): 337–53. https://doi.org/10.1007/s11406-017-9931-z.

Leith, Karen P., and Roy F. Baumeister. 1998. "Empathy, Shame, Guilt, and Narratives of Interpersonal Conflicts: Guilt-Prone People Are Better at Perspective Taking." *Journal of Personality* 66 (1): 1–37. https://doi.org/10.1111/1467-6494.00001.

Lewis, C. S. 1953. "The Humanitarian Theory of Punishment." *Res Judicata* 6: 224–30.

Li, Jing, Wen Wang, Jing Yu, and Liqi Zhu. 2016. "Young Children's Development of Fairness Preference." *Frontiers in Psychology* 7: 1274. https://doi.org/10.3389/fpsyg.2016.01274.

Lindsay-Hartz, Janice. 1984. "Contrasting Experiences of Shame and Guilt." *American Behavioral Scientist* 27 (6): 689–704. https://doi.org/10.1177/000276484027006003.

Lippke, Richard L. 2020. "Retributivism and Victim Compensation." *Social Theory and Practice* 46 (2): 317–38. https://doi.org/10.5840/soctheorpract202033187.

Lipton, Douglas, Robert Martinson, and Judith Wilks. 1975. The Effectiveness of Correctional Treatment: A Survey of Treatment Evaluation Studies. New York: Praeger.

Lotz, Sebastian, Tyler G. Okimoto, Thomas Schlösser, and Detlef Fetchenhauer. 2011. "Punitive versus Compensatory Reactions to Injustice: Emotional Antecedents to Third-Party Interventions." *Journal of Experimental Social Psychology* 47 (2): 477–80. https://doi.org/10.1016/j.jesp.2010.10.004.

Mabbott, John D. 1939. "II. —Punishment." *Mind* XLVIII (190): 152–67. https://doi.org/10.1093/mind/xlviii.190.152.

Mackie, John L. 1982. "Morality and the Retributive Emotions." *Criminal Justice Ethics* 1 (1): 3–10. https://doi.org/10.1080/0731129X.1982.9991689.

Macnamara, Coleen. 2015. "Reactive Attitudes as Communicative Entities." *Philosophy and Phenomenological Research* 90 (3): 546–69. https://doi.org/10.1111/phpr.12075.

Marlowe, Frank W., J. Colette Berbesque, Abigail Barr, Clark Barrett, Alexander Bolyanatz, Juan Camilo Cardenas, Jean Ensminger, et al. 2008. "More 'Altruistic' Punishment in Larger Societies." *Proceedings of the Royal Society of London B: Biological Sciences* 275 (1634): 587–92. https://doi.org/10.1098/rspb.2007.1517.

Martinson, Robert. 1974. "What Works? Questions and Answers about Prison Reform." *The Publica Interest* 35: 22–54.

Matravers, Matt. 2014. "Penal Justice and Social Injustice." In *Encyclopedia of Criminology and Criminal Justice*, edited by Gerben Bruinsma and David Weisburd, 3474–81. New York: Springer.

Mazar, Nina, On Amir, and Dan Ariely. 2008. "The Dishonesty of Honest People: A Theory of Self-Concept Maintenance." *Journal of Marketing Research* 45 (6): 633–44. https://doi.org/10.1509/jmkr.45.6.633.

McAuliffe, Katherine, Peter R. Blake, Nikolaus Steinbeis, and Felix Warneken. 2017. "The Developmental Foundations of Human Fairness." *Nature Human Behaviour* 1 (2): 0042. https://doi.org/10.1038/s41562-016-0042.

McAuliffe, Katherine, Jillian J. Jordan, and Felix Warneken. 2015. "Costly Third-Party Punishment in Young Children." *Cognition* 134: 1–10. https://doi.org/10.1016/j.cognition.2014.08.013.

McCloskey, Henry J. 1957. "An Examination of Restricted Utilitarianism." *The Philosophical Review* 66 (4): 466–85. https://doi.org/10.2307/2182745.

McDonald, William F. 1976. *Criminal Justice and the Victim*. Beverly Hills: Sage.

McGeer, Victoria, and Friederike Funk. 2017. "Are 'Optimistic' Theories of Criminal Justice Psychologically Feasible? The Probative Case of Civic Republicanism." *Criminal Law and Philosophy* 11 (3): 523–44. https://doi.org/10.1007/s11572-015-9381-2.

Mills, Charles W. 2005. "'Ideal Theory' as Ideology." *Hypatia* 20 (3): 165–83. https://doi.org/10.1111/j.1527-2001.2005.tb00493.x.

Molnar, Andras, Shereen J. Chaudhry, and George Loewenstein. 2020. "'It's Not about the Money. It's about Sending a Message!': Unpacking the Components of Revenge." *SSRN Electronic Journal*. https://doi.org/10.2139/ssrn.3524910.

Moore, Michael S. 2010. *Placing Blame*. Oxford: Oxford University Press. https://doi.org/10.1093/acprof:oso/9780199599493.001.0001.

Morris, Herbert. 1968. "Persons and Punishment." *Monist* 52 (4): 475–501. https://doi.org/10.5840/monist196852436.

Mumola, Christopher J. 2000. "Incarcerated Parents and Their Children." In *Bureau of Justice Statistics Special Report*, 1–12. Washington, D.C.: Bureau of Justice Statistic.

Murphy, Jeffrie G. 1973. "Marxism and Retribution." *Philosophy & Public Affairs* 2 (3): 217–43.

Nadelhoffer, Thomas, Saeideh Heshmati, Deanna Kaplan, and Shaun Nichols. 2013. "Folk Retributivism and the Communication Confound." *Economics and Philosophy* 29 (2): 235–61. https://doi.org/10.1017/s0266267113000217.

Nadelhoffer, Thomas, Eddy Nahmias, and Shaun Nichols, eds. 2010. *Moral Psychology: Classical and Contemporary Readings*. Malden, MA: Wiley-Blackwell.

Nahmias, Eddy, and Eyal Aharoni. 2017. "Communicative Theories of Punishment and the Impact of Apology." In *Rethinking Punishment in the Era of Mass Incarceration*, edited by Chris W. Surprenant, 144–61. New York: Routledge. https://doi.org/10.4324/9781315170602-9.

Nelissen, Rob M. A. 2012. "Guilt-Induced Self-Punishment as a Sign of Remorse." *Social Psychological and Personality Science* 3 (2): 139–44. https://doi.org/10.1177/1948550611411520.

Nelissen, Rob M. A., and Marcel Zeelenberg. 2009a. "Moral Emotions as Determinants of Third-Party Punishment: Anger, Guilt, and the Functions of Altruistic Sanctions." *Judgment and Decision Making* 4 (7): 543–553.

Nelissen, Rob M. A., and Marcel Zeelenberg. 2009b. "When Guilt Evokes Self-Punishment: Evidence for the Existence of a Dobby Effect." *Emotion* 9 (1): 118–22. https://doi.org/10.1037/a0014540.

Nichols, Shaun. 2014. "Process Debunking and Ethics." *Ethics* 124 (4): 727–49. https://doi.org/10.1086/675877.

Nichols, Shaun. 2015. *Bound*. Oxford: Oxford University Press. https://doi.org/10.1093/acprof:oso/9780199291847.001.0001.

Nietzsche, Friedrich. 1968. "Zweite Abhandlung: 'Schuld', 'Schlechtes Gewissen' Und Verwandtes." In *Jenseits von Gut Und Böse. Zur Genealogie Der Moral. (1886–1887)*, edited by Giorgio Colli and Wolfgang Müller-Lauter, 305–54. Berlin: De Gruyter. https://doi.org/10.1515/9783111469706.305.

Nino, Carlos Santiago. 1983. "A Consensual Theory of Punishment." *Philosophy and Public Affairs* 12 (4): 289–306.

Nolan, Christopher, director. *The Dark Knight*. Warner Pros. Picture, DC Comics, Legendary Pictures, Syncopy, 2008. 2hr., 32 min.

Ohtsubo, Yohsuke, Masahiro Matsunaga, Hiroki Tanaka, Kohta Suzuki, Fumio Kobayashi, Eiji Shibata, Reiko Hori, Tomohiro Umemura, and Hideki Ohira. 2018. "Costly Apologies Communicate Conciliatory Intention: An FMRI Study on Forgiveness in Response to Costly Apologies." *Evolution and Human Behavior* 39 (2): 249–56. https://doi.org/10.1016/j.evolhumbehav.2018.01.004.

O'Neill, Onora. 1996. *Towards Justice and Virtue*. Cambridge: Cambridge University Press. https://doi.org/10.1017/cbo9780511621239.

Orth, Uli. 2002. "Secondary Victimization of Crime Victims by Criminal Proceedings." *Social Justice Research* 15 (4): 313–25. https://doi.org/10.1023/a:1021210323461.

Orth, Uli. 2003. "Punishment Goals of Crime Victims." *Law and Human Behavior* 27 (2): 173–86. https://doi.org/10.1023/a:1022547213760.

Oswald, Margit E., and Ingrid Stucki. 2009. "A Two-Process Model of Punishment." In *Social Psychology of Punishment of Crime*, edited by Margit E. Oswald, Steffen Bieneck, and Jorg Hupfeld-Heinemann, 173–191. Wiley.

Parfit, Derek. 2011. *On What Matters. Volume One*. Oxford: Oxford University Press. https://doi.org/10.1093/acprof:osobl/9780199572816.001.0001.

Pereboom, Derk. 2001. *Living without Free Will*. Cambridge: Cambridge University Press. https://doi.org/10.1017/cbo9780511498824.

Pereboom, Derk. 2013. "Free Will Skepticism and Criminal Punishment." In *The Future of Punishment*, edited by Thomas A. Nadelhoffer, 49–78. Oxford: Oxford University Press. https://doi.org/10.1093/acprof:oso/9780199779208.003.0003.

Pereboom, Derk. 2014. *Free Will, Agency, and Meaning in Life.* Oxford: Oxford University Press. https://doi.org/10.1093/acprof:oso/9780199685516.001.0001.

Petersen, Michael Bang, Aaron Sell, John Tooby, and Leda Cosmides. 2012. "To Punish or Repair? Evolutionary Psychology and Lay Intuitions about Modern Criminal Justice." *Evolution and Human Behavior* 33 (6): 682–95. https://doi.org/10.1016/j.evolhumbehav.2012.05.003.

Pillutla, Madan M., and J. Keith Murnighan. 1996. "Unfairness, Anger, and Spite: Emotional Rejections of Ultimatum Offers." *Organizational Behavior and Human Decision Processes* 68 (3): 208–24. https://doi.org/10.1006/obhd.1996.0100.

Poama, Andrei. 2015. "Punishment without Pain. Outline for a Non-Afflictive Definition of Legal Punishment." *Philosophy and Public Issues* 5 (1): 97–134.

Poama, Andrei. 2018. "Corrective Justice as A Principle of Criminal Law: A Prolegomenon." *Criminal Law and Philosophy* 12 (4): 605–23. https://doi.org/10.1007/s11572-017-9447-4.

Pölzler, Thomas. 2018. *Moral Reality and the Empirical Sciences.* New York and London: Routledge. https://doi.org/10.4324/9781315145211.

Pölzler, Thomas, and Jennifer Cole Wright. 2019. "Empirical Research on Folk Moral Objectivism." *Philosophy Compass* 14 (5): e12589. https://doi.org/10.1111/phc3.12589.

Price, Michael E., Leda Cosmides, and John Tooby. 2002. "Punitive Sentiment as an Anti-Free Rider Psychological Device." *Evolution and Human Behavior* 23 (3): 203–31. https://doi.org/10.1016/s1090-5138(01)00093-9.

Primorac, Igor. 1981. "Is Retributivism Analytic?" *Philosophy* 56 (216): 203–11. https://doi.org/10.1017/s003181910005004x.

Primoratz, Igor. 1989. "Punishment as Language." *Philosophy* 64 (248): 187–205. https://doi.org/10.1017/s0031819100044478.

Proeve, Michael J., David I. Smith, and Diane Mead Niblo. 1999. "Mitigation without Definition: Remorse in the Criminal Justice System." *Australian and New Zealand Journal of Criminology* 32 (1): 16–26. https://doi.org/10.1177/000486589903200103.

Prooijen, Jan-Willem van. 2010. "Retributive versus Compensatory Justice: Observers' Preference for Punishing in Response to Criminal Offenses." *European Journal of Social Psychology* 40 (1): 72–85. https://doi.org/10.1002/ejsp.611.

Rachlinski, Jeffrey J., and Andrew J. Wistrich. 2017. "Judging the Judiciary by the Numbers: Empirical Research on Judges." *Annual Review of Law and Social Science* 13 (1): 203–29. https://doi.org/10.1146/annurev-lawsocsci-110615-085032.

Radzik, Linda. 2009. *Making Amends. Atonement in Morality, Law, and Politics.* Oxford: Oxford University Press. https://doi.org/10.1093/acprof:oso/9780195373660.001.0001.

Rawls, John. 1955. "Two Concepts of Rules." *The Philosophical Review* 64 (1): 3–32. https://doi.org/10.2307/2182230.

Rawls, John. 1964. "Legal Obligation and the Duty of Fair Play." In *Law and Philosophy*, edited by Sidney Hook, 3–18. New York: New York University Press.

Rawls, John. 1999. *A Theory of Justice. Revised Edition.* Cambridge, MA: Harvard University Press.

Roberts, Julian, Mike Hough, Jonathan Jackson, and Monica M. Gerber. 2012. "Public Opinion Towards the Lay Magistracy and the Sentencing Council Guidelines: The Effects of Information on Attitudes." *British Journal of Criminology* 52 (6): 1072–91. https://doi.org/10.1093/bjc/azs024.

Romanowski, K. A. 1988. Crime and Confession: An Analysis of the Relationship between Contrition, Sentence Severity and Recidivism. Unpublished Doctoral Dissertation: University of Michigan.

Rosebury, Brian. 2011. "Moore's Moral Facts and the Gap in the Retributive Theory." *Criminal Law and Philosophy* 5 (3): 361–376. https://doi.org/10.1007/s11572-011-9117-x.

Ruback, Barry R., Alison C. Cares, and Stacy N. Hoskins. 2008. "Crime Victims' Perceptions of Restitution: The Importance of Payment and Understanding." *Violence and Victims* 23 (6): 697–710. https://doi.org/10.1891/0886-6708.23.6.697.

Rubin, Edward L. 2003. "Trial by Battle, Trial by Argument." *Arkansas Law Review* 56: 261–94. https://doi.org/10.2139/ssrn.328642.

Rustagi, Devesh, Stefanie Engel, and Michael Kosfeld. 2010. "Conditional Cooperation and Costly Monitoring Explain Success in Forest Commons Management." *Science* 330 (6006): 961–65. https://doi.org/10.1126/science.1193649.

Sarin, Arunima, Mark K. Ho, Justin W. Martin, and Fiery A. Cushman. 2021. "Punishment Is Organized around Principles of Communicative Inference." *Cognition* 208: 104544. https://doi.org/10.1016/j.cognition.2020.104544.

Sauer, Hanno. 2018. *Debunking Arguments in Ethics.* Cambridge: Cambridge University Press.

Sauer, Hanno. 2021. "Against Moral Judgment. The Empirical Case for Moral Abolitionism." *Philosophical Explorations*, 1–18. https://doi.org/10.1080/13869795.2021.1908580.

Saulnier, Alana, and Diane Sivasubramaniam. 2018. "Restorative Justice: Reflections and the Retributive Impulse." In *Advances in Psychology and Law*, edited by M. K. Miller and B. H. Bornstein, 3:177–210. Springer. https://doi.org/10.1007/978-3-319-75859-6_6.

Sayre-McCord, Geoffrey. 2001. "Criminal Justice and Legal Reparations as an Alternative to Punishment1." *Philosophical Issues* 11 (1): 502–29. https://doi.org/10.1111/j.1758-2237.2001.tb00055.x.

Sayre-McCord, Geoffrey. 2002. "In Defense of Reparations: A Reply to Estlund and Gaus." Edited by Enrique Villanueva. *Legal and Political Philosophy, Social, Political & Legal Philosophy*, In Defense of Reparations: A Reply to Estlund and Gaus, 1: 371–83.

Schmader, Toni, and Brian Lickel. 2006. "The Approach and Avoidance Function of Guilt and Shame Emotions: Comparing Reactions to Self-Caused and Other-Caused Wrongdoing." *Motivation and Emotion* 30 (1): 43–56. https://doi.org/10.1007/s11031-006-9006-0.

Seip, Elise C., Wilco W. van Dijk, and Mark Rotteveel. 2014. "Anger Motivates Costly Punishment of Unfair Behavior." *Motivation and Emotion* 38 (4): 578–88. https://doi.org/10.1007/s11031-014-9395-4.

Shapland, Joanna. 1984. "Victims, The Criminal Justice System and Compensation." *The British Journal of Criminology* 24 (2): 131–49. https://doi.org/10.1093/oxfordjournals.bjc.a047436.

Shelby, Tommie. 2022. *The Idea of Prison Abolition.* Princeton, New Jersey: Princeton University Press. https://doi.org/10.1515/9780691229775.

Sherman, Lawrence W., Heather Strang, Caroline Angel, Daniel Woods, Geoffrey C. Barnes, Sarah Bennett, and Nova Inkpen. 2005. "Effects of Face-to-Face Restorative Justice on Victims of Crime in Four Randomized, Controlled Trials." *Journal of Experimental Criminology* 1 (3): 367–95. https://doi.org/10.1007/s11292-005-8126-y.

Sherman, Lawrence W., Heather Strang, Evan Mayo-Wilson, Daniel J. Woods, and Barak Ariel. 2015. "Are Restorative Justice Conferences Effective in Reducing Repeat Offending? Findings from a Campbell Systematic Review." *Journal of Quantitative Criminology* 31 (1): 1–24. https://doi.org/10.1007/s10940-014-9222-9.

Shoemaker, David. 2015. *Responsibility from the Margins.* Oxford: Oxford University Press. https://doi.org/10.1093/acprof:oso/9780198715672.001.0001.

Sigall, Harold, and Nancy Ostrove. 1975. "Beautiful but Dangerous: Effects of Offender Attractiveness and Nature of the Crime on Juridic Judgment." *Journal of Personality and Social Psychology* 31 (3): 410–14. https://doi.org/10.1037/h0076472.

Simmons, A. John. 2010. "Ideal and Nonideal Theory." *Philosophy & Public Affairs* 38 (1): 5–36. https://doi.org/10.1111/j.1088-4963.2009.01172.x.

Singer, Peter. 2005. "Ethics and Intuitions." *The Journal of Ethics* 9 (3–4): 331–52. https://doi.org/10.1007/s10892-005-3508-y.

Sinnott-Armstrong, Walter, ed. 2008a. Moral Psychology, Volume 1. The Evolution of Morality: Adaptations and Innateness. Cambridge, MA: MIT Press.

Sinnott-Armstrong, Walter, ed. 2008b. Moral Psychology, Volume 2. The Cognitive Science of Morality: Intuition and Diversity. Cambridge, MA: MIT Press.

Sinnott-Armstrong, Walter, ed. 2008c. Moral Psychology, Volume 3. The Neuroscience of Morality: Emotion, Brain Disorders, and Development. Cambridge, MA: MIT Press.

Sinnott-Armstrong, Walter, ed. 2014. *Moral Psychology, Volume 4. Free Will and Moral Responsibility.* Cambridge, MA: MIT Press.

Sjöström, Arne, Zoe Magraw-Mickelson, and Mario Gollwitzer. 2017. "What Makes Displaced Revenge Taste Sweet: Retributing Displaced Responsibility or Sending a Message to the Original Perpetrator?" *European Journal of Social Psychology* 48 (4): 490–506. https://doi.org/10.1002/ejsp.2345.

Smith, David Livingstone. 2011. *Less than Human: Why We Demean, Enslave and Exterminate Others.* New York: St. Martin's Press.

Smith, David Livingstone. 2020. *On Inhumanity.* Oxford: Oxford University Press. https://doi.org/10.1093/oso/9780190923006.001.0001.

Sommers, Tamler. 2016. "The Three Rs: Retribution, Revenge, and Reparation." *Philosophia* 44 (2): 327–42. https://doi.org/10.1007/s11406-016-9706-y.

Sosis, Richard, and Eric R. Bressler. 2003. "Cooperation and Commune Longevity: A Test of the Costly Signaling Theory of Religion." *Cross-Cultural Research* 37 (2): 211–39. https://doi.org/10.1177/1069397103037002003.

Spamann, Holger. 2020. "Lawyers' Role-Induced Bias Arises Fast and Persists Despite Intervention." *The Journal of Legal Studies* 49 (2): 467–85. https://doi.org/https://doi.org/10.1086/710306.

Spamann, Holger, and Lars Klöhn. 2016. "Justice Is Less Blind, and Less Legalistic, than We Thought: Evidence from an Experiment with Real Judges." *The Journal of Legal Studies* 45 (2): 255–80. https://doi.org/10.1086/688861.

Starmans, Christina, Mark Sheskin, and Paul Bloom. 2017. "Why People Prefer Unequal Societies." *Nature Human Behaviour* 1 (4): 0082. https://doi.org/10.1038/s41562-017-0082.

Stephenson, Wendell. 1990. "Fingarette and Johnson on Retributive Punishment." *The Journal of Value Inquiry* 24 (3): 227–33. https://doi.org/10.1007/bf00149435.

Strang, Heather, Lawrence Sherman, Caroline M. Angel, Daniel J. Woods, Sarah Bennett, Dorothy Newbury-Birch, and Nova Inkpen. 2006. "Victim Evaluations of Face-to-Face Restorative Justice Conferences: A Quasi-Experimental Analysis." *Journal of Social Issues* 62 (2): 281–306. https://doi.org/10.1111/j.1540-4560.2006.00451.x.

Strawson, P. F. 1962. "Freedom and Resentment." *Proceedings of the British Academy* 48: 1–25.

Stuewig, Jeffrey, June P. Tangney, Caron Heigel, Laura Harty, and Laura McCloskey. 2010. "Shaming, Blaming, and Maiming: Functional Links Among the Moral Emotions, Externalization of Blame, and Aggression." *Journal of Research in Personality* 44 (1): 91–102. https://doi.org/10.1016/j.jrp.2009.12.005.

Sundt, Jody, Emily J. Salisbury, and Mark G. Harmon. 2016. "Is Downsizing Prisons Dangerous?" *Criminology & Public Policy* 15 (2): 315–41. https://doi.org/10.1111/1745-9133.12199.

Sverdlik, Steven. 1988. "Punishment." *Law and Philosophy* 7 (2): 179–201. https://doi.org/10.1007/bf00144155.

Tadros, Victor. 2009. "Poverty and Criminal Responsibility." *The Journal of Value Inquiry* 43 (3): 391–413. https://doi.org/10.1007/s10790-009-9180-x.

Tanaka, Hiroki, Ayano Yagi, Asuka Komiya, Nobuhiro Mifune, and Yohsuke Ohtsubo. 2015. "Shame-Prone People Are More Likely to Punish Themselves: A Test of the Reputation-Maintenance Explanation for Self-Punishment." *Evolutionary Behavioral Sciences* 9 (1): 1–7. https://doi.org/10.1037/ebs0000016.

Tangney, June P. 1991. "Moral Affect: The Good, the Bad, and the Ugly." *Journal of Personality and Social Psychology* 61 (4): 598–607. https://doi.org/10.1037/0022-3514.61.4.598.

Tangney, June P., Rowland S. Miller, Laura Flicker, and Deborah Hill Barlow. 1996. "Are Shame, Guilt, and Embarrassment Distinct Emotions?" *Journal of Personality and Social Psychology* 70 (6): 1256–69. https://doi.org/10.1037/0022-3514.70.6.1256.

Tangney, June P., Jeff Stuewig, and Logaina Hafez. 2011. "Shame, Guilt, and Remorse: Implications for Offender Populations." *Journal of Forensic Psychiatry & Psychology* 22 (5): 706–23. https://doi.org/10.1080/14789949.2011.617541.

Tangney, June P., Jeff Stuewig, and Debra J. Mashek. 2007. "Moral Emotions and Moral Behavior." *Annual Review of Psychology* 58 (1): 345–72. https://doi.org/10.1146/annurev.psych.56.091103.070145.

Tangney, June P., Jeffrey Stuewig, and Andres G. Martinez. 2014. "Two Faces of Shame: Understanding Shame and Guilt in the Prediction of Jail Inmates' Recidivism." *Psychological Science* 25 (3): 799–805. https://doi.org/10.1177/0956797613508790.

Tangney, June P., and Ronda L. Dearing. 2002. *Shame and Guilt*. New York and London: Guilford Press.

Tiberius, Valerie. 2015. *Moral Psychology*. New York and London: Routledge. https://doi.org/10.4324/9780203117569.

Tomasello, Michael. 2016. *A Natural History of Human Morality*. Cambridge, Massachusetts: Harvard University Press. https://doi.org/10.4159/9780674915855.

Trickett, Alan, Dan Ellingworth, Tim Hope, and Ken Pease. 1995. "Crime Victimization in the Eighties: Changes in Area and Regional Inequality." *The British Journal of Criminology* 35 (3): 343–59. https://doi.org/10.1093/oxfordjournals.bjc.a048520.

Trivers, Robert L. 1971. "The Evolution of Reciprocal Altruism." *The Quarterly Review of Biology* 46 (1): 35–57.

Tunick, Mark. 1992. *Punishment. Theory and Practice*. Berkeley: University of California Press.

Twardawski, Mathias, Karen T. Y. Tang, and Benjamin E Hilbig. 2020. "Is It All about Retribution? The Flexibility of Punishment Goals." *Social Justice Research* 33: 195–218. https://doi.org/10.1007/s11211-020-00352-x.

Tyler, Tom R. 1987. "Procedural Justice Research." *Social Justice Research* 1 (1): 41–65. https://doi.org/10.1007/bf01049383.

Tyler, Tom R. 1990. *Why People Obey the Law*. New Haven, CT: Yale University Press.

Vel-Palumbo, Melissa, Michael Wenzel, and Lydia Woodyatt. 2019. "Self-punishment Promotes Reconciliation with Third Parties by Addressing the Symbolic Implications of Wrongdoing." *European Journal of Social Psychology* 49 (5): 1070–86. https://doi.org/10.1002/ejsp.2571.

Vyver, Julie van de, and Dominic Abrams. 2015. "Testing the Prosocial Effectiveness of the Prototypical Moral Emotions: Elevation Increases Benevolent Behaviors and Outrage Increases

Justice Behaviors." *Journal of Experimental Social Psychology* 58: 23–33. https://doi.org/10.1016/j.jesp.2014.12.005.

Walen, Alec. 2020. "Retributive Justice." In *The Stanford Encyclopedia of Philosophy*, edited by Edward N. Zalta. Vol. Fall 2020 Edition. https://plato.stanford.edu/archives/fall2020/entries/justice-retributive/.

Walker, Nigel. 1993. *Why Punish? Theories of Punishment Reassessed*. Oxford: Oxford University Press.

Walker, Nigel. 1999. "Even More Varieties of Retribution." *Philosophy* 74 (4): 595–605. https://doi.org/10.1017/s0031819199000704.

Wall, Jesse. 2018. "Public Wrongs and Private Wrongs." *Canadian Journal of Law & Jurisprudence* 31 (1): 177–96. https://doi.org/10.1017/cjlj.2018.8.

Wallbott, Herald G., and Klaus R. Scherer. 1995. "Cultural Determinants in Experiencing Shame and Guilt." In *Self-Conscious Emotions: The Psychology of Shame, Guilt, Embarrassment, and Pride*, edited by J. P. Tangney and K. W. Fischer, 465–87. Guilford Press.

Walters, Mark A. 2014. Hate Crime and Restorative Justice: Exploring Causes, Repairing Harms. Oxford: Oxford University Press.

Walters, Mark A, Jenny L Paterson, and Rupert Brown. 2020. "Enhancing Punishment or Repairing Harms? Perceptions of Sentencing Hate Crimes Amongst Members of a Commonly Targeted Victim Group." *The British Journal of Criminology* 61 (1): 61–84. https://doi.org/10.1093/bjc/azaa062.

Weisburd, David, Tomer Einat, and Matt Kowalski. 2008. "The Miracle of the Cells: An Experimental Study of Interventions to Increase Payment of Court-Ordered Financial Obligations*." *Criminology & Public Policy* 7 (1): 9–36. https://doi.org/10.1111/j.1745-9133.2008.00487.x.

Westen, Peter. 2016. "Retributive Desert as Fair Play." In *Legal, Moral, and Metaphysical Truths*, edited by Kimberly Ferzan and Stephen Morse, 63–78. Oxford: Oxford University Press. https://doi.org/10.1093/acprof:oso/9780198703242.003.0005.

Western, Bruce. 2006. *Punishment and Inequality in America*. New York: Russell Sage Foundation.

Wicker, Frank W., Glen C. Payne, and Randall D. Morgan. 1983. "Participant Descriptions of Guilt and Shame." *Motivation and Emotion* 7 (1): 25–39. https://doi.org/10.1007/bf00992963.

Wright, John Paul, Stephen G. Tibbetts, and Leah E. Daigle. 2015. *Criminals in the Making: Criminality across the Life Course*. London: SAGE. https://doi.org/10.4135/9781483399300.n4.

Wringe, Bill. 2013. "Must Punishment Be Intended to Cause Suffering?" *Ethical Theory and Moral Practice* 16 (4): 863–77.

Wringe, Bill. 2016. *An Expressive Theory of Punishment*. London: Palgrave Macmillan. https://doi.org/10.1057/9781137357120.

Wringe, Bill. 2019. "Punishment, Jesters and Judges: A Response to Nathan Hanna." *Ethical Theory and Moral Practice* 22 (1): 3–12. https://doi.org/10.1007/s10677-018-9966-7.

Yang, Fan, You-Jung Choi, Antonia Misch, Xin Yang, and Yarrow Dunham. 2018. "In Defense of the Commons: Young Children Negatively Evaluate and Sanction Free Riders." *Psychological Science* 29 (10): 1598–1611. https://doi.org/10.1177/0956797618779061.

Yarkoni, Tal. 2020. "The Generalizability Crisis." *Behavioral and Brain Sciences*, 1–37. https://doi.org/10.1017/s0140525x20001685.

Zaibert, Leo. 2018. "Prolegomena to Any Future Axiology." In *Rethinking Punishment*, by Leo Zaibert, 32–58. New York: Cambridge University Press. https://doi.org/10.1017/9781108151740.003.

Index of Names

Aharoni, Eyal   55, 57, 61, 89, 109 f., 206

Bagaric, Mirko   112 f., 135, 139, 156, 158, 163 f.
Bennett, Christopher   89, 102–105
Bentham, Jeremy   25, 139, 155, 179
Boonin, David   3, 5, 14, 19 f., 22, 26 f., 29 f., 45, 65–68, 84–86, 141, 153, 188–190, 193–195, 200, 208
Braithwaite, John   34, 114 f., 156, 159
Brooks, Thom   43, 167–171, 204

Carlsmith, Kevin   55 f., 139
Caruso, Gregg   3, 5, 15, 21 f., 69, 78, 104
Christie, Nils   115, 118 f., 126

Dagger, Richard   36, 61, 67, 69, 71, 73–79, 84–87, 163, 192
Duff, Antony   9, 14, 43, 60, 64, 66, 68, 84, 89, 91–93, 95–97, 99, 101, 106, 109, 111, 148 f., 155 f., 158 f., 164, 185, 199, 202
Duus-Otterström, Göran   65, 68–71, 79 f.

Garvey, Stephen   9, 14, 89, 91–93, 99–101, 109–111

Hampton, Jean   19, 60, 120 f., 123 f., 126, 128–130
Hanna, Nathan   14, 19, 22, 26 f., 86, 129, 131
Hart, H. L. A.   16, 22, 64, 75, 165
Hirsch, Andrew von   67, 93–95, 102 f., 105–107, 149, 164, 172, 178–182
Hörnle, Tatjana   125, 127 f., 131 f., 135, 167–171
Husak, Douglas   16, 45, 49, 127, 163–166, 196, 198 f., 202–207

Moore, Michael   36, 45–54, 57, 122, 163

Nichols, Shaun   35 f., 48, 61

Radzik, Linda   16, 29 f., 72, 89, 91–93, 111, 116, 120, 124
Rawls, John   43, 64, 165

Sayre-McCord, Geoffrey   25, 65

Wringe, Bill   14, 20, 26–28, 89, 123, 128

Index of Subjects

Amends   50, 91, 99, 114, 182
Anger   53f., 100, 112
Anthropology   3, 35

Backward-looking   5, 7, 118
Blame   18, 52, 85f., 102, 104–106, 126
Brute retributivism   7f., 43, 45–48, 54, 58, 61

Censure   5, 9, 16–18, 23f., 27, 29, 31, 37f., 43, 59, 81, 84–87, 89f., 92f., 97–99, 101–111, 114, 117, 123, 129, 131f., 160, 164, 166, 171, 173, 175, 179f., 182, 184, 206
Communication   18, 24, 32, 102, 106, 109–111, 115, 128, 132, 144, 149, 177, 185, 189, 192, 207
Communicative punishment   105, 108
Consequentialism   9, 24f., 31–34, 38, 58, 76, 89f., 96, 98, 101, 107f., 111–114, 117, 127, 151, 157–159, 163, 168, 181, 184
Cooperation   8f., 36f., 43, 47f., 64, 66, 68f., 71, 73–79, 82f., 127, 136, 171–173, 197
Corrective approaches   12, 14, 18, 21, 25, 28–31, 33f., 39, 44, 65, 71, 73, 84f., 87, 132, 135, 140–142, 176, 185–190, 192f., 196, 201, 203f., 206f., 212
Corrective justice   7, 27, 81, 129, 193, 205, 208
Corrective sanction   5–12, 14f., 18, 21–34, 37–39, 60, 65, 79, 84, 86f., 90, 100, 102, 108–112, 114, 116f., 123, 128, 131–134, 136, 140–142, 145, 147, 154f., 160, 164, 166, 172–175, 177f., 181f., 184–186, 189–192, 195f., 198f., 201–203, 205–208
Criminological data   10, 25, 32, 35, 39, 140–143, 154, 156, 160, 173, 180f.
Criminology   35, 191

Debunking   35f., 47, 159
Desert   7, 45, 103, 139, 163f., 182
Deterrence   5, 10f., 23f., 31, 55, 103, 107, 110, 139–141, 143–151, 153, 155–160, 163–165, 168, 171, 173–177, 184, 188f., 191, 194, 208, 211

Economic games   36f., 56–58, 82f., 110
Empirical   3–5, 7f., 10, 12–15, 35–39, 46f., 49f., 52, 58f., 63, 68, 77f., 82f., 89f., 96, 98, 100f., 123, 132, 135f., 140, 143, 146, 156, 160, 163f., 166, 169f., 180, 185–187, 205f., 208–212
Epistemic   7f., 11, 31–34, 36, 46f., 59–63, 89f., 105–111, 117, 121, 128–134, 136, 154, 206, 212
Evolutionary   3, 14, 18, 35f., 47f., 61, 63
Expressivism   16, 18, 85, 100, 102f., 120–124, 128, 131, 168, 173

Fairness theory   8, 36, 43, 45, 64–81, 87, 157, 176
Feelings of guilt   36, 46, 48–55, 58, 63, 92–96, 99–101, 108, 111–117, 166
Forward-looking   5, 10, 63, 81, 92, 101, 191
Free will   3, 5, 104

General deterrence   11, 140, 147, 151, 153–155, 160
Guilt   49f., 52, 90–92, 94, 99f., 104, 111–115, 135, 158, 174, 195

Hybrid   11f., 75, 98, 164–167, 171, 175, 184, 202

Instrumental   45, 70, 211
Instrumentalization   11, 151–155
Interdisciplinary   5, 209
Intrinsic   10, 38, 45, 61, 84, 101f., 104–107, 120, 127, 165, 173
Intrinsic worth   45, 61, 102, 104, 120, 211
Intuition   7–9, 35f., 48, 50, 52f., 55, 61, 74, 82, 85f., 89, 93–95, 99–101, 104, 118, 122f., 132, 149, 152, 157–159, 181

Justice   5, 7, 10, 23f., 31, 38, 45, 56–59, 62, 64f., 97, 106, 110, 115, 119f., 124–127, 132, 134, 136, 145, 160, 164, 170, 173f., 177, 180, 182f., 186–189, 192, 194f., 198f., 205f., 210

Laypeople   7, 17, 36, 55–57, 61, 139, 171, 179, 205
Liberal   9, 90f., 93–98, 115–117, 130, 148

Mala in se   66f., 70f., 73–75, 80f., 95f., 202
Mala prohibita   201–203
Mens rea   93
Moral outrage   36, 48, 50, 52–55, 58

Penance   9, 23, 31, 37f., 43f., 46, 89–101, 107–112, 114–117, 160, 164, 171, 173–176, 184
Pluralism   12, 56, 95, 163f., 167, 171f., 174, 178, 183
Principle of least infringement   22–32, 34, 176f., 191
Prison   17, 20, 22, 26f., 29, 33f., 58, 60, 74, 86, 131, 133, 141–145, 153f., 156, 174f., 178, 181, 187, 190, 194, 197, 206f.
Proportionality   23, 66–68, 72, 74–77, 80f., 90, 96–98, 106, 116f., 123, 130, 135, 142, 163f., 166–171, 174f., 178–184
Punishment   3–12, 14–39, 43–45, 47, 50–52, 54–68, 70–72, 75–81, 84–87, 89–103, 105–114, 116–119, 122f., 125, 127–136, 139–145, 147f., 151, 153–160, 163–169, 171, 173–175, 177–182, 185–192, 194–201, 203–212

Regret   94, 182
Reparation   25, 28, 30, 50, 72, 87, 89, 92, 99f., 106, 109, 123

Repentance   92, 95, 101, 164
Restitution   6, 23f., 26, 28–30, 32–34, 50f., 54, 57–59, 71f., 84–86, 108, 110, 118f., 123, 128f., 131–134, 136, 141f., 145, 174, 176–178, 183–206
Restorative justice   5, 9, 12, 18, 20, 24, 30, 33, 39, 55, 90, 100, 108, 110–112, 114–117, 126, 133–136, 145f., 151, 168, 172–175, 181–183, 191–193, 195, 201, 206, 208, 211
Retributivism   5, 7–9, 23f., 35f., 43–52, 54–64, 70, 76, 89f., 99, 101, 106f., 110, 113, 120–122, 128f., 159, 163–165, 167–169, 205, 211

Sentimentalism   46, 48
Social psychology   112, 117
Specific deterrence   11, 140

Utilitarianism   15f., 24f., 35, 45, 48, 55, 59, 101, 139, 155–158, 163–167, 179, 181

Victim   4, 7–10, 16, 18f., 21, 23–27, 29–34, 37–39, 43, 50f., 53–58, 60f., 69–73, 76f., 79–82, 84, 87f., 91–93, 95, 98–100, 104–108, 110, 112, 115f., 118–136, 141f., 145, 154f., 160, 166, 169f., 172–178, 181–196, 198–208, 210–212
Victimless crimes   7, 70, 201, 203f.
Victim's rights   5, 23f., 30–32, 43f., 46, 71, 87, 110, 118f., 128, 164, 170f., 173, 175f., 184

www.ingramcontent.com/pod-product-compliance
Lightning Source LLC
Chambersburg PA
CBHW020228170426
43201CB00007B/360